Citizenship, Gender and Diversity

Developed out of FEMCIT, a research project funded under the Sixth Framework of the European Commission examining gendered citizenship, multiculturalism and the impact of contemporary women's movements in Europe, the series also welcomes submissions from scholars around the globe working in this area on projects with either a European or international focus.

More information about this series at
http://www.springer.com/series/14900

Berit Gullikstad • Guro Korsnes Kristensen • Priscilla Ringrose
Editors

Paid Migrant Domestic Labour in a Changing Europe

Questions of Gender Equality and Citizenship

Editors
Berit Gullikstad
Interdisciplinary Studies of Culture
Norwegian University of Science and
Technology
Trondheim, Norway

Priscilla Ringrose
Interdisciplinary Studies of Culture
Norwegian University of Science and
Technology
Trondheim, Norway

Guro Korsnes Kristensen
Interdisciplinary Studies of Culture
Norwegian University of Science and
Technology
Trondheim, Norway

Citizenship, Gender and Diversity
ISBN 978-1-349-70400-2   ISBN 978-1-137-51742-5 (eBook)
DOI 10.1057/978-1-137-51742-5

Library of Congress Control Number: 2016937721

© The Editor(s) (if applicable) and The Author(s) 2016
Softcover reprint of the hardcover 1st edition 2016 978-1-137-51741-8
The author(s) has/have asserted their right(s) to be identified as the author(s) of this work in accordance with the Copyright, Designs and Patents Act 1988.
This work is subject to copyright. All rights are solely and exclusively licensed by the Publisher, whether the whole or part of the material is concerned, specifically the rights of translation, reprinting, reuse of illustrations, recitation, broadcasting, reproduction on microfilms or in any other physical way, and transmission or information storage and retrieval, electronic adaptation, computer software, or by similar or dissimilar methodology now known or hereafter developed.
The use of general descriptive names, registered names, trademarks, service marks, etc. in this publication does not imply, even in the absence of a specific statement, that such names are exempt from the relevant protective laws and regulations and therefore free for general use.
The publisher, the authors and the editors are safe to assume that the advice and information in this book are believed to be true and accurate at the date of publication. Neither the publisher nor the authors or the editors give a warranty, express or implied, with respect to the material contained herein or for any errors or omissions that may have been made.

Cover illustration: © Pick and Mix Images / Alamy Stock Photo

Printed on acid-free paper

This Palgrave Macmillan imprint is published by Springer Nature
The registered company is Macmillan Publishers Ltd. London

To our dear colleague Trine Annfelt

Preface

We are in the final stages of writing this book, just as Europe is facing an extreme humanitarian catastrophe, one which the world has not yet seen the end of, and even less has found the solution to. As a result of intolerable conditions in their home countries, almost 600,000 migrants are estimated to have crossed the Mediterranean Sea to Europe so far this year, according to the International Organization for Migration (IOM). The war in Syria, which began more than 4 years ago and shows no sign of ending, continues to be by far the biggest driver of this migration flow. Ongoing violence in Afghanistan, massive human rights violations in Eritrea, and poverty in Kosovo are leading people to flee their countries in an attempt to establish new and better lives elsewhere. In contrast to previous migration to Europe over the past quarter century, when there have been a substantial influx of women, the migrants currently entering Europe are predominantly young men.

How will this group of migrants settle in to their new countries? And how can the European countries that receive migrants, with a range of different backgrounds and competences, facilitate a form of citizenship that ensures that the individuals get what they need, at the same time as being able to participate fully in society? A key to participation is work, providing that it is carried out according to regulations and with a decent salary. What many of the chapters in this book illustrate is that this is not the case for many migrant workers. Lacking or weak citizenship status is a factor that may contribute to forcing migrants into low-status and lowly paid jobs that are part of a deregulated labour market. Paid domestic labour is one notable sector that is largely deregulated, and that does not necessarily ensure social participation for the workers.

As outlined in several places in this book, the increased supply of labour made possible by globalisation and new European policies is closely imbricated in the re-emergence of paid migrant domestic labour across Europe. The social stratification this has produced signals the re-emergence of an old phenomenon, namely the return of the servant society. This current refugee crisis raises some crucial question in this regard: Will the increasing number of migrants fuel the new servant society? Will new migrants compete with settled migrants for the already established jobs in the domestic sphere, potentially leading to even worse working conditions? And will the increased availability of low-cost labour lead to the creation of more jobs in the paid domestic labour sector? How will this potentially new kind of domestic labourer (both in regards to gender, nationality/ethnicity/'race' and social class) impact on the cultural perceptions of this work? How do we create a labour market which is not segregated along the lines of gender, class and ethnicity, as paid domestic work currently seems to be?

An important consideration here is what changes in the regulation of this labour market will come into play, and whether and how the rights of this new type of migrant as citizen and worker will be defended in the Europe of the future. We hope that this book will contribute to an increased interest in social and economic inequalities along the axes of gender, class and nationality/ethnicity/'race', as well as more awareness of the majoritising and minoritising processes at work in today's Europe, and not least give insights into of the ever-present possibilities for negotiations and agency. We also hope that its empirical investigations will contribute to the development of more inclusive policies which actively challenge the inequalities which this book brings to light, in the interests of creating a more equal Europe.

Autumn 2015
Trondheim, Norway

Acknowledgements

This book emerged out of the multidisciplinary research project 'Buying and Selling (gender) Equality: Feminized Migration and Gender Equality in Contemporary Norway', funded by the Research Council of Norway (RCN) under the research programme 'Welfare, Work and Migration' (VAM). In addition to the funding of the research project based at the Centre for Gender Studies at the Norwegian University of Science and Technology, the RCN monies also covered the establishment of a European network in the field of paid migrant domestic labour. We thank the Research Council of Norway for their generous economic and administrative support, and the VAM programme in particular for initiating inspiring and valuable network activities throughout the project's life cycle.

This book is the outcome of this European research network that has included participants from six European countries, whose research material spans nine national contexts. The members of the network have come together in Trondheim, Norway, on three occasions to discuss each other's research material and to comment on each other's drafts and chapters. Our discussions on paid migrant domestic labour at these network meetings brought to light both similarities and differences of policies and culture across national borders, and made us all aware of dimensions and particularities that we might otherwise not have considered.

The organisation of the network involving meetings in Norway means that all contributors have been involved in each other's thinking and analyses, and that everyone has contributed actively both to the conceptualisation of the book and to the final product. As editors, we are most thankful for the fruitful discussions in the network and at the workshops, and the highly inspiring and instructive lessons that came out of them. We would like to thank Dr. Malin Noem Ravn and Associate Professor Helle Stenum who were part of the network, attended the workshop, and as such contributed to the book. Thank you too, to Dr. Elisabeth Stubberud for indispensable assistance in final phase of the book project. Last, but not least we would like to thank Professor Emerita Trine Annfelt who was central in the development and planning of the 'Buying and Selling Gender Equality' project, and who has acted as an invaluable advisor and motivator all the way until the finish line. We dedicate this book to Trine.

Contents

1 Paid Migrant Domestic Labour, Gender Equality, and Citizenship in a Changing Europe: An Introduction   1
Berit Gullikstad, Guro Korsnes Kristensen, and Priscilla Ringrose

2 Neoliberal Citizenship and Domestic Service in Finland: A Return to a Servant Society?   31
Lena Näre

3 The Au Pair Scheme as 'Cultural Exchange': Effects of Norwegian Au Pair Policy on Gender Equality and Citizenship   55
Berit Gullikstad and Trine Annfelt

4 Paid Domestic Work in Spain: Gendered Framings of Work and Care in Policies on Social Citizenship   79
Elin Peterson

5 Gendered Work and Citizenship: Diverse Experiences of Au Pairing in the UK   101
Rosie Cox and Nicky Busch

6 From Intimate Relations to Citizenship? Au Pairing
and the Potential for Citizenship in Norway 125
Elisabeth Stubberud

7 Citizenship and Maternalism in Migrant Domestic
Labour: Filipina Workers and Their Employers
in Amsterdam and Rome 147
Sabrina Marchetti

8 Paid Migrant Domestic Labour in Gender-Equal Norway:
A Win–Win Arrangement? 169
Guro Korsnes Kristensen

9 *The Intouchables*: Care Work, Homosociality
and National Fantasy 195
Priscilla Ringrose

10 Unequal Fatherhoods: Citizenship, Gender,
and Masculinities in Outsourced 'Male' Domestic Work 217
Ewa Palenga-Möllenbeck

11 Buying and Selling Gender Equality:
Concluding Reflections 245
Guro Korsnes Kristensen, Berit Gullikstad, and Priscilla Ringrose

Index 257

Notes on Contributors

Trine Annfelt is Professor Emerita of Gender Studies at the Centre for Gender Studies, Department of Interdisciplinary Studies of Culture, Norwegian University of Science and Technology (NTNU), Trondheim, Norway. She has worked for many years on issues related to gender and ethnicity/'race' in the Norwegian multicultural welfare state. More recently, her research has been focused on majoritising/minoritising processes and on the meanings these processes have for gender equality and integration. Her latest articles are 'Kjønnslikestilling i inkluderingens tjeneste? ('Gender mainstreaming policy—in the service of inclusion?') in *Tidsskrift for kjønnsforskning* (2013), 'Mot et ikke-diskriminerende sosialt arbeid' ('Towards a non-discriminatory social work') in *Fontene forskning* (2014) and 'Et Kolumbi egg? Au pairordningen og diskursen om kulturutveksling' ('Columbi egg? The au pair scheme and the cultural exchange discourse') in *Tidsskrift for kjønnsforskning* (2015).

Nicky Busch is Lecturer in the Department of Geography, Environment and Development Studies, Birkbeck, University of London, London, UK. She has been researching low-paid and informal childcare in the UK for nearly 10 years and has published a range of journal articles and book chapters on the subject. Between 2012 and 2014 she was working with Dr. Rosie Cox on the Economic and Social Research Council (ESRC)-funded project 'Au Pairing After the Au Pair Scheme: New Migration Rules and Childcare in Private Homes in the UK'. She is currently working on a monograph based on the findings from this project to be published by Zed Books in 2016.

Rosie Cox is Reader in Geography and Gender Studies at the Department of Geography, Environment and Development Studies, Birkbeck, University of London, London, UK. She has a long-standing research interest in paid domestic labour and has published widely on the topic. She is author of *The Servant Problem: Domestic Employment in a Global Economy* (I.B. Tauris, 2006) and recently edited the collection *Au Pairs' Lives in Global Context: Sisters or Servants?* (Palgrave, 2015). Between 2012 and 2014 she was working with Dr. Nicky Busch on the Economic and Socia Research Council-Funded project 'Au Pairing After the Au Pair Scheme' examining the effects of deregulation of au pairing in the UK.

Berit Gullikstad is Associate Professor of Gender Studies at the Centre for Gender Studies, Department of Interdisciplinary Studies of Culture, Norwegian University of Science and Technology (NTNU), Trondheim, Norway. She holds a PhD in Modern History from the Norwegian University of Science and Technology. Her main field of research is working life (historical and contemporary) with a special focus on gender/ethnicity and intersectional approaches. In the last years her research has focused on Norwegian policies on migration and gender equality. Gullikstad has led a number of research projects and participated in international EU projects (FEMCIT) and international networks (NordWel). Her recent book is a co-edited book on intersectionality: *Likestilte norskheter. Om kjønn og etnisitet* (Tapir Akademisk forlag, 2010).

Guro Korsnes Kristensen is Researcher at the Centre for Gender Studies, Department of Interdisciplinary Studies of Culture, Norwegian University of Science and Technology (NTNU), Trondheim, Norway. She holds a PhD in Interdisciplinary Studies of Culture. Kristensen's research is broadly focused on gender, migration, family life and working life. Kristensen is the coordinator of the research project 'Buying and Selling (gender) Equality: Feminized Migration and Gender Equality in Contemporary Norway'. She has published several journal articles and book chapters in the fields of gender and multiculturalism. In 2009, she won the *Norwegian Journal of Gender Studies* 'Article of the Year' prize. Her recent publications include 'A Fair Deal? Paid Domestic Labour in Social Democratic Norway', in Triandafyllidou, A. and S. Marchetti (eds.), *Employers, Agencies and Immigration: Paying for Care* (Routledge, 2015).

Sabrina Marchetti is Associate Professor at the Department of Philosophy and Cultural Heritage, Ca' Foscari University of Venice, Venice, Italy. Marchetti holds a PhD from Utrecht University and has worked as a research associate at the Robert Schuman Centre for Advanced Studies of the European University Institute in Florence. She is mainly specialised in issues of gender, welfare, labour and migration, with a specific focus on the question of migrant domestic work. Amongst her publications are *Black Girls. Migrant Domestic Workers and Colonial Legacies* (Brill, 2014) and the co-edited volume, *Employers, Agencies and Immigration: Paying for Care* (Ashgate, 2015).

Lena Näre is Assistant Professor of Sociology in the Department of Social Research, University of Helsinki, Helsinki, Finland. She is also Editor-in-Chief of *Nordic Journal of Migration Research*. She holds a DPhil in Migration Studies from the University of Sussex and a PhD in Sociology from the University of Helsinki. Her research focuses on social inequalities, migration, gender, care work and ethnographic methods. She is currently leading two research projects: one on migrant youth employment and the other on irregular migration and precarious work. Her recent publications include a co-edited book with Katie Walsh entitled *Transnational Migration and Home in Older Age* (Routledge, 2016).

Ewa Palenga-Möllenbeck is Postdoctoral Researcher in the Department of Gender Studies, Goethe-University, Frankfurt, Germany. Her research interests include migration, transnationalism, gender studies, care work, diversity and qualitative research methods. She has published widely in books and international journals on gender, care and migration. Her monograph *Pendelmigration aus Oberschlesien. Lebensgeschichten in einer transnationalen Region Europas* (Bielefeld, 2014) is based on her PhD thesis. Recent publications include 'Global care chains' (with Helma Lutz), in *The Routledge Handbook of Immigration and Refugee Studies* (Triandafyllidou (ed.) 2015) and the co-edited volume *Family Life in an Age of Migration and Mobility: Global Perspectives Through the Life Course* (Palgrave, 2016).

Elin Peterson is Postdoctoral Researcher in the Department of Social Work, Stockholm University, Stockholm, Sweden. She holds a PhD in Political Science from the University Complutense, Madrid, Spain. Her research interests include gender, social policy, domestic and caring work, eldercare, and migration. She is currently working on the research project 'Eldercare policy and struggles for recognition in European care regimes'. The project focuses on eldercare in two very different European care regimes: Sweden and Spain. It involves interviews with organisations working to promote the interests of paid and unpaid carers. The purpose is to contribute to a deeper understanding of the challenges that eldercare policies deal with in ageing Europe, focusing on how care-giving work is valued and reflecting on the consequences for those who give and receive care. She is the author of the chapter 'License to care? Migrant domestic workers in

Spanish employment and family policy' in *Migrant domestic workers and family life: International perspectives* (Kontos and Bonifacio (eds.), Palgrave, 2015).

Priscilla Ringrose is Professor of Gender Studies and French Literature at the Centre for Gender Studies, Department of Interdisciplinary Studies of Culture, and Department of Language and Literature, Norwegian University of Science and Technology (NTNU), Trondheim, Norway. She is currently leading the Norwegian Research Council-funded project 'Buying and Selling (gender) Equality: Feminized Migration and Gender Equality in Contemporary Norway' program (VAM). Her publications focus on the gendered and/or racialised contact zones between individuals and cultures in situations of war and migration, both in the European and Middle Eastern contexts. She is the author of *Assia Djebar: In dialogue with feminisms* (2006, Rodopi).

Elisabeth Stubberud is Senior Adviser at KUN, Centre for Gender Equality, Norfold, Norway. She holds a PhD in Gender Studies from the Department of Interdisciplinary Studies of Culture, Norwegian University of Science and Technology. Her research interests include migration, critical race theory, domestic work, cultural representations, film studies, feminist and postcolonial theory, intersectionality, and intimacy and affect. Recent publications include her doctoral thesis *Au pairing in Norway: The production of a (non-)worker*, which explores the relationship between gender equality, global feminised migration, and racialisation and gendering of labour. She has also published on issues of au pairing, work and affective labour, the cultural representation of au pairs, and racism and film in Scandinavia.

1

Paid Migrant Domestic Labour, Gender Equality, and Citizenship in a Changing Europe: An Introduction

Berit Gullikstad, Guro Korsnes Kristensen, and Priscilla Ringrose

The aim of this book is to provide empirically based investigations of paid migrant domestic labour and au pairing, as they are unfolding in nine different European countries—explored through the concepts of gender equality and citizenship. The book will contribute to rethinking these two concepts within feminist research and policy development, in the light of their central importance to policy making and identity making in today's Europe.

B. Gullikstad (✉) • G.K. Kristensen
Department of Interdisciplinary Studies of Culture,
Centre for Gender Studies, Norwegian University of Science
and Technology (NTNU), Trondheim, Norway

P. Ringrose
Department of Interdisciplinary Studies of Culture
and Department of Language and Literature, Centre for Gender Studies,
Norwegian University of Science and Technology (NTNU),
Trondheim, Norway

© The Editor(s) (if applicable) and The Author(s) 2016
B. Gullikstad et al. (eds.), *Paid Migrant Domestic Labour
in a Changing Europe*, DOI 10.1057/978-1-137-51742-5_1

The contributions focus on exploring the ways in which gender equality and citizenship as values, norms, and practices are discursively produced, negotiated in social relations, and played out in political processes in a variety of European contexts. In doing so, they interrogate universalist assumptions and understandings of both gender equality and citizenship. When citizenship is examined together with gender equality, it is often done in a manner which primarily relates to women. We aim to examine these two concepts from a perspective that does not (implicitly) address them as primarily or exclusively relating either to women or to men. We investigate gender equality and citizenship from a localised and historicised perspective, which takes into account the complexity and fluidity of paid migrant domestic work. This approach implies that gender equality and citizenship can be studied as complex and interrelated phenomena. Citizenship is gendered in different ways across different geographic contexts. At the same time, access to gender equality, through policy incentives, for example, may vary depending on citizenship rights, within as well as across contexts. This means that empirical and theoretical investigations that take account of both gender equality and citizenship have the potential to shed new light on both phenomena and on the ways in which they are connected.

This raises a number of questions which we address in this book: In what ways do citizenship and gender equality take on different forms and meanings in localised contexts of the paid domestic labour sector in Europe? How do gender equality and citizenship as values, norms, and practices contribute to producing privileged or precarious positions? And in what ways can the relations between gender equality and citizenship be understood across geographical contexts, within the sphere of paid domestic labour?

The empirical investigations are situated in Finland, France, Germany, Italy, the Netherlands, Norway, Poland, Spain, and the UK. The field of paid domestic labour investigated in this collection covers both men and women as buyers and sellers of eldercare and childcare, au pair work, cleaning, repair, and gardening services. In some chapters, the focus is on policy developments and political discourses and debates, in others it is on lived life and interpersonal relations. What is common to all these contributions is that the focus is primarily on cultural meaning production, whether in the context of political systems, social structures, or everyday practices.

The book looks to a Europe characterised by extensive and rapid changes which are to a certain extent commonly experienced but which at the same time manifest themselves differently in different national and local contexts. European policy is concerned with promoting values such as (gender) equality and (migrant) inclusion (Lewis, 2006), not least by developing the 'adult worker model' (Lister et al., 2007). Yet, at the same time, national welfare systems are being eroded and care facilities are increasingly privatised. The entrenchment of neoliberal policies, combined with the persistence of (post)colonial processes (Keskinen, Tuori, Irni, & Mulinari, 2009), represents the background to the steady increase in the demand for paid domestic work and au pairing which is primarily, but not exclusively, being performed by migrant women (Anderson, 2007; Anthias, Morokvasic-Müller, & Kontos, 2013; Cox, 2006; ILO, 2013; Isaksen, 2010; Lutz, 2008, 2011; Palenga-Möllenbeck, 2013; Triandafyllidou, 2013).

Paid Migrant Domestic Labour

Paid domestic labour has re-emerged on the European scene in the last decades. It has never been 'ectinct', but in many countries it declined significantly before increasing again (Kilkey, Perrons, & Plomien, 2013, p. 20). This increase is particularly of note in the Nordic countries, where extensive welfare systems and a political and cultural ideal of social equality have rendered paid domestic labour, which is bought and sold on the private market, both unnecessary and unwanted—at least officially (Bikova, 2010; Isaksen, 2010; Kristensen, 2015; Stenum, 2010). In other parts of Europe, it may make more sense to speak of changes in already established practices, especially where there have been, for example, changes in migration practices leading to new, or different, groups of migrants from Europe or elsewhere offering domestic services. Another important change concerns what Triandafyllidou and Marchetti describe as the 'proletarisation' of paid domestic work. By this they mean that services, which used to be considered a 'luxury that only few households could afford', are now being purchased by employers from the middle and lower middle classes who regard it as 'not a luxury but a necessity' (Triandafyllidou & Marchetti, 2015, p. 231).

The particular nature of domestic labour has been widely commented on, among others by Joan Tronto, who points to three of its distinguishing features, namely relating to the institutional setting, to the workplace, and to the relations involved (Tronto, 2002, pp. 37–39). The institutional setting of the household is very different from that of a commercial setting (Anderson, 2000; Isaksen, 2010; Lutz, 2011; Parreñas, 2001). A crucial point to note here is that paid domestic labour is often organised in a way that evades state policy and regulation. The fact that this labour is carried out in private households, as well as being work that is traditionally done by members of the household, makes it appear informal, and this affects employment procedures, work instructions, and wages (Anderson, 2000). Furthermore, since domestic labour usually takes place in private homes, it is often not regarded as employment at all, but rather as help, as an 'extra pair of hands'. The au pair arrangement, for example, is commonly not organised and regulated as work, but defined as 'cultural exchange', with the au pair receiving board, lodging, and 'pocket money' instead of a salary (Cox, 2015; Stubberud, 2015a, 2015b). Similarly, as far as home cleaning services are concerned, the widespread occurrence of unregulated arrangements and the concomitant lack of political will to address them is evidence of the fact that such services are considered as less 'proper' than other kinds of labour (Gavanas & Callemann, 2013; Lutz, 2011).

Tronto (2002) further argues that relationships within a household are considerably more intimate than those played out within market settings. This may mean that domestic workers may be assigned the status of quasi-family members, entangling workers' lives with the lives of employers without taking account of the unequal power dynamics of the relationship. Moreover, domestic workers are often expected to reflect varied aspects of their employers' lives, such as values in raising children and tastes regarding food- and cleaning products (Tronto, 2002), as well as to generally adapt to their employers' habits (Näre, 2011). Furthermore, the fact that the work is done, not in a public space, but in someone else's private sphere, also means that the level of control that employers expect to exert over domestic workers is often very great, and non-compliance can be emotionally and psychologically charged.

A third factor that distinguishes domestic service from other market relations, as argued by Tronto (2002), is that it often creates ongoing relationships between employers and employees, and that the quality of these relationships effectively functions as a measuring tool for the quality of the work that is done. This implies a personalisation of relationships, which blurs the distinction between the person that does the work and the work itself, in other words the boundaries between the individual and his or her work are broken down and the worker is defined by the work that is being done (Stubberud, 2015a, p. 77). While these concerns also exist in market relations, they are presumed to be paradigmatic of domestic relations, and thus, constitute a central aspect of domestic labour.

To Tronto's list of differences between domestic work and market relations, we add three more aspects: gender, class and ethnicity/'race'. Domestic work is frequently described as gendered in the sense that some aspects of this labour have traditionally been carried out by women while other aspects have traditionally been carried out by men. The term 'domestic work' is generally applied in a traditionally feminised sense to work revolving around cooking, caring, and cleaning (Anderson, 2000). However, there are also certain types of domestic work that have masculine connotations, which should be studied alongside traditional 'women's work' (Kilkey et al., 2013; Palenga-Möllenbeck, 2013). A substantial difference here, however, is that 'masculine' jobs are generally better paid and that those who perform these jobs are rarely live-in domestic workers (Kilkey et al., 2013). There are however exceptions, as demonstrated in research on Sri Lankan men working as cleaners and carers in Naples, Italy (Näre, 2010), and in Ringrose's analyses of the movie *The Intouchables* (Chap. 9). According to Triandafyllidou and Marchetti (2015, p. 231), employers also maintain the traditional gender divide since female employers tend to manage female employees' domestic work, often positioning themselves as 'mothers' or even 'daughters' of their employees.

As far as class is concerned, the differences in social background between buyers and sellers of paid domestic work have tended to become less marked, as Triandafyllidou and Marchetti point to when they claim that buying these services is no longer a luxury that only a few households can afford (2015, p. 231). In line with this, Stubberud argues that the au pair scheme or rather domestic work itself produces a hierarchical relationship that exists independently of potential similarities between the au pair and the host family (Stubberud, 2015a, p. 21). Doing paid domestic work often means working for low wages in a profession with low status, and doing work that is highly demanding, as Anderson's concept of 'dirty work' indicates (Anderson, 2000; see also Lan, 2006; Näre, 2011). Futhermore, due to the feminization of migration, domestic labour has also become part of a global market and, as such, is saturated with ethnicity/|race|. In general, there is a tendency for those buying domestic labour to be positioned within the Global North/West, and those selling it within the Global South/East (Lutz, 2007). The combination of this structural inequality and the characteristics of domestic labour described above contributes to the (re)production of ethnic/|racial| hierarchies. These hierarchies can be identified both in national policies, in relationship between buyers and sellers, and across sellers of domestic work. For example Cox and Busch|s chapter illustrates how in the context of au pairing in the UK (Chapt. 5), there is a hierarchical relation between au pairs from different EU states. Au pairs originating from new EU members and/or from states where there is higher unemployment tend to be pressured to perform more |work| tasks and are less likely to participate in cultural exchange.[1]

Altogether, the structural and cultural aspects of domestic labour, combined with is gendered, classed and ethnic/|racial| dimensions produce a situation where low paid migrants undertaking undervalued yet physically and mentally demanding work are at risk of exploitation. Their citizenship rights are connected to the precarious work they do and they are particularly vulnerable to the working conditions of contemporary Europe.

Gender, Gender Equality, and Citizenship

Scholarship on paid migrant domestic labour, including the research perspectives mentioned above, has primarily investigated paid domestic work from a gendered perspective, more or less explicitly viewing it

---

[1] Only five European countries have ratified the Domestic Workers Convention. http://www.ilo.org/dyn/normlex/en/f?p=1000:11300:0::NO:11300:P11300_INSTRUMENT_ID:2551460

as gendered labour associated with women's subordinate position in the family and in society (Cox, 2012; Lutz, 2011). As an extension of this kind of thinking, domestic work has also been researched from the perspective of gendered citizenship (Lister et al., 2007). The cluster of paid migrant domestic work, gender equality, and citizenship, which is the book's main focus, has primarily been thematised as a woman's question (e.g. Grossman & McClain, 2009; Isaksen, 2010; Lister et al., 2007; and Yeates, 2012, for a critique). The contributions in this book engage with this cluster as both a woman's and a man's question, while conceptualising gender as intertwined with other socially differentiating categories such as ethnicity, 'race', sexuality, and socio-economic class (Cho, Crenshaw, & McCall, 2013; Davis, 2008; Manalansan, 2006; Purkayvastha, 2012). Moreover, by engaging with an understanding of gender that takes into account and destabilises differences within categories, we open up for an investigation of paid migrant domestic labour that demands to be studied from a localised, historicised, and contextual perspective. As such, the volume has the potential to demonstrate the ways in which this kind of work takes on different forms and allows for different experiences in different contexts.

Gender equality has become both a widespread value and a norm which is variously integrated into European political welfare strategies and thinking. This is particularly evident in policies related to the family, where the paternity leave quota, childcare leave-sharing regulations, and the development of day care facilities facilitate the implementation of the 'adult worker model' or the 'dual earner/dual carer model' for gender equality. These concepts translate the ambition of gender equality into equal opportunities for women and men primarily through women's participation in working life but also through men's participation in family life.

These types of policies, which can be characterised as forms of gender mainstreaming, are common in European Union (EU) countries (Lutz, 2007). Gender mainstreaming in the EU context is defined as 'the integration of a gender perspective into every stage of each intervention: preparation, design, implementation, monitoring and evaluation of policies, regulatory measures and spending programmes' (The European Institute for Gender Equality). As an umbrella term, it is meant to provide substance for new gendered policy developments and political practices

(Christensen & Breengaard, 2011; Walby, 2005), aimed at achieving gender justice and gender equality. Gender mainstreaming policies seek to challenge patriarchal and gender-blind norms in theory and in policy, and to mobilise actors in the public sector and civil society. As a concept and practice, gender mainstreaming summons up the ideal of gender justice for all, that is to say a universalisation of justice regardless of gender.

Gender mainstreaming is, however, contested as both a theoretical and a political concept. One of the problematics it presents is the way that 'gender' is itself conceptualised within its framework. Critics argue that this policy development nevertheless sanctions the assimilation to a male norm and the perpetuation of the gender dichotomy (Eveline & Bacchi, 2005). Scholars working with theories of intersectionality have also criticised both the concept and policies of gender mainstreaming, seeing it as a reinvention of feminism, which effectively neutralises its discursive power by creating a depoliticised alternative to addressing female subordination. While this critique has itself been instrumental in the development of new political strategies of 'diversity policy' and 'equal opportunities for all' (Christensen & Breengaard, 2011; Einarsdottir & Thorvaldsdottir, 2007; Nentwich, 2006; Squires, 2005; Verloo, 2006; Yuval-Davis, 2006), these policies have not been successful in challenging binary understandings of gender. Empirical studies in a variety of European contexts have demonstrated just how much policy development has been imbricated in essentialist and dichotomist understanding of gender, in the name of gender mainstreaming (Annfelt & Gullikstad, 2013; Christensen & Breengaard, 2011; Eveline & Bacchi, 2005). Several of the chapters in this volume, including Peterson's analysis of Spanish policy making in the fields of family, domestic work, and care for children, the elderly, and disabled persons, illustrate this point (Chap. 4).

Like the concept of gender, the notion of citizenship is highly contested and the debate around it has resulted in many and contrasting definitions (Dobrowolsky & Tastsoglou, 2006; Lister, 2003, Lister et al. 2007). In everyday speech citizenship is often related to basic rights and duties connected to the right to reside in a country, to have a passport, and to vote in elections. As such, citizenship is understood as a limited and stable legal and political category that defines a list of duties and rights, but which also encompasses a series of practices. However, citizenship is a concept that has moved beyond the legal and political relationship between the individual and the nation state, involving participation in civil society, including rights and duties, to also encompassing belonging and participation (Isin, Nyers, & Turner, 2013; Kymlicka, 1995; Roseneil, Halsaa, & Sümer, 2012).

These divergent views point to two radically different traditions in citizenship thinking. One tradition follows in the wake of Marshall, with an emphasis on social difference. His vision of citizenship is aimed towards the achievement of a more equal and inclusive society (Dobrowolsky & Tastsoglou, 2006; Eggebø, 2012; Lister et al., 2007). Feminist research has pointed to the need to include the category of gender, alongside class, as key to fulfilling Marshall's vision. The feminist critique of citizenship has been based on the fact that the concept of citizenship has not interrogated the public/private divide, and that in particular the private realm has not been problematised (Lister, 2003, Lister et al. 2007). By focusing exclusively on the public sphere, this approach has the effect of making woman disappear out of sight, with both their rights and duties largely overlooked. In other words, when the private sphere is not included within the framework of citizenship, it follows that inequalities in the spheres of family life—reproduction, sexuality, caring, and domestic work—cannot be addressed.

The feminist critique of the concept of citizenship has led to the rethinking of the notions of political, social and economic citizenship, and also to the development of new dimensions, such as bodily citizenship and intimate citizenship (Halsaa, Roseneil, & Sümer, 2012). Citizenship has acquired many and varied meanings, and can be understood as a lived experience (Hall & Williamson, 1999; kennedy–macfoy, 2012), or in terms of the results of 'acts' of citizenship (Isin & Nielsen, 2008; Pajnik & Bajt, 2013), or as multilayered 'package' of practices, rights, and identities which are always historical, local, and contextual (Joppke, 2007; Yuval-Davis, 1999).

The other tradition in citizenship thinking has pointed to the fact that the feminist and multiculturalist critique of citizenship has its own 'blind spots', namely that it primarily operates within the framework of the nation state (Eggebø, 2012). This critique sets itself up against such a notion of citizenship as primarily being concerned with those who are already citizens, as not allowing for the question of formal non-citizenship, and as assuming that those who do not 'belong' are excluded from citizenship (Bosniak, 2009). The concept of 'denizen' has been introduced to designate individuals who have citizenship rights without having the formal status of a national citizen (Hammar, 1990). Another concept that has been developed is that of 'partial citizenship' (Bauböck, 2011; Bosniak, 2009; Parreñas, 2001). Both concepts point to citizenship as not a definitive, either/or position (Bosniak, 2009, p. 138). People can enjoy partial citizenship, or they may be the subject of citizenship in some respects but not in others (Bosniak, 2009, p. 139). Predelli, Halsaa, and Thun argue that the word 'citizenship' is 'out of place' and point to the importance of 'remaking' both the concept and practices of lived citizenship, in order to promote inclusion, participation, justice, and equality (Predelli et al., 2012, p. 220).

In this volume we understand citizenship both as public rights and duties that are claimed by and/or attributed to citizens as markers of recognition and belonging, and as practices and identities chosen, constructed, and performed by citizens in their daily lives (Dobrowolsky & Tastsoglou, 2006; Lister et al., 2007; Roseneil et al., 2012). This notion of citizenship is understood 'as social relations and participatory practices within all spheres of life, be they political, economic, social, cultural, religious, bodily, domestic or intimate' (Predelli et al., 2012, pp. 190, 220). We approach citizenship as a multilayered, historical, local, and contextual concept which is tightly bound up with other phenomena such as neoliberalism, migration, gender equality and diversity policies, and processes of racialisation and minoritisation (Anderson & Shutes, 2014; Benhabib & Resnik, 2009; Halsaa et al., 2012; Lister et al., 2007; Somers, 2008; Strasser, 2012; Tastsoglou & Dobrowolsky, 2006).

While Marshall's concept of citizenship has been criticised and developed, his main legacy to the various conceptualisations of citizenship is the founding idea that citizenship is about equality. As such his conceptualisation is allied to a universal notion of equality, a founding aspect of modernity. In this volume, we ask whether citizenship has been robbed of this founding principle (see Näre, Chap. 2). Näre argues that neoliberalism has signalled an ideological shift and a reformulation of citizenship away from egalitarianism and universalism and towards the increased 'marketisation' and 'contractualisation' of rights (Somers, 2008) and not least, the increased acceptance of inequalities in labour markets and private households.

Throughout Europe, gender equality for women is connected to social and economic citizenship through the 'adult-worker-model' policies (Lister et al., 2007). At the same time there are increasing political initiatives across Europe aimed at encouraging fathers' greater participation in care work (Moss & Kamerman, 2009). This is particularly the case in Nordic countries where the dual-earner–dual-carer model represents a political ideal (Ellingsæter & Leira, 2006). But is it possible to realise this ideal? And is the employment of migrant domestic workers the solution for realising it? These questions are central in the contributions which examine employers' arguments for buying paid migrant domestic services in Norway and in Germany (Kristensen, Chap. 8; Palenga-Möllenbeck, Chap. 10).

Some strands of research in the field of domestic labour have investigated the increased demand for paid household services in relation to women's increased participation in the labour market. This research has pointed to the fact that thanks to paid migrant domestic labour, Western middle-class women can achieve gender equality and economic citizenship in line with men by taking part in the labour market (Kvist & Peterson, 2010; Macklin, 1994; Tronto, 2002; see Bosniak, 2009 for a discussion). In the Nordic countries the connection between gender equality and citizenship (as cultural values and as policies) is particularly close (Lister, 2008; Predelli et al., 2012, p. 220). As Ellingsæter and Leira affirm 'gender equality is now integral to Scandinavian citizenship' (2006, p. 7). This connection is the backdrop to Norwegian au pair policy and to the public debate which it has pre-empted. Looking at official policies related to this scheme, Gullikstad and Annfelt (Chap. 3) ask what the implications are of maintaining the definition of au pairing as cultural exchange for the political values of equality and citizenship. Focusing on gender equality and citizenship as complex phenomena whose meanings are negotiated, challenged, or reproduced in specific contexts, the contributions in this volume are sensitive to the ways in which various differences coalesce to produce minoritised and majoritised positions.

Majoritising and Minoritising Processes

Since research on paid migrant domestic work has tended to focus on the working conditions of migrant workers, on the perspectives of their employers, and on the policies regulating the transactions between them, there has been little scholarship around the wider processes of majoritising and minoritising in which domestic labour is imbricated. The postcolonial critique of research on global care chains exemplifies this deficiency. This research field, which focuses on women's perspectives, and is particularly concerned with the connections between women and caring in a global context, perceives gender exclusively in terms of the relation between women and men (Hochchild, 2000; Isaksen, 2007; Parreñas, 2001). In other words, this global care chain research does not analyse conflicts of class and 'race'/ethnicity between women (Lewis, 2006).

In this volume, analytical perspectives which address these wider processes are considered crucial to the investigation of domestic labour. In particular we refer to the work of Avtar Brah (2003), who questions the tendency to equate numerical number and minority. According to Brah, this equation assumes an understanding of minorities and majorities as stable and fixed entities, which reduces the power inequalities between majority and minority to a question of quantity. Brah reminds us that both 'the elite' and 'the ethnic other' can be a minority in numerical terms. By introducing the verb 'minoritising' she clarifies that the term 'minority', in the sense that it is used in so-called multicultural societies, relates to processes that make something into 'otherness'. This means that the concept of minoritising covers discourses, attitudes, and practices that produce othering processes. Furthermore, a 'minority' is not understood as a group that exists on the basis of inherent characteristics, but rather refers to certain markers, such as black skin, blond hair, or the hijab, that are discursively and socially constructed as border markers and as testimonials to how 'they' and 'we' are, by nature or as a fact of culture (Narayan, 1997). Just as the signs that are associated with different groups, categories and positions can change, so can the categories and their positions within the different axes of power. This means that it is not a given that 'migrant women/men' will remain in this category forever. Stubberud thematises this capacity for exceeding categories by asking how au pairs in Norway negotiate their intimate relations with members of their host families and with partners outside the family in order to get access to formal and informal citizenship and become part of Norwegian society (Chap. 6). From a different starting point, the film *The Intouchables* problematises how a black male care worker succeeds in transcending his minority subject position by entering into a homosocial relation with his employer (Ringrose, Chap. 9).

We argue that research on what Brah labels 'minoritising' must be accompanied by a majority-inclusive approach (Staunæs, 2003). This approach perceives majority and minority as categories that are produced, sustained, and subverted in relation to each other, majority being positioned as 'the first' and minority as 'the other' (Søndergaard, 2000; Staunæs, 2003). Furthermore, we understand the constructions of 'firstness' and 'otherness' as unstable categories, whereby a hegemonic majority grants itself the power to define borders. As such, the white, Western middle-class woman is reproduced as Woman, that is, given her position as 'the first', while the 'the third-world' woman is reproduced as 'the other' (Lewis, 2006; Mohanty, 1988). In this volume, we are concerned with which markers work as borders between 'us' and 'them', and further, with investigating to what extent gender equality is one such border marker. What other axes of difference does gender equality and/or citizenship intertwine with, and what are the effects of these intersections? How do understandings and practices produce positions of majority and minority? These are perspectives that have inspired several of the contributors. While Cox and Busch analyse how the intertwining of migration regulations, the deregulation of the au pair scheme and prejudices among the au pair employers, produces inequalities amongst au pairs in the UK (Chap. 5), Marchetti discusses how the matrix of migration regimes and citizenship produces differences among Filipina domestic workers in Amsterdam and Rome (Chap. 7).

Finally, we approach the constructions of minority and majority as resulting from the way categories intersect, intermingle, overrule, capture, differentiate, and transgress each other (Staunæs, 2003). This means that we have tried to go beyond the additive models of oppression and focus on how different categories, such as 'race'/ethnicity and gender, and local categories such as 'Norwegian families' and 'migrant woman' are constructed. The concept of intersectionality aims at capturing how categories in complex ways are dynamically and mutually intertwined with each other in hierarchical patterns, and how subjectivities are constructed in these intersections of multiple dimensions and axes of power (Gullikstad, 2010; Kristensen, 2010; Ringrose, 2013; Stubberud, 2015a). In this book, the concept of intersectionality has mainly served as a sensitising concept drawing attention to processes whereby certain people are positioned as not just different, but also as troubled and in some instances marginalised, and other people are positioned as majoritised. Furthermore, the concept has enabled the contributors to become more aware of how the 'doings' and intermingling of categories work in specific contexts, and of what the effects these 'doings' have on different people in different contexts, as well as to identify the ways in which categories such as minority and majority are saturated by 'race'/ethnicity, gender, class, and nation.

Regimes and Relations

The book is organised in two parts, plus an overall introduction and a concluding chapter. The chapters all share the same ambition, that is to examine the ways in which gender equality and citizenship as values, norms, and practices take on different forms and meanings in a range of localised contexts across Europe, and to explore the relations between gender equality and citizenships that are produced in these contexts. The two parts are distinguished by the empirical material they draw on. While the contributions in part one mostly draw on policy documents, media discourses, and parliamentary debates and acts, the contributions in part two are predominantly based on a variety of interview material, including interviews with individual employers, with couples who are joint employers, and with employees and the partners of employees.

Regimes

In the first section of the book on 'Regimes', we look at the ways in which the intersections of regimes, including care, migration, welfare, gender, labour, and taxation regimes, have impacted on domestic labourers and their employers in a variety of European contexts. As the various chapters in this section show, the effects of policies and legislation have been exclusionary in many national contexts, while in others, they have had, paradoxically, both inclusionary and exclusionary consequences. The chapters explore the ways in which different regimes combine to produce employers and employees as very different types of citizens, demonstrating that in doing so they pose a serious challenge to the European ideal of gender equality.

European-level supranational actors, such as the European Commission and the EU, have actively promoted the employment of domestic workers in private households since the early 1990s (Morel, 2015). This development has led to various European countries adopting national policies that encourage the employment of domestic workers. Even in Nordic countries with comparatively strong welfare states (Esping-Andersen, 2000; Lister, 2008), the use of private household services has become an increasingly popular option for those trying to balance paid work and care responsibilities (Gavanas & Callemann, 2013; Isaksen, 2010). Finland, for example, instituted the tax subsidy system for household services in 2001.

Lena Näre's 'Neoliberal Citizenship and Domestic Service in Finland: A Return to a Servant Society?' (Chap. 2) focuses on the consequences of the resurgence of domestic labour spearheaded by such policies in the light of neoliberalism. She looks at the increasing employment of household workers in a context in which private markets are regarded as the best answer to structural problems, such as employers' increased demands for flexibility and long working hours. In this same context, because of their vulnerable citizenship status and limited options, migrant workers are forced to accept low-paid jobs in stratified labour markets.

Näre examines the prevalence of domestic work as part of the return to a servant society which is radically destabilising the grand narrative of Western modernisation as progress towards more egalitarian societies based on a differentiated division of labour. Her chapter focuses on how the use of domestic services has been justified in parliamentary debates on tax credits on domestic services and in interviews with representatives of private cleaning companies. It argues that an ideological shift has taken place in the Nordic countries in that the employment of a cleaner is no longer stigmatised, but has rather become normalised especially among dual-earner families and those of older age. This shift is explored as indicative of a wider social change that Näre terms 'neoliberal citizenship' (i.e. the marketisation and 'contractualisation' of citizenship), which has paved the way for increased privatisation of services and for the privatisation of risk and responsibility according to neoliberal ideals.

In Norway, as in Finland, there has been steady increase in the demand for cleaners and au pairs. Up until 2004, au pairs were categorised as migrant workers but have since been re-categorised as students. In 'The Au Pair Scheme as "Cultural Exchange": Effects of Norwegian Au Pair Policy on Gender Equality and Citizenship' (Chap. 3), Berit Gullikstad and Trine Annfelt note that despite these changes in the status of the au pair, the 1969 European agreement on the au pair placement as cultural exchange has continued to hold. Meanwhile Norway has gone from being a sending country to being a wealthy destination and receiving country, with most au pairs coming from the Global South.

These authors' research is contextualised against a national backdrop where gender equality is considered an intrinsic aspect of citizenship. Their chapter analyses the way in which gender equality and inclusion, as primary dimensions of citizenship in Norwegian contemporary policies, are at stake when it comes to female work migration and the au pair scheme in particular. The analysis is based on Norwegian government policies relating to the au pair scheme examined via government and parliamentary policy documents, administrative regulations and rules, and media statements. The authors argue that the perpetuation of the 'cultural exchange' basis for au pairing produces representations of au pairs as young people on an educational journey and not as migrant women with agency. Furthermore, under-communicating the work dimension of the au pair programme in official documentation makes the needs and interests of the au pair invisible. They conclude that the 'win–win situation' invoked by the authorities enables gender equality to be reproduced as a national concern, while at the same time making migrant women's rights disappear from view.

With Elin Peterson's contribution 'Paid Domestic Work in Spain: Gendered Framings of Work and Care in Policies on Social Citizenship' (Chap. 4), we move south to Spain, which unlike its Nordic counterparts is conceptualised as a non-caring state where the family care model prevails. But while Spanish households with low incomes continue to rely on informal care provided by family members, well-off families are increasingly turning to market-provided services. As a result, caring for older people in private homes has become a common source of employment for migrant women.

In her study of Spanish domestic labour, Peterson analyses domestic workers' social citizenship status and the role and value attributed to paid domestic work in public policy. In particular, she examines key documents, such as acts, bills, and parliamentary debates relating to three policy areas, namely the regulation of household employment, the dependent care policy, and the policies facilitating the reconciliation of work and family life. The policies can all be seen as extending social citizenship in Spain—strengthening social- and labour-related rights for employees in the household service sector, announcing new social rights and support for dependent people, and introducing improved rights for combining work and care for small children. However, Peterson demonstrates that the very policies that aim for a more inclusive citizenship also have exclusionary effects, at the expense of migrant domestic workers.

In 'Gendered Work and Citizenship: Diverse Experiences of Au Pairing in the UK' (Chap. 5), Rosie Cox and Nicky Busch also focus on exclusion, this time on the exclusionary aspects of the UK migration regime. The authors show that the UK migration regime combines with other factors to produce inequalities between au pairs. Drawing on findings from the interviews with au pairs and employers from 15 European countries, they examine the different experiences of citizenship of au pairs in the UK who all ostensibly have equal citizenship rights as EU nationals. While au pairing in the UK was largely deregulated when the Au Pair Visa was abolished in 2008, since then the UK government has provided no definition of au pairing or guidance on how au pairs should be treated, while specifically excluding au pairs from the categories of 'worker' and 'employee' and explicitly denying them rights to the National Minimum Wage and other labour protections.

Cox and Busch show how deregulation of the au pair sector has allowed a hierarchy of au pairs to develop with only those from the most prosperous states able to access the most 'au pair-like' conditions. They demonstrate that those nationals of new EU member states and those who face low pay or high unemployment at home are more likely to accept 'work-like' conditions without opportunities for cultural exchange. They conclude that between them, the prejudices and preferences of host families, UK migration rules, and the very different opportunities available to au pairs in their home countries work to produce a gap between the putative equality of formal EU citizenship, which is shared by all, and the practical and lived experience of citizenship as migrants in the UK.

Relations

The second part of the book, 'Relations', focuses on the many relations which are at play when domestic labour and care work are undertaken. These include relations between employers (couples who engage cleaners), between employers and employees, between employees and their partners, between employees and their romantic interests, and between employees and their extended family. The contributions relate to a variety of types of domestic labour and care work performed by both men and women in several European contexts. These include Polish handymen in Germany, European and South-Asian au pairs in Norway, Filipina domestic labourers in Italy and the Netherlands, and migrant care workers in France. While all the chapters engage with relational dynamics, Kristensen's contribution (Chap. 8) predominantly relates to the employer's perspective, three others focus mainly on the relations between employers and employees (Marchetti, Chap. 7; Ewa Palenga-Möllenbeck, Chap. 10; and Ringrose, Chap. 9), while the first contribution in this section (Stubberud, Chap. 6) is mostly concerned with the relation between employees and their dating interests.

All the chapters in this section provide evidence of the complex forms of negotiations which take place between employers and employees. In doing so they demonstrate how these negotiations in many different ways produce both the employee and the employer as certain kinds of citizens, imbricated in divergent understandings of both gender and gender equality.

In the first contribution in this section, 'From Intimate Relations to Citizenship? Au Pairing and the Potential for Citizenship in Norway' (Chap. 6), Elisabeth Stubberud points out that no contemporary exploration of citizenship can be complete without considering the changing ways in which people's intimate relations, family relations, and networks of friends and acquaintances, as well as their gender, affect the way in which they do citizenship.

In this context, Stubberud's chapter explores au pairs' intimate relations and their potential to facilitate access to formal as well as informal citizenship. Stubberud looks in particular at the ways in which intimate relations come into play when au pairs are looking for more secure long-term citizenship, in a context where au pairing has become a migration route, even though it was never intended as such. She points to the many challenges involved in playing the role of both 'family member' (big sister) and 'employee' when both your formal and informal citizenship rights and belongings depend on your relation with the host family. Given that the relation with the host family and the au pair contract only provide for a limited kind of citizenship, Stubberud explores other immediate and long-term alternative options available to the au pair via relationships outside the 'host' family.

Drawing on au pairs' narratives of dating and on their relations to host families, she demonstrates that access to citizenship is both highly gendered and intertwined with personal and intimate relationships with host families/employers, as well as with partners or potential partners. Yet, while au pairs' narratives of dating suggest a greater degree of agency than those of their 'working' relationships with host families - whom they depend on for both formal and informal citizenship, she argues that they still entail a sense of cruel optimism since formal citizenship is always governed from above.

As several of the contributions point out, the common configuration of domestic workers and au pairs within fictive family relations has important consequences for their formal and informal citizenship. While in the context of Stubberud's research, the discourse of the Norwegian au pair scheme places the au pair in a symbolic family structure in which she is figured as a 'big sister', the following chapter invokes the mother–daughter dynamic. In 'Citizenship and Maternalism in Migrant Domestic Labour: Filipina Workers and Their Employers in Amsterdam and Rome' (Chap. 7), Sabrina Marchetti examines the fictive family relation in terms of maternalism. For her research, Marchetti interviewed Italian and Dutch women and their Filipina employees who are privately employed by them to clean their homes in the cities of Rome and Amsterdam. She notes that while the employers in this study enjoy full citizenship rights, the employees are often undocumented migrants or partial citizens. However, despite this asymmetry, both employers and employees perceived their relation to be 'special' and immune from what they regarded as the typical exploitative dimensions of domestic labour.

Marchetti's study shows that these employer–employee relationships are embedded in a maternalistic setting, where the employers' willingness to help their employees with their legal and bureaucratic challenges ultimately serves to reinforce their own superior socio-economic position as non-migrant women. This is because this help is predicated on a victimising depiction of their employees as transnational mothers who are dependent on their goodwill to maintain their caring commitments. Filipina employees on the other hand, while benefitting from and soliciting the supportive role of their employers, end up performing unpaid tasks as a mark of gratitude. Marchetti's study shows how employers and employees reciprocally exchange favours, creating a space of citizenship negotiations which enables resistance against superimposed legal conditions but at the same time produces a context in which disparaging representations of Filipinas, as migrant women and mothers, are strengthened.

The next chapter, Guro Korsnes Kristensen's 'Paid Migrant Domestic Labour in Gender Equal Norway: A Win–Win Arrangement?' (Chap. 8) also focuses on an employer–employee relation that is imagined as positive, this time by employers who regard domestic labour as a win–win situation for both sides. Kristensen's study is predicated on a national context where gender equality is at the core of cultural identity. Norway's main strategies in achieving gender equality has been to strengthen women's economic independence through increasing their labour market participation and to normalise men's involvement in domestic work and care work. As Kristensen notes, running in parallel to this normative and political focus on gender equality, more and more Norwegian families, particularly those with young children, are employing migrant women to help out with domestic work. On the one hand, these migrant women achieve economic and social independence through paid work, but on the other hand, they are excluded from basic citizenship rights due to unclear and ambiguous au pair arrangements and poorly regulated or illegal employments.

Kristensen's chapter draw on on qualitative interviews with parents of young children who are either hiring or intending to employ a domestic cleaner or an au pair. It looks at the ways in which the implementation of the Norwegian model of gender equality is closely related to specific forms of citizenship and to specific notions of 'the good citizen'. It argues that paid migrant domestic labour has smoothed the implementation of both the dual-earner and the dual-carer aspects of the gender equality ideal. It also demonstrates that the employers, by focusing on the migrant women's empowerment (in the country of origin) rather than their exploitation and subordination (in Norway), create a win–win narrative in which paid migrant domestic labour is made compatible with the Norwegian citizenship ideals of gender equality and social equality.

While Kristensen's chapter shows that migrant domestic labour helps to maintain an idealised view of the gender equal Norwegian citizen, Priscilla Ringrose's 'The Intouchables: Care Work, Homosociality, and National Fantasy' (Chap. 9) looks at how an idealised vision of the French nation is produced in Olivier Nakache and Éric Toledano's award winning 2011 movie The Intouchables. The film's appeal rests on the standard exploitation of an unlikely friendship between a mismatched pair, a wealthy disabled white Frenchman and his black male migrant carer, who is keen to distance himself from what he perceives to be the feminised tasks associated with care work. In addition to casting a spotlight on the power relations at work in the central employer–employee relation, the film also engages with the relations between care workers and their families, as well as with carers' involvement in their employers' dating interests.

Ringrose argues that the context of the film, contemporary France, with its republican model of citizenship and vexed relation to immigration, raises particular questions about the racial and gendered framing of the central employee–employer relation. She suggests that the framing of the employer–employee relation in the film simply functions as a form of 'protective fiction', a fantasy narrative support that gives consistency to the notion of a united French nation, free from the dissentions of class and 'race'. This fantasy is imagined at the interface between reality and horror, as the 'psychic glue' (Rose, 1998, p. 3) which 'protects the nation/al from the horrors of the "real" that threaten the disintegration of the self; [and which] it keeps it whole' (Fortier, 2008, p. 12).

Ringrose suggests that the homosocial relation that emerges between employee and employers in *The Intouchables* serves to protect the viewer from the real, whether that is the real lives of (most) disabled people, immigrants or care workers, or the structural conditions that circumscribe them. As such, the relation does not ultimately challenge the unequal power dynamics of the assimilative model of citizenship. Instead, it sanitises both care work and immigration, and in so doing succeeds in complying with colonialism.

The last chapter in this section, 'Unequal Fatherhoods: Citizenship, Gender, and Masculinities in Outsourced "Male" Domestic Work' (Chap. 10) by Ewa Palenga-Möllenbeck, also engages with male domestic work and notions of masculinity. But while *The Intouchables* focuses on the ways in which male domestic workers negotiate what they perceive to be the feminised aspect of this work, Palenga-Möllenbeck's study is concerned with the ways in which male household workers negotiate fatherhood. The chapter looks in particular at migrant Polish handymen and on the German employers who outsource 'male' domestic work to them. For 25 years, these Polish handymen have been dominating the supply side of a firmly established semi-legal market for domestic work. While German policy-makers consider the outsourcing of domestic work to be a viable solution to the work–family balance for some parts of the population and to unemployment for others, this chapter shows that there are serious side effects to this type of outsourcing. In particular, it engenders and rigidifies inequality between Western and Eastern Europe in terms of access to social reproductive work.

Palenga-Möllenbeck draws on interviews with Polish handymen and their partners and with German employers (fathers and/or mothers) who contract handymen. She shows that this kind of outsourcing enables German men to deal with domestic work selectively and spend 'quality time' with their families. On the other hand, the Polish handymen, unlike their employers, cannot fully live up to the expectations of modern fatherhood. As absent fathers and breadwinners, they reproduce a patriarchal model of family life and have unequal access to intimate relations. This means that the supposedly 'modern' and gender-equal lifestyle of German middle-class fathers is dependent on the mobility and precarious working and living conditions of Polish fathers and, paradoxically, on the gender-unequal relations in their own families.

The concluding chapter provides a synthesis of the main findings from the empirical material. In particular it shows how the contributors' analysis of the complex intersections of gender, nationality/ethnicity/'race', and social class which this multifaceted material brings to play casts a critical light on the political and cultural discourses of gender equality and citizenship unfolding in different localised contexts across Europe.

References

Anderson, B. (2000). *Doing the dirty work. The global politics of domestic labour*. London and New York: Zed Books.
Anderson, B. (2007). A very private business. Exploring the demand for migrant domestic workers. *European Journal of Women's Studies, 14*(3), 247–264.
Anderson, B., & Shutes, I. (Eds.) (2014). *Migration and care labour. Theory, policy and politics*. Houndsmill, Basingstoke, Hamshire: Palgrave Macmillan.
Annfelt, T., & Gullikstad, B. (2013). Kjønnslikestilling i inkluderingens tjeneste. *Tidsskrift for kjønnsforskning, 37*(3–4), 309–328.
Anthias, F., Morokvasic-Müller, M., & Kontos, M. (2013). Introduction: Paradoxes of integration. In F. Anthias, M. Morokvasic-Müller, & M. Kontos (Eds.), *Paradoxes of integration: Female migrants in Europe*. International Perspectives on Migration 4. Dordrecht: Springer Science+Business Media. doi:10.1007/978-94-007-4842-2_1.

Bauböck, R. (2011). Temporary migrants, partial citizenship and hypermigration. *Critical Review of International Social and Political Philosophy,* *14*(5), 665–693.
Benhabib, S., & Resnik, J. (Eds.) (2009). *Migrations and mobilities. Citizenship, borders and gender.* New York: New York University Press.
Berg, A.-J., Flemmen, A. B., & Gullikstad, B. (Eds.) (2010). *Likestilte norskheter: Om kjønn og etnisitet.* Trondheim: Tapir akademisk forlag.
Bikova, M. (2015). In a minefield of transnational social relations—Filipino au pairs between moral obligations and personal amibitions. In R. Cox (Ed.), *Au pair's lives in a global context. Sister or servant?* Basingstoke: Palgrave Macmillan.
Bikova, M. (2010). The snake in the grass of gender equality. In L. W. Isaksen (Ed.), *Global care work: Gender and migration in Nordic societies.* Lund: Nordic Academic Press.
Bosniak, L. (2009). Citizenship, non-citizenship, and the transnationalization of domestic work. In S. Benhabib & J. Resnik (Eds.), *Migrations and mobilities. Citizenship, borders and gender.* New York: New York University Press.
Brah, A. (2003). Diaspora, border and transnational identities. In R. Lewis & S. Mills (Eds.), *Feminist postcoloninal theory.* Edinburgh: Edinburgh University Press.
Cho, S., Crenshaw, K. W., & McCall, L. (2013). Toward a field of intersectionality studies: Theory, applications, and praxis. *Signs, 38*(4), 785–810.
Christensen, H. R., & Breengaard, M. H. (2011). Mainstreaming gender, diversity and citizenship: Concepts and methodologies. *FEMCIT. WP7 Working Paper No. 4.* Copenhagen: University of Copenhagen.
Cox, R. (2006). *The servant problem: Domestic employment in a global economy.* London: Tauris.
Cox, R. (2012). Invisible Au pairs: Gendered work and migration regimes. In R. Sollund (Ed.), *Transnational migration, gender and rights.* Advances in Ecopolitics (Vol. 10, pp. 33–52). Bingley: Emarald Group Publishing.
Cox, R. (Ed.) (2015). *Au pair's lives in a global context. Sister or servant?* Basingstoke: Palgrave Macmillan.
Davis, K. (2008). Intersectionality as buzzword. A sociology of science perspective on what makes a feminist theory successful. *Feminist Theory, 9*(1), 67–85.
Dobrowolsky, A., & Tastsoglou, E. (2006). Crossing boundaries and making connections. In E. Tastsoglou & A. Dobrowolsky (Eds.), *Women, migration and citizenship. Making local, national and transnational connections.* Aldershot, Burlington: Ashgate.
Eggebø, H. (2012). *The regulation of marriage migration to Norway.* Doctoral dissertation, University of Bergen.

Einarsdottir, T., & Thorvaldsdottir, T. (2007). Gender equality and the intersectional turn. *Kvinder, køn & forskning, 16* Vol 16 (1), 20–31.
Ellingsæter, A.-L., & Leira, A. (2006). Introduction: Politicising parenthood in Scandinavia. In A.-L. Ellingsæter & A. Leira (Eds.), *Politicising parenthood in Scandinavia*. Bristol: The Polity Press.
Esping-Andersen, G. (2000). *A welfare state for the 21st century. Ageing societies, knowledge-based economies, and the sustainability of the European welfare state.* Unpublished paper.
Eveline, J., & Bacchi, C. (2005). What are we mainstreaming when we mainstream gender? *International Feminist Journal of Politics, 7*(4), 496–512.
Fortier, A.-M. (2008). *Multicultural horizons: Diversity and the limits of the civil nation*. London: Routledge.
Gavanas, A., & Callemann, C. (Eds.) (2013). *Rena hem på smutsiga villkor? Hushållstjänster, migration och globalisering*. Göteborg/Stockholm: Makadam Förlag.
Grossman, J. L., & McClain, L. C. (2009). Introduction. In L. C. McClain & J. L. Grossman (Eds.), *Gender equality. Dimensions of women's equal citizenship*. Cambridge: Cambrigde University Press.
Gullikstad, B. (2010). Når likestilling blir ulikhet. Interseksjonalitet i arbeidslivet. In A.-J. Berg, A. B. Flemmen, & B. Gullikstad (Eds.), *Likestilte norskheter. Om kjønn og etnisitet*. Trondheim: Tapir akademisk forlag.
Hall, T., & Williamson, H. (1999). *Citizenship and community*. New York: Youth Work Press.
Halsaa, B., Roseneil, S. and S. Sümer (Eds.). (2012) *Remaking citizenship in multicultural Europe: Women's movements, gender and diversity*. Basingstoke: Palgrave Macmillan.
Hammar, T. (1990). *Democracy and the nation state: Aliens, denizens and citizens in a world of international migration*. Aldershot: Avebury.
Hochchild, A. R. (2000). The nanny chain. *The American Prospect, 11*(4), 32–36.
Hondagneu-Sotelo, P. (2001). *Doméstica: Immigrant workers cleaning and caring in the shadows of affluence*. Berkeley: University of California.
ILO. (2013). *Domestic workers across the world. Global and regional statistics and the extent of legal protection*. Geneva: International Labour Office.
Isaksen, L. W. (2007). Gender, care work and globalisation. Local problems and global solutions in the Norwegian welfare state. In M. Griffin-Cohen & J. Brodie (Eds.), *Remapping gender in the new global order*. London and New York: Routledge.

Isaksen, L. W. (2010). Introduction: Global care work in Nordic societies. In L. W. Isaksen (Ed.), *Global care work: Gender and migration in Nordic societies*. Lund: Nordic Academic Press.
Isin, E. F., & Nielsen, G. M. (2008). *Acts of citizenship*. New York: Zed Books.
Isin, E. F., Nyers, P., & Turner, B. S. (2013). *Citizenship between past and future*. New York: Taylor & Francis.
Joppke, C. (2007). Transformation of citizenship: Status, rights, identity. *Citizenship Studies, 11*(1), 37–48.
kennedy-mcfoy, M. (2012). Remaking citizenship from the margins: Migrant and minoritized women's organizations in Europe. In B. Halsaa, S. Roseneil, & S. Sümer (Eds.), *Remaking citizenship in the multicultural Europe: Women's movements, gender and diversity*. Basinstoke: Palgrave Mcmillan.
Keskinen, S., Tuori, S., Irni, S., & Mulinari, D. (Eds.) (2009). *Complying with colonialism. Gender, race and ethnicity in the Nordic region*. Farnham: Ashgate.
Kilkey, M., Perrons, D., Plomien, A. with Hondagneu-Soleto, P., & Ramirez, H. (2013) *Gender, migration and domestic work. Masculinities, male labour and fathering in the UK and USA*. Houndmills: Palgrave Macmillan.
Kristensen, G. K. (2010). Trad eller trendy med tre. Om barnetall, likestilling og "norskhet". In A.-J. Berg, A. B. Flemmen, & B. Gullikstad (Eds.), *Likestilte norskheter. Om kjønn og etnisitet*. Trondheim: Tapir akademisk forlag.
Kristensen, G. K. (2015). A fair deal? Paid domestic labour in social democratic Norway. In A. Triandafyllidou & S. Marchetti (Eds.), *Employers, agencies and immigration: Paying for care*. Franham: Ashgate.
Kvist, E., & Peterson, E. (2010). What has gender equality got to do with it? An analysis of policy debates surrounding domestic services in the welfare states of Spain and Sweden. *Nordic Journal of Feminist and Gender Research, 18*(3), 185–203.
Kymlicka, W. (1995). *Multicultural citizenship. A liberal theory of minority rights*. Oxford: Oxford University Press.
Lan, P.-C. (2006). *Global cinderellas: Migrant domestics and newly rich employers in Taiwan*. Durham, NC: Duke University Press.
Lewis, G. (2006). Imaginaries of Europe: Technologies of gender, economics of power. *European Journal of Women Studies, 2*, 87–103.
Lister, R. (2003). *Citizenship: Feminist perspectives*. New York: New York University Press.
Lister, R. (2008). Gender, citizenship and social justice in the Nordic welfare states: A view from the outside. In K. Melby, A.-B. Ravn, & C. C. Wetterberg (Eds.), *Gender equality and welfare politics in Scandinavia. The limits of political ambition?* Bristol: The Policy Press.

Lister, R., Williams, F., Anttonen, A., Bussemaker, J., Gerhard, U., Heinen, J., et al. (2007). *Gendering citizenship in Western Europe: New challenges for citizenship research in a cross-national context*. Bristol: Policy Press.

Lutz, H. (2007). The intimate "other". Migrant domestic workers in Europe. In E. Berggren, et al. (Eds.), *Irregular migration, informal labour and community: A challenge for Europe* (pp. 226–241). Maastricht: Shaker Publishing.

Lutz, H. (2008). *Migration and domestic work: A European perspective on a global theme*. Farnham: Ashgate.

Lutz, H. (2011). *The new maids. Transnational women and the care economy*. London: Zed Books.

Macklin, A. (1994). On the outside looking in: Foreign domestic workers in Canada. In W. Giles & S. Arat-Koc (Eds.), *Maid in the market: Women's paid domestic labour*. Halifax: Fernwood Publishing.

Manalansan, M. (2006). Queer intersections: Sexuality and gender in migration studies. *International Migration Review, 40*(1), 224–249.

Mohanty, C. T. (1988). Under 'Western eyes': Feminist scholarship and colonial discourses. *Feminist Review*, (30), 65–88.

Morel, N. (2015). Servants for the knowledge-based economy? The political economy of domestic services in Europe. *Social Politics, 22*(2), 170–192.

Moss, P., & Kamerman, S. (Eds.) (2009). *The politics of parental leave policies*. Bristol: The Policy Press.

Narayan, U. (1997). Contesting cultures. Westernization, respect for cultures and third world feminists. In L. Nicholson (Ed.), *The second wave. A reader in feminist theory*. New York: Routledge.

Näre, L. (2010). Sri Lankan men working as cleaners and carers: Negotiating masculinity in Naples. *Men and Masculinities, 13*(1), 65–86.

Näre, L. (2011). The moral economy of domestic and care labour: Migrant workers in Naples, Italy. *Sociology, 45*(3), 396–412.

Nentwich, J. C. (2006). Changing gender: The discursive construction of equal opportunities. *Gender, Work & Organization, 13*(6), 499–521.

Pajnik, M., & Bajt, V. (2013). Civic participation of migrant women: Employing strategies of active citizenship. In F. M. Anthias, et al. (Eds.), *Paradoxes of integration: Female migrants in Europe*. Dordrecht: Springer.

Palenga-Möllenbeck, E. (2013). New maids—New butlers? Polish domestic workers in Germany and commodification of social reproductive work. In B. Aulenbacher & C. Innreiter-Moser (Eds.), *Making the difference—Critical perspectives on the configuration of work, diversity and inequalities*. Special issue of *Equality, Diversity and Inclusion: An international Journal, 32*(6), 557–574.

Parreñas, R. (2001). *Servants of globalization. Women, migration and domestic work*. Standford: Stanford University Press.
Predelli, L. N., Halsaa, B., & Thun, C. (2012). 'Citizenship is not a word I use': How women's movements activists understand citizenship. In B. Halsaa, S. Roseneil, & S. Sümer (Eds.), *Remaking citizenship in multicultural Europe: Women's movements, gender and diversity*. London: Palgrave.
Purkayvastha, B. (2012). Intersectionality in a transnational world. Symposium on Patricia Hill Collins. *Gender & Society, 26*(1), 55–66.
Ringrose, P. (2013). Migrants of the new Norway: Sara Johnsen's Upperdog. *Tidsskrift for kjønnsforskning, 37*(1), 26–45.
Rose, J. (1998). *States of fantasy*. Oxford: Clarendon Press.
Roseneil, S., Halsaa, B., & Sümer, S. (2012). Remaking citizenship in multicultural Europe: Women's movements, gender and diversity. In B. Halsaa, S. Roseneil, & S. Sümer (Eds.), *Remaking citizenship in multicultural Europe: Women's movements, gender and diversity*. London: Palgrave.
Somers, M. (2008). *Genealogies of citizenship*. Cambridge: Cambridge University Press.
Søndergaard, D. M. (2000). Destabiliserende diskursanalyse: veje ind i poststrukturalistisk inspirert empirisk forskning. In H. Haavind (Ed.), *Kjønn og fortolkende metode. Metodiske muligheter i kvalitativ forskning*. Oslo: Gyldendal Akademisk.
Squires, J. (2005). Is mainstreaming transformative? Theorizing mainstreaming in the context of diversity and deliberation. *Social Politics, 12*(3), 366–388.
Staunæs, D. (2003). Where have all the subjects gone? Bringing together the concepts of intersectionality and subjectification. *Nordic Journal of Women's Studies, 10*(2), 101–110.
Stenum, H. (2010). Au-pair migration and new inequalities. The transnational production of corruption. In L. W. Isaksen (Ed.), *Global care work: Gender and migration in Nordic societies*. Lund: Nordic Academic Press.
Strasser, S. (2012). Rethinking citizenship: Critical encounters with feminist, multicultural and transnational concepts of citizenship. In B. Halsaa, S. Roseneil, & S. Sümer (Eds.), *Remaking citizenship in multicultural Europe: Women's movements, gender and diversity*. London: Palgrave.
Stubberud, E. (2015a). *Au pairing in Norway. The production of a (non-) worker*. PhD thesis, Department of Interdisciplinary Studies of Culture, Faculty of Humanities, Norwegian University of Science and Technology.
Stubberud, E. (2015b). "It's not much": Affective (boundary) work in the Au pair scheme. In R. Cox (Ed.), *Au pair's lives in a global context. Sister or servant?* Basingstoke: Palgrave Macmillan.

Tastsoglou, E., & Dobrowolsky, A. (Eds.) (2006). *Women, migration and citizenship. Making local, national and transnational connections*. Aldershot: Ashgate.

The European Institute for Gender Equality. Retrieved from http://eige.europa.eu/gender-mainstreaming/what-is-gender-mainstreamingwebsite of EIGE

Triandafyllidou, A. (2013). *Irregular migration in Europe. Who cares?* Farnham/Burlington: Ashgate.

Triandafyllidou, A., & Marchetti, S. (2015). Paying for care: Advantages and challenges for the employers. In A. Triandafyllidou & S. Marchetti (Eds.), *Employers, agencies and immigration: Paying for care*. Farnham/Burlington: Ashgate.

Tronto, J. C. (2002). The "nanny" question in feminism. *Hypatia, 17*(2), 34–49.

Verloo, M. (2006). Multiple inequalities, intersectionality and the European Union. *European Journal of Women's Studies, 13*(3), 211–229.

Walby, S. (2005). Gender mainstreaming: Productive tensions in theory and practice. *Social Politics, 12*(3), 321–343.

Yeates, N. (2012). Global care chains: A state-of-the-art review and future directions in care transnationalization research. *Global Networks, 12*(2), 135–154.

Yuval-Davis, N. (1999). The "multi-layered citizen". *International Feminist Journal of Politics, 1*(1), 119–136.

Yuval-Davis, N. (2006). Belonging and the politics of belonging. *Patterns of Prejudice, 40*(3), 197–214.

2

Neoliberal Citizenship and Domestic Service in Finland: A Return to a Servant Society?

Lena Näre

Introduction

In the 1970s, domestic service was considered a premodern occupation and, as such, contradictory to the egalitarianism and secularism of modern societies. It was deemed to become obsolete (Coser, 1973). However, as the chapters in this volume—and the range of existing international literature on paid domestic and care work in private households—demonstrate (see, for example, Anderson, 2000; Cox, 2004; Isaksen, 2010; Kristensen, 2015; Lutz, 2008, 2011; Palenga-Möllenbeck, 2013; Triandafyllidou & Marchetti, 2015), paid domestic and care work in private households is by no means disappearing, but thriving in the

L. Näre
Department of Social Research, University of Helsinki, Helsinki, Finland

twenty-first century.[1] European-level supranational actors (the European Commission, followed by the European Union (EU)) have actively promoted the employment of domestic workers in private households since the early 1990s (Morel, 2015). This development has led various countries in continental and Northern Europe to adopt national policies that encourage the employment of domestic workers.[2] Thus, also in Nordic countries with comparatively strong welfare states, families and individuals are outsourcing their care and domestic work to other women—and also men—from poorer backgrounds, many of whom are migrants. This development, I argue, can be perceived as a return to a servant society in a global form. It can be understood as radically destabilising the grand narrative of Western modernisation as progressive and linear development towards more egalitarian societies based on a differentiated division of labour (Näre, 2012; see also Bhambra, 2007). This chapter examines the increase in household employment in Europe and, in particular, Finland. Drawing on qualitative research data, it analyses the emergence of a private domestic service sector in Finland, and the ways in which the employment of household workers has been justified.

The use of private household services has become increasingly popular in the Nordic countries as a means to cover for shortages in elder care services, to provide 'flexibility' in childcare in dual-earner families and to pay for more free time with the family by transferring the burden of household work to other people (for example, Bikova, 2010; Fjell, 2010; Gavanas, 2010, 2013; Kristensen, 2015; Määttä, 2008; Platzer, 2006). Increasingly, the providers of domestic services are migrant workers who lack full citizenship rights in the countries where they live and work. The increased demand for household services and the provision of these services by migrant workers who lack full access to social citizenship rights have led to the recommodification of labour in two interconnected

---

[1] This research has been funded by the Kone Foundation and the Academy of Finland project, 'The Shaping of Occupational Subjectivities of Migrant Care Workers: A Multi-Sited Analysis of Glocalising Elderly Care' (2011–2015) (project no. 251239).
[2] Since the 1990s, Germany, Belgium, France, the Netherlands, Denmark, Finland and Sweden have implemented national policies that aid the private employment of domestic and care workers, including tax rebates, voucher systems and employer social contribution exemptions (Morel, 2015).

ways. First, families and individuals are increasingly dependent on private markets to combine paid work and reproductive labour. Second, labour migrants who are not full citizens are much more dependent on labour markets, as their right to stay in a country depends on a valid work contract. Both processes of recommodification point towards a reformulation of citizenship according to neoliberal ideals, wherein individuals become increasingly dependent on private markets in their everyday lives. Finland and Sweden are illustrative cases in this regard, because, for a long time, they were considered the most egalitarian societies in the world, with low-income differences and a largely universal welfare state. However, since the mid-1980s, income differences in Finland and Sweden have been the fastest growing among the Organisation for Economic Co-operation and Development (OECD) countries (Cingano, 2014, p. 9).

The chapter argues that the introduction of public support for privatised forms of welfare such as the tax credit is part of a wider process of rearticulating citizenship according to neoliberal ideals. It discusses the notion of neoliberal citizenship as a new articulation of citizenship that is increasingly market and contract based (Somers, 2008). It draws on the conceptualisation of citizenship as a deeply gendered concept (Lister, 2003) and a dynamic and changing set of complex relationships between individuals and the state (Halsaa, Roseneil, & Sümer, 2012; Stasiulis & Bakan, 1997), and also as a complex socio-juridical apparatus that is part of the global state system (Anderson, 2013).

The impact of neoliberal structural adjustment programmes in the countries of the Global South is more readily recognised than the fact that the same neoliberal policies have also transformed the welfare states in the Global North—including Finland. In migration 'sending countries' of the Global South, such as the Philippines, neoliberal economic restructuring has reduced the state provision of social care and education and increased individuals' burden to pay for health care and education in private markets (Misra, Woodring, & Merz, 2006; Rodriguez, 2010). These welfare deficits, combined with debt-ridden and weak national economies, many of which originated in the colonial era, have created unemployment and underemployment in the Global South. On the other hand, in the Global North, working life has become more fragmented, precarious and intense due to very similar neoliberal doctrines, so that efforts to combine family and care responsibilities with the demands of working life have become more and more taxing on individuals and families. The erosion of public care provisions and the transfer of the care burden from the state to individual families—the increasing commodification of care (Lister et al., 2007; Williams & Brennan, 2012)—are neoliberal policies that have taken place in the Nordic countries. The result has been an increased demand for various domestic and care services in private households in the North and an increased supply of female and male workers in search of better employment opportunities and greater welfare and educational security from the South (Misra et al., 2006; Sassen, 2003). Hence, the introduction of the tax subsidy system, which gives private employment of household services political and moral legitimacy, calls for a rethinking of gendered citizenship in the welfare state context.

In what follows, I first discuss in more detail how I approach citizenship in this chapter, after which I discuss the increase in domestic services in Finland followed by a presentation of the data and methods. The first empirical section discusses the way in which paid domestic work has been debated in the Finnish Parliament in relation to the introduction of tax rebates for household services in Finland. The second section analyses the ways in which representatives of household service agencies discuss the demand for paid domestic work in Finland.

The Marketisation of Citizenship: Conceptualising Neoliberal Citizenship

Recent literature on paid domestic and care work has signalled the importance of taking into account migration, employment and welfare regimes (Williams, 2014; Williams & Gavanas, 2008) when analysing the increase in domestic and care work in the contemporary world. I would argue—with the authors in this volume—that as important as it is to analyse the changes in policies and practices, it is also important to understand how these changes relate to wider changes in citizenship and gender (in)equalities. An analysis of migrant care and domestic work at the intersections of migration, employment and welfare regimes must be connected to an understanding of citizenship and the gendered and racialised forms of exclusion and inclusion that it carries. The full participation of middle-class women in working life (that is, the fulfilment of their economic and social citizenship in society) depends increasingly on the domestic and care labour performed by migrant women who often lack full membership status in the countries where they reside (Bosniak, 2009).

This chapter analyses practices and discourses of paid domestic and care work employment in Finland. It argues that these changes are indicative of a wider ideological shift and formulation of citizenship—a move from egalitarianism and universalism towards increased 'marketisation' and 'contractualisation' of rights (Somers, 2008) and increased acceptance of inequalities in labour markets and private households.

In my understanding of citizenship, I draw on an Arendtian notion of citizenship as the 'right to have rights', as developed by Margaret Somers (2008). Citizenship as the 'right to have rights' combines two types of rights: first, the foundational right to membership in a political community as the social inclusion in civil society; and second, a bundle of rights including social, cultural and economic rights (Somers, 2008, pp. 5–6). Both types of rights must include human rights. Moreover, Somers expands the notion of citizenship from the relationship between the individual and the state to encompass 'a triadic assemblage of shifting institutional and discursive relationships and struggles for power among state, market and civil society' (Somers, 2008, p. 20). However, these relationships between the individual and the state limit citizenship to a specific nation state context, but citizenship ought to be conceptualised more broadly as part of a global state system, as Bridget Anderson (2013) has argued.

Alongside Somers, I lean on the feminist critique of mainstream political theory's conceptualisation of citizenship as a universal, ahistorical concept and a container of rights and duties. Feminists have emphasised the gendered and embodied dimensions of citizenship and the fact that it is necessarily a historical construction (Lister, 2003). This grounded approach to citizenship directs us to investigate the ways in which citizenship is understood and practised and the institutional and discursive relationships among state, market and civil society that constitute the realm and regime of citizenship at a given time and in a given place. I argue that the metadiscourse framing citizenship today is neoliberalism. Here, neoliberalism is not only understood as a political and economic philosophy, but also as a governmental practice and an articulation of the relations between the state, the market and citizenship (see, for example, Wacquant, 2012, p. 71). Specifically, neoliberalism introduces

> market and quasi-market arrangements into areas of social life which had hitherto been organised in other ways—the corporatisation and privatisation of state agencies, the promotion of competition and individual choice in health, education and other areas of what Marshall regarded as the proper sphere of social policy, the use of financial markets (...) to regulate the conduct of states, and so on. (Hindess, 2002, p. 140)

In a similar fashion, Wendy Brown (2003, p. 199) has argued that extending 'economic rationality to formerly non-economic domains and institutions extends to individual conduct, or more precisely, prescribes citizens-subject conduct in a neo-liberal order'.

Neoliberal citizenship then refers to a move from a relationship between citizens and the state that is based on membership, to a relationship that is conditional and organised according to market logic[3] and an exchange similar to what Somers (2008, p. 2) terms the 'contractualization of citizenship', but which I would prefer to call the 'marketisation of citizenship', to emphasise individuals' increased dependence on private markets. Somers writes about the contractualisation of citizenship as follows:

> Contractualization of citizenship distorts the meaning of citizenship from that of a shared fate among equals to that of conditional privilege. The growing moral authority of both market and contract makes social inclusion and moral worth no longer inherent rights but rather earned privileges that are wholly conditional upon the ability to exchange something of equal value. (Somers, 2008, p. 3)

---

[3] By the logic of the market, I understand various 'discursive and material practices closely aligned with market liberalism and articulated around notions of flexibility, individual freedom and responsibility' (Fournier, 2000, p. 77).

2 Neoliberal Citizenship and Domestic Service in Finland ...

In other words, contractualisation of citizenship means that social inclusion is based on exchange, rather than on membership-based parity. Neoliberal articulations of citizenship signify that individuals are increasingly bearing the risks and responsibilities for the consequences of their actions, regardless of the causes and social constraints on their action, such as limited public care or welfare benefits (Brown, 2003).

Hence, neoliberalism is a wider discourse and mode of governance that affects the way in which citizen-subjects are perceived. Formulations of neoliberal citizenship go hand in hand with a reimagining of the state as a market actor (Brown, 2003). A neoliberal understanding of the state and citizenship is deeply ingrained with specific articulations of labour and processes of labour power (see Clarke, 2004). An important labour process, which has become the norm in most parts of the world, is the two-earner family norm. Disturbingly, as Nancy Fraser (2009) has argued, here, second-wave feminism's critique of the family wage has been part and parcel in providing a justification for such development:

> [Second-wave feminism's] critique of the family wage now supplies a good part of the romance that invests flexible capitalism with a higher meaning and a moral point. Endowing their daily struggles with an ethical meaning, the feminist romance attracts women at both ends of the social spectrum: at one end, the female cadres of the professional middle classes, determined to crack the glass ceiling; at the other end, the female temps, part-timers, low-wage service employees, domestics, sex workers, migrants, EPZ workers and microcredit borrowers, seeking not only income and material security, but also dignity, self-betterment and liberation from traditional authority. At both ends, the dream of women's emancipation is harnessed to the engine of capitalist accumulation. (Fraser, 2009, pp. 110–111)

It is the disturbing convergence between the emancipatory goals of second-wave feminism and neoliberal capitalism, I argue, that limits the discursive space from which the employment of migrant workers as domestic and care workers is criticised. The ideal of gender equality, which is best realised when women participate equally in labour markets, can easily obscure the fact that this achievement is increasingly dependent on other women workers from migrant and poorer backgrounds taking on the care and domestic responsibilities of those women who strive towards gender equality in labour markets and in households (see Gullikstad and Annfelt; Kristensen; Peterson; all this volume). This is also why the introduction of state mechanisms that support household services can be argued in the name of promoting gender equality, as the discussion below demonstrates.

Paid Household Services in Europe and Finland

There has been an expansion in the domestic and care sector across the European (EU-15) countries. Although domestic service is more prevalent in Southern European familistic welfare regimes, the sector has expanded also in the Northern and continental European countries with conservative and universal welfare state models. According to the European Union Labour Force Survey in 2000–2010, the employment of domestic and care services increased from 5509 to 7531 million (an increase of 36.7 %), while the number of personal care workers increased from 5033 to 7128 million (an increase of 41.6 %; Abrantes, 2014). The countries with the highest growth rates of over 100 % were Sweden and Belgium for domestic work, and Austria, Finland, Luxembourg, Spain and Ireland for personal care (Abrantes, 2014). The share of women in these occupations has stayed more or less the same, with over 80 % of domestic workers and almost 90 % of personal caregivers in Europe being women (Abrantes, 2014). These figures tell us clearly that gendered division of domestic and care labour has remained intact and that there has been a significant expansion in these occupations, also in the Nordic countries where the comparatively strong welfare state model meant that labour was, for a long time (at least in part), decommodified. Historically, the development of the 'Nordic' welfare state model enforced women's labour market participation by creating public services and welfare benefits which allowed women to combine wage work and family life. Women were then doubly 'dependent' on the welfare state: for public sector jobs in the segmented labour markets of the Nordic countries and for public services and benefits that made combining work and family life possible in the first place. In other words, in Nordic countries, citizens entitled to social security have been able to 'maintain a livelihood without reliance on the market' (Esping-Andersen, 1990, p. 22).

One reason for the increase in the domestic service sector in Europe is the active policies promoted by the EU since the early 1990s. The EU has promoted the creation of the domestic service sector in member countries by arguing for increased employment opportunities in the low-wage sector on the one hand, and for facilitating women's labour market opportunities on the other hand (Morel, 2015). As Morel (2015) notes, the decision to subsidise the demand rather than the supply of services in a sector in which work takes place in the privacy of the household and in which there are fewer possibilities for work regulations signifies that the state is actively deregulating the labour market and supporting the privatisation of domestic and care services. This development, I argue, contributes to the marketisation of citizenship according to neoliberal ideals.

In Finland, the tax subsidy system was adopted first regionally in 1997, and nationally in 2001. This was based on a report from the Finnish Social Democrat–led government in 1995 on how the labour supply could be increased through improved incentives for work (Hiilamo, 2015). The following year, a household survey was conducted that concluded that as many as 8 % of the households claimed to have purchased domestic services, with two-thirds not having paid taxes or social contributions on those services (Hiilamo, 2015). Hence, the main arguments for introducing the scheme that derived from these findings were that there was potentially a high demand for domestic services, which signified potential work opportunities for the unemployed, and that the sector was mainly informal and should be regularised. There was a rare consensus over the need for the tax reform, and it entered into force immediately after the government proposal was passed in parliament, which very seldom happens in Finland (Hiilamo, 2015). Compared to other European countries in which similar schemes have been introduced, Finland has included a wider range of services within the tax credit system: household repairs, maintenance jobs and even information and communications technology (ICT)-related equipment installation and maintenance conducted in the household. In practice, the tax deduction means that individual taxpayers can deduct a proportion of the costs of domestic services from their personal income taxes. The minimum deductible cost has been 100 euros and the maximum amount that can be deducted annually has varied from 2000 to 3000 euros per taxpayer. The tax deduction can also be used for services purchased for the taxpayers' parents or grandparents.

There has been a steady increase in the popularity of the tax credit. The use of the credit system has increased exponentially from 32 million euros in 2001, when the system came into force nationwide, to over 476 million euros in 2011 (Häkkinen Skans, 2011). Tax deduction for household services is most frequent among the elderly (individuals over the age of 75 years), entrepreneurs, two-parent households and highly educated people (Häkkinen Skans, 2011). The use of the tax deduction in Finland is still rather modest, and, according to the most recent available figures, only 14 % of the 2.5 million Finnish households benefited from the tax deduction for domestic costs in 2011 (Aalto, 2015).

However, what is more significant is the change in attitudes that the tax deduction has brought about. According to survey findings, the purchase of household services is considered a normal part of daily life (Aalto & Varjonen, 2010; Varjonen, Aalto, & Leskinen, 2007). For older people, the purchase of domestic services is justified by the need to compensate for their personal loss of capacity to perform domestic tasks (Varjonen et al., 2007). The flip side of the coin is the lack of sufficient public home care services. While prior to New Public Management reforms, public home care was time based so that a caregiver could visit a person in need of a specific amount of time in which s/he could then do the necessary cleaning, cooking and nursing; home care is now performance based and care services are reduced to the minimum. Public home services only include personal care (for example, medication or hands-on help with daily life), while, for instance, cleaning and Meals on Wheels services are considered support services and not included in the basic care services. Support services are publicly subsidised by the national tax credit, and municipalities also provide vouchers that can be used to pay for private services. According to my research, it is precisely these cuts in public provision that the elderly are compensating for in the private markets (for similar results in Sweden, see Gavanas, 2013).

While older people are purchasing services because of reduced capability to perform domestic tasks themselves, in upper-middle- and middle-class families the tax credit is seen as a way to pay for more free time and decrease tensions over the division of domestic work between spouses (Aalto & Varjonen, 2010; Varjonen et al., 2007). The upper middle class has been particularly affected by the intensification of work. While at the low-skilled end of the labour markets, neoliberalism has led to a devaluation of work and increased underemployment, on the highly skilled end and in the middle, work has intensified, working days have become longer and demands for flexibility have increased. These jobs have started to resemble self-employment, wherein free time and work time are blurred, leading to a growing demand for domestic services. In Finland, part-time work is not common, so individuals who have children in most cases also work full-time.

Data and Methods

The research draws on a qualitative study of the private cleaning and caring service sectors in Finland, including an analysis of the parliamentary debate on the tax credit in Finland and qualitative interview data collected in 2011–2012. The data include 30 in-depth interviews with representatives of private cleaning and home care companies (N = 13) and with migrant cleaners and caregivers from various backgrounds (from the Philippines, Estonia, Congo, Latvia and Kenya) who all worked in private households (N = 17). The private household service agencies were mostly small- and medium-sized companies employing anywhere between three and fifteen workers. Some were entrepreneurs in a larger franchising-based cleaning company, while others were cooperatives. All but one—the head of the franchising cleaning company—of the interviewed people were directly in charge of recruiting cleaners and dealt directly with customers, and they all had frequent contact with both the cleaners and the customers.

For the purposes of this chapter, I concentrate on the interviews with the representatives of Finnish cleaning and home care companies and on the parliamentary debate in order to trace the ways in which gender (in)equality and citizenship were articulated. The data regarding the parliamentary debate include statements by Members of Parliament (MPs) on the tax credit for household services in Finland in 1997, when the tax rebate was first introduced to some parts of the country, as well as in 2000, when the credit was expanded to all of Finland. I also analysed written questions by MPs addressed to the government regarding the tax credit since 2001. The data for the parliamentary debate were collected from the website of the Finnish Parliament (www.eduskunta.fi), and contains, in total, 138 statements by Finnish MPs and Cabinet Ministers.

Articulations of Neoliberal Citizenship in the Tax Credit Debate

The analysis of the parliamentary debate on the tax credit demonstrates that there were two main arguments supporting the system: first, that introducing the tax credit system would increase the use of services and employment and reduce the grey economy in these sectors; and second, that the tax credit would support the 'Finnish' norm of gender equality in dual-earner families and would be beneficial for women and children's well-being. For example, below are two quotes from the debate:

> I think that we all need to work with all possible means towards people having the strength to go to work, because the Finnish model is that both the father and the mother of the family go to work. Many have working hours that are of the kind that you cannot put your child into a day care, and full-day day care models are very expensive. This is one way to help the care of old and infirm people and children in their homes. (Tuija Nurmi, MP of the National Coalition Party [Finnish Centre-Right Party])

> Mothers would have much more strength if they did not have to wash all the clothes, cook all the food. They would have more time with their children, the afternoon problems, care problems of small schoolchildren would be resolved in a much better way. Nobody can estimate how much this would save in the future. (Hanna Markkula-Kivisilta, MP of the National Coalition Party)

In the parliamentary debate, the increased flexibility demands of working life and the intensification of labour were taken for granted and not questioned. The answer, according to the MPs, was not to criticise the rules of the game—the 'spirit of capitalism', as Boltanski and Chiapello (2007) would put it—but to deal with demanding working life by supporting a marketised solution of the private employment of caregivers in households. According to neoliberal ideology, this is typically called a 'win–win' situation: it solves a problem (deficit of public care provisions) by creating more jobs in private markets. What such a solution overlooks, however, is that it also transforms the basis of social citizenship rights. Instead of perceiving citizens as having rights because their membership in a political community entitles them to public services, citizens are expected to bear the responsibility for their care needs and to resort to private markets to resolve their demand for care. Instead of a relationship between citizens and the state based on parity, neoliberal citizenship introduces an exchange relation according to market logic, or, what is here termed the 'marketisation of citizenship'.

Moreover, according to the parliamentary debate, the answer to the care deficit in private households was not to have men participate more equally in the households, but to employ other women to compensate for the burden middle-class women had in taking care of children as well as being employed full-time. Women's care responsibility in the household was not questioned. Significantly, the parliamentary debate focused on those who bought household services and much less was said about those who provided household services. A telling exception was the statement made by MP Hanna Markkula-Kivisilta:

> It would not be completely vain that this system would create jobs for not only young people who aim to work in the care sector, but also for those slightly ageing women who are now very difficult to employ and who would be very happy to work, for instance, part time in somebody's home instead of feeling completely useless after they have, for instance, been dismissed from banks. For them, the 50- to 60-year-old women, it is so hard to find a job.

According to Markkula-Kivisilta, the introduction of the tax credit would emancipate not only the employed women who needed flexible caregivers to work full-time in the labour markets, but also those ageing women who were the victims of the recent financial crisis and the recession it created, and who were, due to ageism, 'difficult to employ'. Neoliberalism delivers a solution to the problems it creates. Markku-Kivisilta's statement also supports Fraser's (2009) claim about the affinities between neoliberalism and feminist claims for women's emancipation at both the higher and lower ends of the labour market. These affinities make it difficult to criticise neoliberal capitalism from a purely feminist perspective, because the question becomes easily framed from the individual woman's perspective rather than from a societal point of view. Hence, it is easy to agree with the benefits of purchasing domestic services in freeing women for the labour markets at both ends of the social spectrum—what is typically termed a win–win situation in neoliberal 'newspeak'. Yet, calling it a win–win situation overlooks the wider consequences of the solution: the increased privatisation of services and the privatisation of risk and responsibility according to neoliberal ideals.

Interestingly, the MPs did not mention migrants as potential employees in the household. This reflects the fact that labour migration had not yet become a significant phenomenon in Finland in 2000, when the debate took place. Although the share of migrants in Finland is still relatively low compared to the average of the other 27 EU countries, the growth rate of immigration, particularly to the capital city of Helsinki, is among the highest amongst the OECD countries (OECD, 2010).[4] Moreover, these figures do not include thousands of temporary and posted workers who work in Finland but live in neighbouring countries, Estonia in particular. Further, although labour migration to Finland is a relatively recent phenomenon, dating back to the mid-2000s, especially a migrant division of care work is rapidly emerging in the metropolitan areas of Finland (Näre, 2013). Migrant workers are also over-represented in elder care in the city of Helsinki, and more than 60 % of bus drivers in the metropolitan area are of a foreign background (Näre, 2013). Construction and cleaning are other sectors in which migrancy-based divisions have emerged. Most household cleaning and home caring in Finland is provided by private companies, or, in the case of elder care, by public services or companies that stem from the non-profit, third sector. Increasingly, customers of household services are turning to agencies when employing caregivers and cleaners, rather than employing them directly. This is why it is useful to turn to the employers and representatives of private and third-sector–

---

[4] Of the population of 5.4 million people, 4.5 % spoke another mother tongue than one of the three official languages (Finnish, Swedish or Sami), and 3.4 % of the population living in Finland were foreign nationals (Statistics Finland, 2011). These figures are small compared to the average of the other 27 EU countries (6.4 %).

related companies in order to analyse further the discourse on private employment of domestic and care work in Finland.

From Egalitarianism to Neoliberalism: Everyday Practices of Gendered Neoliberal Citizenship

The interviews with the representatives of home cleaning companies confirm the findings in the above analysis. First, an ideological shift has occurred in Finland, which has made employment of a cleaner a normal practice that is no longer stigmatised, as survey data have revealed (Varjonen et al., 2007). This is apparent in the interviewees' reflections of the different attitudes that younger professionals have, relative to older customers. Representatives of cleaning companies affirmed that, while older people—especially older women—might resist hiring a cleaner as they equal it to servant labour, younger professional generations no longer make this connection:

> When you think about the retirees among our customers (…) you can clearly see the changes in the society (…) that when you have seen the war and (…) then worked physically hard to build your living standards, it is really difficult to accept somebody to come home to do maid's work (*piikomaan*), while an IT-specialist in his/her[5] thirties who buys this kind of service, s/he is already a professional buyer in that s/he just buys this service for his/her home and that's it. That there is not that big of a drama there and s/he also appreciates the work [done by the cleaner]. (Head of a big franchising company offering cleaning services)

> Yes, it has become so that if before, for instance, a grandmother wanted to order [a cleaner] she would explain several times that last year she had cleaned everything herself and that she is reluctant for somebody to come and clean her house, like a servant comes. That it's embarrassing. But now, many are really willing for somebody to come to clean, because then you have more time to do other things. (Owner of a cleaning company)

---

[5] The Finnish language does not distinguish between genders. The third person, *hän*, which the interviewee uses, does not reveal whether the interviewee is referring to a man or a woman.

In both quotes, the choice of words referring to domestic work is revealing: *piikoa*, an old-fashioned word for doing maid's work, and *palvelija*, which means servant, are used to describe the way in which older generations feel about hiring cleaners (*siivooja*). For the older generation, hiring a home cleaner involves a 'drama', as the first quote suggests. The drama relates to hiring a servant or a maid because, for the older customers, the employment of a cleaner in one's home signifies an inherent acceptance of inequality. Younger generations do not make this association. For young professionals, hiring a house cleaner is buying a service like any other. Young professionals have become professional customers of household services. One of the interviewees, who had been working in the sector since the late 1990s, said she had noticed a change, in that the customers had also become more demanding in their requirements and that basic cleaning was no longer sufficient; they wanted more 'quality service in that the standards of cleanliness have risen' (head of a cooperative offering cleaning services). Moreover, the tendency is that, when the services are paid for, the clients start to expect more (Kristensen, this volume).

The gendered dimension of domestic service emerged slightly differently when the interviewees spoke of the older generation and the young professionals. When speaking of the older customers, the cleaning company representatives said that the need to purchase domestic services emerged when the older women were no longer able to do household work in the home. Consider, for instance, how a manager of a cleaning company explained the company's different groups of customers:

> We have some aged retirees and the demand [for household labour] occurs especially in a situation when the wife is quite ill and too tired to clean and then it's the husband who calls, then that is the situation when a man calls and says that I need help. As long as the lady is up for it, until then [cleaning] is not a problem. (Human resource manager in a cleaning company)

For the younger professional couples, the gender order emerged in a slightly different way. Similar to the survey findings (Varjonen et al., 2007), the representatives of the cleaning agencies argued that the demand in dual-earner couples emerged from the conflict that a more equal division of domestic work potentially created among the couples and in their families:

2 Neoliberal Citizenship and Domestic Service in Finland ...

They need time for themselves. That's the thing that they don't use that little free time...the kids have a lot of hobbies and the adults they have the work, plus their own hobbies possibly, so they leave that little time that you can breathe that you don't have to think about cleaning the house and I would say that it releases (...) a huge stress from the person and the fighting within the family over who cleans, that now it's your turn and that I don't have time (...) so it does bring happiness to the family (laughs) this kind of harmony and peace. (A human resource manager in a cleaning company)

The above interviewee addresses several interesting dimensions of domestic services in their quote. There is the idea that doing domestic work is a likely cause of conflict within families. The moral justification for hiring a cleaner in dual-earning families is the well-being of children: by saving time that was previously dedicated to domestic chores, parents have more time to dedicate to their children and to their children's hobbies. The interview evokes a strong individualistic discourse of happiness and personal well-being. The work of cleaning is considered an unnecessary part of family life—a source of conflict—and thus outsourcing it is expected to bring harmony and peace to the family. Then there is, again, the assumed acceptance of a taxing work life, which is not questioned—a finding that also emerged from the analysis of the parliamentary debate. The interviewee, in fact, continues to describe a change in lifestyle, in that working people have less available time than before. Finally, the interviewees also pointed out how the introduction of the tax credit had made domestic services accessible to a wider range of people—not only those who were rich:

Of course (...) if somebody buys services for their home they have to be (...) they have to have proper income, that you don't constantly live by the last cent but of course this tax credit makes it that with a middle range income, and even below middle income you have the possibility to use these services. So this wealthier group of people they would use [the services] even without the tax credit, but this middle income and those who are at the lower end of the middle range income, they can use services because this tax credit exists. (Head of a cleaning company)

This quote highlights the significance of the tax credit in making domestic services more affordable to a wider range of people. More significantly,

I would argue, the tax credit, as any law, by its mere existence operates as a moral validation for outsourcing domestic work in private households. It is thus a significant form of neoliberal governance that transforms the organisation of everyday practices of domestic work, and, by doing so, is involved in (re)producing a novel formulation of citizenship according to neoliberal logic.

Conclusions

The data discussed in this chapter reflect the social change that has occurred in Finland, including the recommodification of domestic services and the reintroduction of market arrangements into spheres of everyday life and the domestic space from which they were absent for several decades. A significant shift in attitudes is exemplified by the finding that, while the older generation attaches the uncomfortable meanings of hiring a maid or a servant to buying domestic services, for young professionals the main question is where they might find the best quality of service. For the younger generation, the outsourcing of domestic services as a means for coping with an intensified work life signals a neoliberal answer to a problem caused by neoliberalism. The increased flexibility and productivity demands that young professionals face, as well as the increased difficulty in combining professional and family life, are resolved by outsourcing domestic chores rather than resisting the intensification of work life or demanding better public services. In a similar way, the finding that buying domestic services is a means for resolving conflicts over the division of labour and for liberating working women for the labour markets, as argued in the parliamentary debate, not only demonstrates the gender implications of domestic service, but also brings to mind Fraser's (2009) point on the affinities between feminist emancipatory goals and neoliberal capitalism. Critiquing the outsourcing of domestic labour becomes difficult if the gender equality argument is only reflected from the middle-class women's perspective. In fact, I would suggest that a way to formulate a convincing critique is to point out the deeper changes in the relationship between the citizen and the state that are implicated in domestic service.

Thus, a key argument of this chapter is that the way in which domestic work and the reproductive labour of care and household work is organised tells us a great deal about the relationship between the citizen and the state. As argued already by Coser in 1973, the outsourcing of domestic work—or the 'servant occupation', as he called it—can be used as a yardstick in assessing the acceptance of social inequalities in a society. However, as this chapter and the other chapters in this book demonstrate, instead of becoming obsolete with modernisation progress, as Coser thought it would, domestic service is thriving. It is globalising, spreading and becoming more acceptable even in societies with long egalitarian ideologies and welfare state traditions, such as the Nordic countries. Significantly, domestic service is not thriving because of some kind of organic growth in demand and supply. On the contrary, an active political economy has supported and advanced the increase in this sector in various ways and on various levels, including the supranational level of the EU (Morel, 2015). It is also increasing due to national policy reforms such as the implementation of the tax credit and cash-for-care arrangements, as the case of Finland demonstrates.

Recent research has shown that a higher prevalence of paid domestic labour is associated with greater income inequality and a higher proportion of migrant workers (Jokela, 2015). Thus, the return of a servant society can be seen to reflect the emergence of old lifestyles in a new form and to go hand in hand with a wider increase in economic inequalities, globally. The private employment of domestic work is then indicative of a wider social change that is taking place in high-income countries, as well as in Nordic countries. I have traced this social transformation in the Nordic context as a move from egalitarianism to neoliberalism and propose to call this transformation a formulation of a neoliberal citizenship. This does not mean that there is a simple return to the past, but that a form of a servant society is emerging in a new, neoliberal form. This, I have argued, is indicative of a deeper societal transformation and a new articulation of citizenship according to neoliberal logic. By introducing a tax credit for domestic services, Nordic countries (except for Norway, Iceland and the Faroe Islands) and other continental European countries are, in fact, articulating citizenship that is 'marketised' and 'contractualised' according to neoliberal logic. Thus, unlike domestic service in the past, which was a private affair outside of state regulation, or which was regulated very little, contemporary states of high-income countries have introduced systems—such as the tax credit in the Nordic countries or cash-for-care schemes—that encourage and facilitate the private employment of household and care services. Finally, this chapter can also be taken as a call for an urgent rethinking of the tenets of neoliberal global economics and for the need to create discursive spaces of critique. A serious critique of neoliberalism must also include a rethinking of how citizenship should be thought about and formulated, both now and in the future. The choice is between promoting formulations of citizenship that are non-contractual and non-market based or formulations of neoliberal citizenship that include an acceptance of differential access to social rights based on individuals' economic status.

References

Aalto, K. (2015). The Finnish tax reduction for domestic costs: Consumption patterns. In N. Morel & C. Carbonnier (Eds.), *The political economy of household services in Europe*. Basingstoke: Palgrave Macmillan.
Aalto, K., & Varjonen, J. (2010). Käyttäjäkokemuksia kotitalouspalveluista: mistä laadulle takuu? [User experiences of household services: Who can guarantee the quality?]. *Working Papers 122/2010*. National Consumer Research Centre, Helsinki.
Abrantes, M. (2014). What about the numbers? A quantitative contribution to the study of domestic services in Europe. *International Labour Review, 153*(2), 223–243.
Anderson, B. (2000). *Doing the dirty work? The global politics of domestic labour*. London: Zed Books.
Anderson, B. (2013). *Us and them? The dangerous politics of immigration control*. Oxford: Oxford University Press.
Bhambra, G. (2007). *Rethinking modernity. Postcolonialism and the sociological imagination*. Basingstoke: Palgrave Macmillan.
Bikova, M. (2010). The snake in the grass of gender equality. In L. Widding Isaksen (Ed.), *Global care work. Gender and migration in Nordic societies* (pp. 49–68). Lund: Nordic Academic Press.
Boltanski, L., & Chiapello, E. (2007). *The new spirit of capitalism*. London: Verso.

2 Neoliberal Citizenship and Domestic Service in Finland ...   51

Bosniak, L. (2009). Citizenship, noncitizenship, and the transnationalization of domestic work. In S. Benhabib, V. Coopan, & J. Resnick (Eds.), *Citizenship, borders and gender: Mobility and immobility*. Yale: Yale University Press.

Brown, W. (2003). Neo-liberalism and the end of liberal democracy. *Theory and Event, 7*(1).

Cingano, F. (2014). Trends in income inequality and its impact on economic growth. *OECD Social, Employment and Migration Working Papers*, No. 163. OECD Publishing. doi:10.1787/5jxrjncwxv6j-en

Clarke, J. (2004). *Changing welfare, changing states: New directions in social policy*. London: Sage.

Coser, L. (1973). Servants: The obsolescence of an occupational role. *Social Forces, 52*(1), 31–40.

Cox, R. (2004). *The servant problem. Domestic employment in a global economy*. London: I.B. Tauris.

Esping-Andersen, G. (1990). *The three worlds of welfare capitalism*. Princeton: Princeton University Press.

Fjell, T. I. (2010). Doing gender equality. Cleaners employed in Norwegian middle-class homes. In L. Widding Isaksen (Ed.), *Global care work. Gender and migration in Nordic societies* (pp. 97–114). Lund: Nordic Academic Press.

Fournier, V. (2000). Boundary work and the (un)making of the professions. In N. Malin (Ed.), *Professionalism, boundaries and the workplace* (pp. 67–86). London: Routledge.

Fraser, N. (2009). Feminism, capitalism and the cunning of history. *New Left Review, 56*(March–April), 97–117.

Gavanas, A. (2010). *Who cleans the welfare state? Migration, informalization, social exclusion and domestic services in Stockholm*. Research Report 2010:3. Institute for Future Research, Stockholm.

Gavanas, A. (2013). Elderly care puzzles in Stockholm: Strategies on formal and informal markets. *Nordic Journal of Migration Research, 3*(2), 63–71.

Häkkinen Skans, I. (2011). *Kotitalouspalveluiden verovähennykset Suomessa ja Ruotsissa* [*Tax reductions on domestic services in Finland and Sweden*]. Valmisteluraportit [Preparatory Reports] 11/2011. Government Institute for Economic Research, Helsinki.

Halsaa, B., Roseneil, S., & Sümer, S. (2012). Remaking citizenship in multicultural Europe: Women's movements, gender and diversity. In B. Halsaa, S. Roseneil, & S. Sümer (Eds.), *Remaking citizenship in multicultural Europe: Women's movements, gender and diversity* (pp. 1–20). Basingstoke: Palgrave Macmillan.

Hiilamo, H. (2015). The politics of domestic outsourcing in Finland and Sweden. In N. Morel & C. Carbonnier (Eds.), *The political economy of household services in Europe*. Basingstoke: Palgrave Macmillan.

Hindess, B. (2002). Neo-liberal citizenship. *Citizenship Studies, 6*(2), 127–143.
Isaksen, L. W. (Ed.) (2010). *Global care work. Gender and migration in Nordic societies*. Lund: Nordic Academic Press.
Jokela, M. (2015). Macro-level determinants of paid domestic labour prevalence: A cross-national analysis of seventy-four countries. *Social Policy and Society*. Available at CJO 2014. doi:10.1017/S1474746414000487.
Kristensen, G. K. (2015). A fair deal? Paid domestic labour in social democratic Norway. In A. Triandafyllidou & S. Marchetti (Eds.), *Employers, agencies and immigration. Paying for care* (pp. 207–226). Aldershot: Ashgate.
Lister, R. (2003). *Citizenship: Feminist perspectives* (2nd ed.). New York: New York University Press.
Lister, R., Williams, F., Anttonen, A. I., Bussemaker, J., Gerhard, U., Heinen, J., et al. (2007). *Gendering citizenship in Western Europe. New challenges for citizenship research in cross-national context*. Bristol: Policy Press.
Lutz, H. (2008). *Migration and domestic work. A European perspective on a global theme*. Aldershot: Ashgate.
Lutz, H. (2011). *The new maids. Transnational women and the care economy*. London: Zed Books.
Määttä, A. (2008). Piikana Suomessa [Maid in Finland]. In T. Selin (Ed.), *Filippiinit. Myrskyjen ja mahdollisuuksien saaristo [The Philippines. Archipelago of storms and possibilities]* (pp. 121–138). Helsinki: Like.
Misra, J., Woodring, J., & Merz, S. (2006). The globalization of care work: Neoliberal economic restructuring and migration policy. *Globalizations, 3*(3), 317–332.
Morel, N. (2015). Servants for the knowledge-based economy? The political economy of domestic services in Europe. *Social Politics, 22*(2), 170–192.
Näre, L. (2012). *Moral economies of reproductive labour. An ethnography of domestic and care labour in Naples, Italy*. SSKH Skrifter, Swedish School of Social Science, University of Helsinki.
Näre, L. (2013). Ideal workers and suspects: Employers' politics of recognition and the migrant division of care labour in Finland. *Nordic Journal of Migration Research, 3*(2), 72–81.
OECD (2010). *International migration outlook*. Geneva: OECD.
Palenga-Möllenbeck, E. (2013). New maids—New butlers? Polish domestic workers in Germany and commodification of social reproductive work. *Equality, Diversity and Inclusion: An International Journal, 32*(6), 557–574.
Platzer, E. (2006). From private solutions to public responsibility and back again: The new domestic services in Sweden. *Gender & History, 18*(2), 211–221.

Rodriguez, R. M. (2010). *Migrants for export: How the Philippine state brokers labour to the world*. Minneapolis: University of Minnesota Press.

Sassen, S. (2003). The feminisation of survival: Alternative global circuits. In M. Morokvasic-Müller, U. Erel, & K. Shinozaki (Eds.), *Crossing borders and shifting boundaries. Gender on the move* (pp. 59–78). Opladen: Leske and Budrich.

Somers, M. (2008). *Genealogies of citizenship*. Cambridge: Cambridge University Press.

Stasiulis, D., & Bakan, A. (1997). Negotiating citizenship: The case of foreign domestic workers in Canada. *Feminist Review, 57*(Autumn), 112–139.

Statistics Finland. (2011). *Population structure*. Retrieved June 7, 2012, from http://www.stat.fi/til/vaerak/index_en.html

Triandafyllidou, A., & Marchetti, S. (Eds.) (2015). *Employers, agencies and immigration. Paying for care*. Aldershot: Ashgate.

Varjonen, J., Aalto, K., & Leskinen, J. (2007). *Täsmällistä, ammattitaitoista ja edullista—kuluttajapalautetta kotitalousmarkkinoille [Prompt, professional and inexpensive—Customer feedback to household service markets]*. Kuluttajatutkimuskeskuksen julkaisuja 2/2007. Helsinki: National Consumer Research Centre.

Wacquant, L. (2012). Three steps to a historical anthropology of actually existing neoliberalism. *Social Anthropology, 20*(1), 66–79.

Williams, F. (2014). Making connections across the transnational political economy of care. In I. Shutes & B. Anderson (Eds.), *Migration and care labour. Theory, policy and politics* (pp. 11–30). Basingstoke: Palgrave Macmillan.

Williams, F., & Brennan, D. (2012). Care, markets and migration in a globalising world: Introduction to the special issue. *Journal of European Social Policy, 22*(4), 355–360.

Williams, F., & Gavanas, A. (2008). The intersection of childcare regimes and migration regimes: A three-country study. In H. Lutz (Ed.), *Migration and domestic work. A European perspective on a global theme* (pp. 13–28). Aldershot: Ashgate.

3

The Au Pair Scheme as 'Cultural Exchange': Effects of Norwegian Au Pair Policy on Gender Equality and Citizenship

Berit Gullikstad and Trine Annfelt

(…) this is a good scheme which we must protect. (…) it's a good scheme for language and cultural exchange, and by far most people respect the rules so that it is a win-win situation for the host family and the au pair. (Parliamentary debate 17.06.2013, pp. 4–5)

Introduction

Throughout the 2000s, the au pair scheme has been hotly debated in the Norwegian media and academic research (Bikova, 2008; Hovdan, 2005; Isaksen, 2007, 2010; Løvdal, 2012; Øien, 2009; Sollund, 2010). One reason for this is that the phenomenon of women coming to Norway as au pairs has become much more widespread since the late 1990s. The focus

---

B. Gullikstad (✉) • T. Annfelt
Department of Interdisciplinary Studies of Culture, Centre for Gender Studies, Norwegian University of Science and Technology (NTNU), Trondheim, Norway

© The Editor(s) (if applicable) and The Author(s) 2016
B. Gullikstad et al. (eds.), *Paid Migrant Domestic Labour in a Changing Europe*, DOI 10.1057/978-1-137-51742-5_3

in media debates has partly been on families who have exploited au pairs as cheap labour or subjected them to other criminal offences, and partly on how the au pair scheme is beneficial to au pairs and host families alike. These contradictive positions can be formulated in two apt questions: Does the scheme contribute to unregulated and vague working conditions, making au pairs servants in private families, and does it contribute to the exploitation and abuse of women, particularly young women from the Global South? Or does the au pair scheme give young women a good chance to become familiar with a foreign culture while earning some pocket money and living safely within a family?

A recurring question, also debated in Parliament, has been whether the scheme should be terminated. In June 2013, Parliament decided a new statutory provision which made it possible to punish families who abused the scheme by temporarily disqualifying or banning these families from hosting au pairs (Regjeringen, 2013a). But, as the quotation that introduces this chapter shows, politicians still want to keep the au pair scheme, as they believe it is good for cultural and language exchange and creates a win–win situation for both parties. In this chapter, we examine how the au pair scheme has been constituted and represented in political documents during the 40-year period since Norway ratified the European agreement on au pairing in 1971. During this period, Norway has gone from being a sending country—sending young Norwegian women to serve as au pairs in Europe and the USA in order to learn foreign languages—to being a wealthy destination and receiving country, with most au pairs coming from the Global South. At the same time, Norwegian society has also changed from a male breadwinner model to a dual-earner/dual-carer model in the organisation of family–work life.

International research on au pairing has documented the way in which increasing socio-economic differences between sending and receiving countries have strengthened the au pair scheme as domestic work (Calleman, 2010; Cox, 2012; Hess & Puckhaber, 2004). In Norway, this development can also be seen to have taken place as the authorities (as the introduction quote shows) strongly underline the cultural dimension of au pairing. Why is it important for Norwegian authorities to maintain the scheme as cultural exchange instead of defining it as paid domestic work performed by migrant women? We argue that this has to be understood in relation to (gender) equality ideology and migration policy. The au pair scheme evokes questions concerning (paid) domestic work and (gendered) migration that are central policy fields today. The question of domestic work is a core point in the policy model for gender equality in Norwegian families, stressing the dual position of earning and caring for both mother and father (Ellingsæter & Leira, 2006). With respect to migration and integration policy, participation—and especially migrant women's participation—in a well-regulated labour market is seen as the main political tool for ethnic inclusion and gender equality (AID, 2007).

Gender equality and ethnic inclusion are values that have become very politically explicit and are framed as inclusive values concerning all of Norwegian society. Though there is no absolute given when it comes to who or eventually how one is included as a member of Norwegian society. Inclusion and exclusion in forms of migration regimes (Benhabib & Resnik, 2009; Walsum & Spijkerboer, 2007; see also Cox and Busch; Marchetti; Stubberud, this volume), gender equality and citizenship are connected to intersectional dimensions of (in)equality (Annfelt & Gullikstad, 2013; Bosniak, 2009; Yuval-Davis, 2008). Using a feminist postcolonial perspective, this chapter analyses the way in which gender and 'race' are interwoven in the rhetorical concepts of au paring as 'cultural exchange' and how the au pair scheme produces 'a win–win situation'. What are the implications or effects for the political values of gender equality and inclusion—as dimensions of citizenship—of maintaining the definition of au pairing as cultural exchange?

We first briefly introduce the intersections of gender equality, migration regime and citizenship in the Norwegian policy context and account for the material and analytical concepts the chapter builds on. Then we draw a historical line from the European Council's Convention 1969 on the au pair scheme, as the rules regulating today's au pair scheme are based on this agreement. The scheme has always featured aspects of education (cultural exchange) and services (work). We show the tensions between these aspects and conclude with a discussion of the effects of these tensions for the citizenship of au pairs and gender equality in contemporary Norway.

Gender Equality and Citizenship in the Norwegian Policy Context

In Norwegian political rhetoric, inclusion and (gender) equality are highly valued. These are referred to as shared values in the so-called 'Norwegian model', which is used as an argumentative tool to promote Norway's global reputation (Regjeringen, 2009, p. 10). These values are also referred to in the majority of policy documents from the last decade concerning the labour market and employment, welfare state development, migration regulation and gender equality, and they are tightly connected to each other, as this quotation from a labour market policy document expresses: 'An inclusive society requires gender equality' (AID, 2007). Attention to the values of inclusion and equality in the employment policy demonstrates how important the work line has become in current political social understanding and policy (Nilssen & Kildal, 2009). Participation in paid work has become the basis for equality between women and men by providing economic independence, which is seen as 'the cornerstone for equality' (AID, 2007). The fight for women's right to paid work during the 1960s and 1970s in Norway—as in most Western European countries—has been more or less met, since the proportion of working women is now almost equal to that of working men (Statistics Norway, 2015), and has also been included as mainstream political rhetoric. Furthermore, the goal of social inclusion policy is 'that everyone living in Norway will participate in working life, in all other societal arenas and have equal opportunities' (AID, 2007). Participation in the labour market is thus the main gateway to citizenship. The previous link between citizenship and the male breadwinner has been replaced by a link between citizenship and 'adult workers' (Lewis, 1992, 1997; Lister et al., 2007), which, in the Norwegian context, can be further defined as 'the gender-equal adult worker'. The first paragraph of the governmental white paper on gender equality published in June 2013 made the link between gender equality, justice and full citizenship: 'Gender equality is fundamentally a question of justice. In a fair society everyone has the opportunity, legally and factually, to participate in the society on equal terms. In other words, justice is to ensure everyone full citizenship (...)'

(Regjeringen, 2013b: pkt. 1.1). In contemporary Norwegian political rhetoric, gender equality has become an integral aspect of citizenship. The concept of citizenship is also closely related to that of migration regimes, and migration regimes capture the combination of formal/legal rules and political/cultural practices that govern the terms of admittance to nation state citizenship for migrants (Lister et al., 2007, p. 4). The Norwegian migration regime has been named 'restricted and controlled', allowing inflows of migrants to manage economic needs, while at the same time fencing out those who are considered superfluous or a burden on society (Hagelund, 2003, p. 10). The establishment and practice of a relatively strict migration regime has taken place within a vocabulary of humanitarianism, justice, equality and decency. The integration policy has been presented as a generous policy aimed at those who have already been granted residency, containing ideals of equality between Norwegians and migrants (Hagelund, 2003, p. 13). At the same time, the national framing of gender equality tends to exclude the migrant population from the 'national we' (Annfelt & Gulliksen, 2013).

Even though the Norwegian gender regime is characterised by the dual-earner/dual-carer model policy, the increase in paid domestic migrant workers and au pairs suggests that equal responsibility for care involves much more than public provision of care to deal with the gendered division of labour in the household (Lister et al., 2007, p. 162). The increased demand for paid household services has been explained as a result of women's increased participation in the labour market, which has been seen as a way to achieve gender equality and citizenship for those participating in paid work outside the household (for a critique, see Lutz, 2002, 2007). Western middle-class women's citizenship has thus been described as increasingly contingent upon the labour of non-citizen women (for a discussion, see Bosniak, 2009, p. 137). Bosniak (2009) argues that these two citizenships are incommensurable because of the national framing of citizenship. While Norwegian women have formal and legal citizenship as members of the state, the situation for migrant women—for example au pairs—is often non-citizenship.

Formal non-citizenship does not necessarily exclude all rights. Referring to Nancy Cott, Bosniak finds that citizenship is not necessarily a definitive, either/or position (2009, p. 138). People can enjoy partial citizenship, or they may be the subject of citizenship in some respects but not in others (Bosniak, 2009, p. 139). It is possible to enjoy aspects of equal or democratic citizenship without being a formal citizen (Bosniak, 2009, p. 144). This is the situation for legal migrant workers in Norway, because welfare rights and social citizenship are connected to paid work and legal residence. Another question is who is admitted to be a migrant worker (Anthias et al., 2013). Such rights may depend on nationality, residence and admittance category. Au pairs in Norway who come from the European Union (EU)/European Economic Area have, since 2004, been categorised as legal migrant workers; therefore, in principle, they enjoy partial citizenship. In contrast, au pairs coming from other countries are categorised as students and must apply for the specific au pair visa, which grants only a few rights. Differences may also be linked to gender and 'race'. Women, in general, appear to have fewer opportunities and harder conditions as migrants (Anderson, 2000; Anthias et al., 2013; Carling, 2002; Øien, 2009; Parreñas, 2001). For example, Norwegian rules intending to prevent the exploitation of Eastern European labour have had the effect of excluding women from these countries from coming to Norway as migrant workers (Friberg & Eldring, 2013, p. 15).

These discussions reveal how citizenship is connected to gender regimes and migration regimes. Female migrant domestic workers and au pairs are at the core of this cluster. An analysis of Norwegian policy on the au pair scheme can therefore shed more light on the way in which citizenship and gender equality, as basic values in Norwegian society, are intertwined with gender and 'race'.

Methodology

The public and political debates over the au pair scheme reveal that it is perceived in various different ways, and that there is a discursive fight going on over the different perceptions. As communicators of perceptions of reality, political actors have a particular opportunity to destabilise, reproduce or strengthen representations of the categories and problems that policy instruments are meant to solve (Bacchi, 1999). Inspired by Bacchi's approach to analysing political documents with the question 'What is the problem represented to be?' (Bacchi, 1999, 2009), we were especially concerned with questions of representation, presupposition, silence and effect.

Since the aim of the chapter is to uncover the effects of the political rhetoric on cultural exchange, the chapter is based primarily on analyses of Norwegian public policy documents during the period from 1971 when the au pair convention was ratified up to 2014. In addition, media statements from regional newspapers and the major Oslo dailies in the period from 2000 to 2014 were used primarily to identify when the debates on au pairing were especially intense and what questions were raised.

Bearing in mind that an au pair, by definition, is a foreign national, we drew on policy documents raising issues relating to immigration, residence and employment in Norway in connection with changes in the Immigration Act. These documents, which are public reports, formed the basis of the bureaucratic and political work on immigration policy, reports to Parliament, propositions from relevant Parliamentary committees, and debates in the committees and in Parliament. In 1975, a few years after the ratification of the au pair convention, Norway introduced the 'Immigration stop', and we analysed the way in which this regulation affected the au pair scheme.

Most of the political documents we analysed were from the past 10–15 years, the period of time when au pair employment became more widespread. As mentioned in the introduction, during this period, the au pair scheme came into the public as well as the political spotlight. Particularly after 2005/2006, policy was clearly influenced by the many inputs from media and research, as well as from reports from the Directorate of Immigration (UDI). The Directorate implements migration policy by processing applications for work and residence permits in Norway, including au pair permits. The UDI makes the rules that pertain to au pairs in dialogue with the governing Ministry. For this research, we referred to annual reports, statistics, evaluation reports and circulars relating to the rules of the au pair scheme.

From Worker to Student: Representations of the Au Pair Category 1971–2013

A rationale for the European Council's agreement in 1969 on the 'au pair' placement was that an au pair does not belong in either the student or worker category, 'but to a special category which has features of both, and that therefore it is useful to make appropriate arrangements for them' (European Agreement on 'Au Pair' Placement, Strasbourg 24.11.1969[1]). The agreement thus formalised 'au pair' as a new but ambiguous category that would include both student and employee. Correspondingly, the receiving family was construed in part as an employer, through the regulation of working hours, and in part as a family, for example, through the use of the term 'pocket money' (EAAP, 1969).

This ambiguous position was constructed through the supranational rights and obligations that the agreement put forward and which national authorities, families and au pairs would have to comply with. The au pair's rights referred to temporary migration for up to two years, welfare benefits in the event of 'sickness, maternity or accident' (Article 9 EAAP, 1969) and working conditions as regulation of working hours and pay. The au pair was also granted the right to time off to attend language courses or, more specifically, vocational training and the practice of his/her religion. The au pair was supposed to be a youth and, in practice, a woman between the ages of 17 and 30, coming from Western Europe. She was expected to put her labour at the family's disposal in exchange for board, lodging and pocket money. Young women were, as such, given the opportunity to travel and experience other countries and possibilities for educational and personal growth. By regulating a barter scheme involving free stay with a family and time for studies against provision of household service, youth of limited means were given the opportunity to both travel and study abroad. Thus, the scheme was thought to promote socio-economic equality or 'social progress', which was declared the intention of the agreement (EAAP, 1969). This can be said to be in line with ideas of the concept of citizenship, as the concept has a vision

---

[1] Hereinafter EAAP 1969.

of a more universally equal and inclusive society (Bosniak, 2009; Lister et al., 2007).

Since the supranational agreement established au pairs as an ambiguous category, similar to both a student and a worker, the national political and executive authorities have options when it comes to interpreting and regulating the au pair scheme. As a consequence, the scheme varies between countries (Cox, 2015). How did the Norwegian authorities understand the au pair institution in the decades after the agreement was ratified? How is it understood today? In the following, we will show how these interpretations have changed from the 1970s up to today.

Until 1971 (the year in which Norway ratified the agreement), the country had a very liberal immigration policy (Carling, 1999, p. 51). In 1975, this policy was drastically modified with the introduction of an (initially temporary) immigration stop. Strict requirements were set for granting new work and residence permits, and there was political agreement that the immigration regulations should not be illusory due to the use of comprehensive dispensation rules (Regjeringen, 1975; St.meld. nr. 39, 1973–74). There was also political agreement that dispensations were needed for some groups of employees. One of the groups that came under the dispensation scheme was that of the au pair. Au pairs were granted a work permit without a needs assessment as the basis for their temporary residence in Norway.

There are two points to note here. Au pairs were thus first granted residence in Norway through a work permit. The similarities the au pair category shared with the worker category were hence decisive. Second, au pair work permits were granted through the dispensation rules. These rules gave rise to heated debates in the committee preparing the case and also in the subsequent debate in Parliament (Regjeringen, 1975; St.meld., 1988; Stortingstidende bind 7, 1974–75: 1992–1979). The debate partly concerned the risk that dispensation for particular groups might allow them to outcompete domestic labour, and it partly concerned the risk that the immigration stop might be undermined. But au pairs were not mentioned in the discussions; thus, they were regarded as a given and non-problematic category in terms of granting work permits.

There was sound logic both in granting au pairs residence through a work permit and in permitting them entry under the dispensation rules. An important intention of the immigration hiatus was to stop the growing labour immigration from third-world countries. The arguments were social problems for both migrants and the majority population, such as bad living conditions for the migrant population, and the fare of pressure in the labour market which could result in lowered wages for all (Carling, 1999; St.meld. nr. 39, 1988, pp. 27–28). Au pair employment naturally fell outside such political concerns, both because au pairs generally came from Western countries and because very few persons in this category wanted to come to Norway (Carling, 1999, pp. 59–60). In the middle of the 1970s, it was obvious that nobody associated au pairs with migrants. As mentioned above, Norway ratified the au pair convention of 1969 and, in doing so, legally obliged the nation to be a receiver country. This may have contributed to giving au pairing dispensation from the immigration stop in 1975.

After 2000, the categorisation of au pairs changed. In political documents and discussions, 'au pair' became positioned closer to the 'student' category through discursive work over time. A clear example of this is the change in the Directorate of Immigration's (UDI) practice. Before 2003, au pair permits were grouped with work permits; after 2003, they were grouped with education permits (Henriksen, 2007, p. 160). The rhetoric in public documents and political debates also changed. Gradually, it became solidified that the purpose of the au pair scheme was cultural exchange. In 2003, the UDI's definition of 'au pair' was more or less the same as that of the agreement from 1969 describing rather precisely the purpose: 'A person who is granted (...) residence (...) to live with a Norwegian family in exchange for service provision. The aim is that the au pairs will improve language skills/vocational knowledge and (...) expand their general education (...)' (UDI, Annual Report, 2003). The UDI's circular from 2012 has a less specified definition of the au pair: 'The European Council's agreement states that (...) the purpose of the scheme is cultural exchange. (...) The au pair stay must (...) primarily have an educational and a cultural purpose' (UDI RS, 2012-015: Item 2.2). The key words in the 2003 definition are 'service provision' and 'language skills/vocational knowledge', while in 2012 these are reduced to the inaccurate notion of 'cultural exchange'.

Some terms also changed. 'Receiver families' became 'host families', and while 'receiver' does not specify whom one receives or for what purpose, 'host families' suggests that these persons are guests, which in turn fits well with 'cultural exchange'. The term 'au pair employment', which we find in the translation of the agreement document from 1969, disappeared—perhaps because it had too many associations with an employer–employee relationship? Another change is the 'sound level'. Au pairs were not a theme in documents and debates on the entry of foreign nationals to the nation until well into the 2000s. After this time, au pairs and the au pair scheme became a recurrent topic in the media and the subject of innumerable statements from politicians, bureaucrats and researchers. The political debate today thus highlights and favours the idea of cultural exchange.

The change in the rhetoric occurred more or less in line with the dramatic influx of au pairs into Norway who came primarily from third-world countries. The change can therefore be seen in connection to migration policies. A question is how the connection with student—cultural exchange—migration is intertwined in the regulation of the au pair scheme and the effect of this intertwining.

Cultural Exchange as a Restricted Gendered Migration Regime

The visa regulations for au pairs in Norway are and have always been tightly connected to the immigration hiatus mentioned above. Up until 1994, au pairs coming from non-Nordic countries had to apply for a visa. After 2004, this became the situation only for au pairs coming from outside the EU/EEA. Over the last 20 years, Norway has become an au pair receiver country. In the late 1970s, the number of au pairs arriving in Norway was low: around 40 per year (Carling, 1999, pp. 59–60). During the 1990s, the number of au pairs amounted to between 250 and 400, annually (UDI Annual Reports). There was, however, a dramatic rise in the number of permits per year in the new millennium, up to almost 1800 in 2007 and later (UDI Annual Reports). The increase in numbers in the years around 2000 was especially due to interest from Eastern European women (Aftenposten, 2002). Au pairs from Eastern Europe, particularly Poland and Lithuania, caused a doubling of the number from 1993 to 2003 (UDI Annual Report, 2002). Since 2004, au pairs from the Philippines have made up the largest group. In 2009 alone, 1300 Filipino au pairs were granted a permit (Thorud, 2010, p. 27). Russia, Ukraine and Belarus are the other major recruitment countries, but with significantly lower numbers (UDI Annual Reports). The actual number of au pairs has probably in all years been substantially higher than the statistics suggest, since the statistics only refer to the number of visa permits issued, and in 2013 it was assumed that there were approximately 3000 au pairs in Norway (Arbeidsliv i Norden, 2013). To the extent that youth from the EU/EEA countries wish to be au pairs in Norway, they do not come under the Norwegian au pair rules with respect to host family requirements, language instruction or working hours (UDI, RS, 2012-15, Item 1). The Norwegian au pair rules explicitly apply to those who come from countries outside the EU/EEA area (ibid.), which is to say primarily from countries in Asia.[2]

During the last decade, the rules for regulating the au pair scheme have become much more specified though the definition of the au pair has become more diffuse. This can be seen as a response to the increased critique from researchers and media that the scheme is 'primarily regular paid work' (UDI, 2011). Specification of the rules and obligations has therefore aimed to underline the au pair scheme as cultural exchange and weaken the connotations to work. The most important requirement is that the family 'should use the Norwegian language in their day-to-day life and have good knowledge about Norwegian society' (UDI, RS, 2012-15, Item 2.2). To ensure this requirement, other requirements are also placed on the family. The regulations describe the normal host family as one in which both adults were born and raised in Norway. There are possible exceptions, but as a general rule 'it is required that the countries of origin of the host parents and the au pair are different' (UDI, RS, 2012-15, Item 3.2.3). The requirement of a different country of

---

[2] Host families having au pairs from countries in the EU/EEA likewise often use the visa au pair contract. See the chapters of Stubberud and Kristensen in this volume.

origin is an argument for preventing unwanted immigration, since family reunification is the most common option—and often the only possible option—for permanent residency for female migrants because of the very restricted migration policy both for migrant workers and refugees/asylum seekers. The rules therefore underline that familial relationships between the au pair and anyone in the host family are prohibited. 'One cannot be an au pair with own ascending or descending family members, or with siblings, cousins, in-laws or uncles/aunts. Nor can an au pair be married or cohabitant with any of the host parents' (UDI, RS, 2012-15, Item 3.2.2). This last sentence about marriage seems odd. Who would apply for an au pair visa if family reunification through marriage were an option? This specification is probably meant to prevent forced marriage, since the au pair can be rather young, but the fact that some au pairs marry their host father (Stubberud, this volume) could also be a reason for this specification.

The rules obviously have a double aim: to underline au pairing as cultural exchange and to regulate and prevent unwanted migration. They are meant to undermine the critique of au pairing as cheap labour and a vehicle for the exploitation of women while also underlining the migration policy. On the other side, it is possible to interpret the cultural exchange policy as an opening for and legitimation of the globalised and feminised migration into domestic services in private homes. The transfer of the au pair scheme from the work permit category to youth exchange schemes/student permits in the migration regulations in 2003 is an example. The change occurred simultaneously with the increased number of au pairs coming from third-world countries and more media debates about au pairing as servitude. But the transfer from one category to another did not mean much in the way of a change of practice, as it still presumed that 'the applicant [the au pair] shall be employed in Norway' and the rules for temporary stay as a student/au pair or worker from the Global South were the same (NOU, 2004, p. 20, ch. 9.4.1.1). Thus, the change of categories can be seen more as a symbolic act to focus the cultural exchange rhetoric than a new barrier for female migrant workers.

The migration policy makes it very difficult for women to immigrate to Norway as workers if they are from countries outside the EU/EEA.

From countries such as the Philippines and Thailand, most women come as spouses of Norwegian citizens (Henriksen, 2007; UDI Annual Report, 2012). There is also much to indicate that the vocationally trained man is favoured (Anthias et al., 2013; Friberg & Eldring, 2013). A glance at the migration flow into Norway, as measured by the number of work permits issued, shows that three out of four of those who come to work in Norway are men (UDI Annual Report, 2013). Permanent work migration into Norway is only allowed if the migrant is an expert needed in Norwegian society. Since very few typical female occupations are considered expert occupations, female nurses make up the only group who come to Norway as experts. For non-professional female workers, the 'front door' is closed. The student categorisation for au pairs opens the 'back door' for both professional (many au pairs are well educated) and non-professional female migrant workers, but without controlled working conditions (Sollund, 2010; Stubberud, 2015a). The effect of focusing on au pairing as cultural exchange is avoiding attention and critique of the migrant work policy. This means continuing to produce this policy as gendered, and thus in opposition to the clearly expressed goal of gender equality.

Cultural Exchange: Preventing Servitude and Mommy Robbery?

Why have these changes in the understanding of au pairs taken place? What is produced and legitimised through the emphasis on cultural exchange as the purpose of the au pair institution? We have pointed out some development trends that show contemporaneity between change in the recruiting countries and changes in the Norwegian discourse about the au pair scheme. We have argued that au pairing in the 1970s and onwards was a marginal phenomenon that did not cause any problems. What was important was finding a practical solution for au pairs' entry into the nation. Before Norway became an attractive receiver country, it did not matter whether the association with 'worker' or with 'student' was foregrounded in the au pair discourse. It was only after such changes took place, and not least after repeated argumentation that au pairs from the Global South came for economic reasons (Arbeidsliv i Norden, 2013; Calleman, 2010; NOU, 2004, p. 20; Sollund, 2010), that the discursive tension over the meaning of au pairing became important. The attuned message from the politicians and bureaucrats about the scheme's purpose and function, as well as the work to prevent immigration, was also in accordance with these changes.

What would happen if the au pair discourse were to be linked more tightly to work? There can only be speculation about this. But it is possible to point out discomfort and problems the authorities might avoid if this link were to remain weak and the discourse about the au pair as a student and cultural exchanger were to stay hegemonic. There is widespread ill will against any policy that supports servitude (Bergens Tidende, 2013; Kluge, 2013; Stortingsdebatt, 1997, 2013). The media has repeatedly brought the debate about servants into the au pair discourse, and the political authorities have opposed the servant discourse by constantly referring to 'students' and 'culture exchange'. The abovementioned Parliamentary debate in June 2013 on the disqualification of host families who abuse the au pair scheme is a good example of this. PM Michael Tetzschner (Conservative Party), for example, stated that the purpose of the scheme is cultural exchange, pointing out that a unanimous Parliamentary committee supported this fact (Stortingsdebatt, 2013, p. 2). All of the speakers in Parliament wholeheartedly endorsed this understanding. The purpose of the amendment was to protect those who come to Norway and to counteract the possibility of the development of '(…) a new class of servants in Norway' (Stortingsdebatt, 2013, pp. 4–5). The Minister of Justice Grete Faremo (Labour Party) concluded the debate by stating that this legal amendment had had its '(…) purpose to tighten and strengthen the cultural aspect of the au pair scheme and to prevent au pairs from being used as cheap labour' (Stortingsdebatt, 2013, p. 6). The political authorities thus focused their attention on preventing the scheme from contributing to a new class of servants. Through the current understanding of what hiring an au pair means, they and the general public do not have to change their understanding of Norway as a nation against servants and exploitation and in favour of caring for others.

It is quite clear that there may be major consequences for au pairs with respect to whether their permit is understood to represent work or cultural exchange. *One* important decision, supposedly connected to the discourse about cultural exchange, has already been made. Women with provider responsibilities for their own children cannot be employed as au pairs, and the given reason for this is that income, rather than cultural exchange, would be the purpose of their stay (Regjeringen, 2012). This restriction may be considered the answer to concerns raised that the au pair scheme contributes to 'mommy robbery', wherein mothers leave their own children to come to Norway to work as an au pair (Isaksen, 2010; Sollund, 2012; Stubberud, 2015b). By tentatively pulling the au pair discourse away from 'worker' and towards 'student/cultural exchange', the exclusion of mothers is legitimised while the discomfort of 'mommy robber' is eliminated. For the au pair, such exclusion can be dramatic. Mothers may still have to go abroad to earn money, but if they go to Norway, they have to hide the fact that they have children.

The effects of making cultural exchange the backbone of the au pair scheme means that the critical eye that should be turned on migration policy and its gendered consequences is omitted. The same applies to the debate about servitude, the need for 'extra hands' and the critical questions this raises about gender equality policy—including both problems relating to equality between ethnically Norwegian women and men and between femininities and the women who inhabit these. By not raising such questions, the au pair policy—wherein the rules are written into a language of protection, partly by strengthening the au pair's rights and partly by putting a lot of obligations on the family—produces an image of the Norwegian society that is concerned with what is good in the form of openness to the world, equality-thinking and considerate behaviour.

A Loophole Which Strengthens Gendered Citizenship

In the final discussion, we follow the themes of gendered citizenship and migration policy. As mentioned above, the vision of a universal equal and inclusive society is clearly expressed in Norwegian policies. If this vision is to be realised, gender must be included in the formulation of policy. In Norwegian politics, much has been done to accomplish this (Annfelt

& Gullikstad, 2013). As discussed earlier, gender equality is spoken of as a national ideal. Comprehensive schemes and great resources have been put in place to ensure that citizens can combine paid employment and caregiving duties. Now the question is whether Norwegian society has reached the end of the line or whether extra hands are required to realise gender equality (Lister et al., 2007). Is the gender equality policy good enough? These issues are relevant for the au pair scheme.

The political statement about the scheme as a 'win–win' situation (for example, the introduction quote) can be interpreted as an implicit criticism of the gender regime: Parents need more relief than authorities offer to realise the combination of childcare and paid employment outside the home, and an au pair can fill in for the gender regime's shortcomings. This solution is also a cheap way for the authorities to solve the problem.

At the same time, use of services in the home, including au pairs, has increased across Europe independently of individual state gender regimes. Migration and the offer of inexpensive labour that thus arises appear, in their own way, to stimulate the purchase of household services. Bearing this in mind the au pair scheme not only points towards a (maybe) imperfect gender regime, but also points towards colonial features in Norwegian society. Keskinen, Tuori, Irni and Mulinari (2009) analyse this development in the Nordic countries as complying with colonialism and show how migration, nationality and power dimensions such as gender and 'race' contribute to such development. The term 'complicity' in postcolonial studies refers to closing a hegemonic discourse about itself, thus maintaining it as precisely hegemonic (Vuorela, 2009). Silent approval and endorsement of hegemonic understandings are part of such discursive work. The rejection of servitude as an aspect of au pairing, combined with the repetition of the scheme's focus on cultural exchange, can be interpreted as part of this work. Both legitimise very poor pay for a type of shift work with highly unclear working hours and the way in which this is determined without the au pair's input. It also legitimises the absence of reflection over the fact that the sender countries are often at the other end of the global economy. At the same time, the discursive work constructing au pairing as cultural exchange contributes to Norway's self-understanding as a gender-equal and considerate nation.

In postcolonial Western societies, migrant women become invisible (Keskinen et al., 2009; Lewis, 2006). When it comes to au pairs in Norway, they are made simultaneously visible and invisible. They are very visible in the media debate, yet they are also made invisible when the policy and rules insist on cultural exchange as the primary goal for the scheme, by maintaining that au pairs should be coming for the sake of culture and that, for them, cultural exchange is a good result of their stay. They become invisible to the extent that the argumentation denies the fact that there are several reasons why au pairs come to Norway. Invisibility can also be inferred from, first, the threat by the authorities to close down the scheme if it continues to break with the condition of cultural exchange, and, second, the provision that mothers must be excluded. In these regulations, au pairs are rendered invisible when the consequences for them of implemented and planned measures are not a subject of discussion. These findings are consistent with Lewis' descriptions of the imaginaries of Europe and the effects of these in today's society (2006). Lewis shows how Europe has talked a common conviction about superiority into existence, and made assumptions about a successful gender order and women's freedom into key evidence of this superiority.

According to Lewis, such symbolic production places Europe and the European 'as the standard of humanity and closes down questions as to whose identity, autonomy, family and privacy are to be respected, at whose cost and with what consequences for Europe's potential for an economy of gender equality' (Lewis, 2006, p. 93). Both the historic heritage and the current design of multicultural Europe create particular relations 'between women inhabiting different femininities differentiated by ethnicity and class', and for Lewis, this means to 'conceive gender as expressive of and constituted by the range of womanhoods that exists on one side of the [gendered] binary' (Lewis, 2006, p. 93). Both the assumption of (our) superiority and the positioning of au pairs as cultural exchangers make the au pairs invisible. The Western and the white are constituted as the essential and the important. Woman's gender equality and need or lack of need for an au pair/housekeeper is made into policy. The Western woman is prioritised, while the migrant woman disappears from the field of vision. In this way, the production of invisibility takes part in the hierarchies and production of inequality between femininities and the women who carry them.

This chapter has asserted that the Norwegian rules under-communicate the work dimension of the au pair scheme, and we have argued that the logic behind this is the wish to close the scheme to migration. In Sweden, the political discourse on au pairs is different, since au pair employment is clearly articulated as work (Arbeidsliv i Norden, 2013). It is thus fully possible both to have a discourse with au pairing as (primarily) work and to maintain the au pair scheme, itself. Seeing the scheme as work was, and is, important to social rights that are linked to economic citizenship. With respect to the citizenship of au pairs, it is interesting that the rights that are beyond what the convention established appear to have come into place after the media and researchers revealed obvious disparities. This includes taking steps to prevent au pairs from becoming literally indebted to their host by borrowing money to pay for their journey (Bikova, 2008), and the change in the Immigration Act that enabled host families to be disqualified (Regjeringen, 2013a). But we see no trace of questioning the au pairs about their needs and interests, and where they form the basis for their citizenship during their stay in Norway. Again, the au pair appears and is maintained as invisible. One could have, for example, made it possible for au pairs to unionise, as they can in Denmark.[3] Unionising, as we know, is seen as fundamental precisely for making visible a group's interests and rights and strengthening their opportunity to compete for these.

Aspects of the debate about servants connect to our previous discussion about the cluster of migration—labour immigration—and restrictive immigration policy. As of today, the au pair scheme more or less functions as 'a loophole used to meet the demand for certain types of domestic labour' (Calleman, 2010, p. 69). We would turn this around and say that the scheme is also a loophole in the migration policy for women. Actively making the au pairs visible by allowing for their unionising or taking other steps may help to strengthen their partial citizenship. Taking their standpoint seriously and acknowledging au pair employment also as an income strategy might help to improve au pairs' life situation as citizens while they are in Norway and perhaps also in their country of origin. Locking the scheme permanently into the cultural exchange framework may be the

---

[3] Oral presentation at the conference 'Au pairordningen, Balansekunst mellom arbeid og kultur', 11.10.2013, Oslo.

most significant impediment to this, since this discourse legitimises the choice of measures that impact and can impact this group hard. Closing this loophole in the migration regulation (which was suggested by prominent Norwegian female politicians during summer 2015) may push these women to countries with fewer regulations for au pairs and housekeepers than in Norway (Cox, 2015; Shechory, Ben-David, & Snoen, 2010) and may also stimulate the market for under-the-table housekeeping services (Friberg & Tyldum, 2007). The hiring of 'au pairs' as 'servants' will, in all probability, not disappear. It is more probable that women from Eastern Europe will replace women from the third world in this capacity. The regulations and the degree of protection inherent in the legislation will, however, be gone (Cox, 2012). This is also an argument for retaining the au pair scheme and strengthening the influence au pairs have over it.

References

Aftenposten. (2002). *Stadig færre vil bli au pairer*. December 2, 2002.
AID. (2007). *Veileder til Utredningsinstruksen. Likestillingsmessige konsekvenser for personer med innvandrerbakgrunn, samer og nasjonale minoriteter*. Oslo: The Ministry of Work and Inclusion.
Anderson, B. (2000). *Doing the dirty work. The global politics of domestic labour*. London: Zed Books.
Annfelt, T., & Gullikstad, B. (2013). Kjønnslikestilling i inkluderingens tjeneste? *Tidsskrift for kjønnsforskning, 37*(3–4), 309–327.
Anthias, F., Morokvasic-Müller, M., Kontos, M. (Eds.) (2013). *Paradoxes of integration. Female migrants in Europe*. Dordrecht: Springer.
Arbeidsliv i Norden [Working life in the Nordic countries] nr. 10-2013. (2013). Retrieved August 27, 2014, from http://www.arbeidslivinorden.org/i-fokus/i-fokus-2013/arbetsmiljoen-foer-unga/article.2013-10-06.0038500062
Bacchi, C. L. (1999). *Women, policy and politics. The construction of policy problems*. London: Sage.
Bacchi, C. L. (2009). *Analysing policy: What's the problem represented to be?* French Forest, NSW: Pearson Australia.
Benhabib, S., & Resnik, J. (Eds.) (2009). *Migrations and mobilities: Citizenship, borders and gender*. New York and London: New York University Press.

3 The Au Pair Scheme as 'Cultural Exchange ...   75

Bergens tidende. (2013). *La dem få bli!* April 28, 2013.

Bikova, M. (2008). *A family member or a family servant. A qualitative study.* Unpublished master thesis, Sosiologisk Inst., University of Bergen.

Bosniak, L. (2009). Citizenship, noncitizenship and the transnationalization of domestic work. In S. Benhabib & J. Resnik (Eds.), *Migrations and mobilities: Citizenship, borders and gender*. New York and London: New York University Press.

Calleman, C. (2010). Cultural exchange or cheap domestic labour? Constructions of "Au pair" in four Nordic countries. In L. W. Isaksen (Ed.), *Global care work. Gender and migration in Nordic societies*. Lund: Nordic Academic Press.

Carling, J. (1999) *Arbeidsinnvandring og familiegjenforening 1967–1980. En oversikt med hovedvekt på statistikk*. Program for kulturstudier nr. 4/NFR. Bergen: Senter for kulturstudier.

Carling, J. (2002). Migration in the age of involuntary immobility. *Journal of Ethnic and Migration Studies*, 28, 5–42.

Cox, R. (2012) invisible Au Pairs: Gendered work and migration regimes. In Sollund, R. (Ed.), *Transnational migration, gender and rights* Advances in Ecopolitics. Vol 10, 33–52. Bingley: Emerald Group Publishing.

Cox, R. (Ed.) (2015). *Au pairs' lives in global context. Sisters or servants?* Basingstoke: Palgrave Macmillan.

Ellingsæter, A. L., & Leira, A. (Eds.) (2006). *Politicising parenthood. Gender relations in welfare states*. Bristol: Policy Press.

European Agreement on "Au Pair" Placement. Strasbourg 24.11.1969. (1969). Retrieved from http://conventions.coe.int/Treaty/en/Treaties/Html/068.htm

Friberg, J. H., & Eldring, L. (Eds.) (2013). *Labour migrants from Central and Eastern Europe in the Nordic countries. Patterns of migration, working conditions and recruitment practices*. Copenhagen: Nordic Council of Ministers.

Friberg, J. H., & Tyldum, G. (Eds.). (2007). *Polania i Oslo. En studie av arbeids- og levekår blant polakker i hovedstadsområdet*. Fafo-rapport 2007:27. Oslo.

Hagelund, A. (2003). *The importance of being decent. Political discourse on immigration in Norway 1970–2002*. Oslo: Unipax.

Henriksen, K. (2007). *Fakta om 18 innvandrergrupper i Norge*. Oslo-Kongsvinger: Statistics Norway.

Hess, S., & Puckhaber, A. (2004). "Big sisters" are better domestic servants? Comments on the booming Au pair business. *Feminist Review*, 77, 65–78.

Hovdan, M. (2005). *Au pair in Norway: A qualitative study*. Unpublished master thesis, University of Bergen.

Isaksen, L. W. (2007). Gender, care work and globalisation. Local problemes and global solutions in the Norwegian welfare state. In M. Griffin-Cohen & J. Brodie (Eds.), *Remapping gender in the new global order*. London and New York: Routledge.

Isaksen, L. W. (Ed.) (2010). *Global care work. Gender and migration in Nordic societies*. Lund: Nordic Academic Press.

Keskinen, S., Tuori, S., Irni, S., & Mulinari, D. (Eds.) (2009). *Complying with colonialism. Gender, race and ethnicity in the Nordic region*. Farnham: Ashgate.

Kluge, L. (2013). Svartelister norske familier. *A-Magasinet*, May 16, 2013.

Lewis, G. (2006). Imaginaries of Europe: Technologies of gender, economics of power. *European Journal of Women Studies, 2*, 87–103.

Lewis, J. (1992). Gender and the development of welfare regimes. *Journal of European Social Policy, 3*, 159–173.

Lewis, J. (1997). Gender and welfare regimes: Further thoughts. *Social Politics, 2*, 160–177.

Lister, R., Williams, F., Anttonen, A., Bussemaker, J., Gerhard, U., Heinen, J., et al. (2007). *Gendering citizenship in Western Europe. New challenges for citizenship researching a cross-national context*. Bristol: The Policy Press.

Løvdal, L. (2012). *Au pairer i Norge. Rettigheter og rettighetsinformasjon*. Oslo: IMDI.

Lutz, H. (2002). At your service madame! The globalization of domestic service. *Feminist Review, 70*, 89–104.

Lutz, H. (2007). The intimate "other". Migrant domestic workers in Europe. In E. Berggren, et al. (Eds.), *Irregular migration, informal labour and community: A challenge for Europe*. Maastricht: Shaker Publishing.

Nilssen, E., & Kildal, N. (2009). New contractualism in social policy and the Norwegian fight against poverty and social exclusion. *Ethics and Social Welfare, 3*(3), 302–321.

NOU. (2004). *20 Ny utlendingslov* [New Immigration Act]. Oslo: Lobo Media AS.

Øien, C. (2009). *On equal terms? An evaluation of the Norwegian Au pair scheme*. Oslo: Fafo-report 2009:29. Retrieved from http://www.fafo.no/pub/rapp/20119/index.html

Parreñas, R. S. (2001). *Servants of the globalisation: Women, migration and domestic work*. Stanford: Stanford University Press.

Regjeringen (the Government). (1975). Innst. S. nr. 85, 1974–75. Innstilling fra kommunal- og miljøvernkomitéen om innvandringspolitikken.

Regjeringen. (2009). *Interesser, ansvar og muligheter*. Melding til Stortinget nr. 15 2008–2009. Oslo: Regjeringen/UD.

Regjeringen. (2012). GI-12/2011 *Instruks vedrørende endringer i au pairordningen*. Oslo: Justisdepartementet [The Ministry of Justice and Public Security]. Retrieved August 15, 2013, from http://www.regjeringen.no/nb/dep/jd/dok/rundskriv/2011/gi-122011--instruks-vedrorende-endringer.html?id=668958

Regjeringen. (2013a). Prop. 154 L (2012–2013) *Endringer i utlendingsloven (misbruk av aupairordningen mv)*. Retrieved September 24, 2013, from http://www.regjeringen.no/nb/dep/jd/dok/regpubl/prop/2012-2013/prop-154-l-20122013/2.html?id=726043

Regjeringen. (2013b). *Likestilling kommer ikke av seg selv*. Melding til Stortinget 44. Oslo: Regjeringen/BLID.

Shechory, M., Ben-David, S., & Snoen, D. (Eds.) (2010). *Who pays the prize? Foreign workers, society, crime and the law*. New York: Nova Science Publishers.

Sollund, R. (2010). Regarding Au pairs in the Norwegian welfare state. *European Journal of Women's Studies, 17*(2), 143–161.

Sollund, R. (2012). Arbeidsmigrantene. *Dagbladet*, January 25, p. 52.

Statistics Norway. (2015). Retrieved from https://www.ssb.no/aku

St.meld. nr. 39. (1973–74). *Om innvandringspolitikken*. Oslo: Kommunal- og arbeidsdepartementet (KAD).

St.meld. nr. 39. (1987–1988). *Om innvandringspolitikken*. Oslo: Regjeringen/KAD.

Stortingsdebatt (Parliamentary debate). (1997, June 6). Sak 5.

Stortingsdebatt (Parliamentary debate). (2013, June 17). Sak 18. Retrieved September 24, 2013, from http://www.stortinget.no/no/Saker-og-publikasjoner/Publikasjoner/Referater/Stortinget/2012-2013/130617/18/

Stortingstidende, bind 7, 1974–75: 1992–1979.

Stubberud, E. (2015a). "It's not much". Affective (boundary) work in the Au pair scheme. In R. Cox (Ed.), *Au pair's lives in global contexts. Sisters or servants?* Basingstoke: Palgrave Macmillan.

Stubberud, E. (2015b). Framing the Au pair: Problems of sex, work and motherhood in Norwegian Au pair documentaries. *NORA—Nordic Journal of Feminist and Gender Research, 23*(2), 125–139.

Thorud, E. (2010) *International Migration 2009–2010. Sopemi-report from Norway*. Oslo: Ministry of Justice and Police.

UDI. (2011). *Nye regler for au au pairordningen*. Oslo: Utlendingsdirektoratet. Retrieved from https://www.udiregelverk.no/no/rettskilder/departementets-rundskriv-og-instrukser/2011-012-GI/

UDI. (2012). Rundskriv 2012-015. Retrieved from https://www.udiregelverk.no/no/rettskilder/udi-rundskriv/rs-2012-015/

UDI Annual Reports (1996–2013). Oslo: Utlendingsdirektoratet.
Vuorela, U. (2009). Colonial complicity: The "postcolonial" in a Nordic context. In S. Keskinen, et al. (Eds.), *Complying with colonialism. Gender, race and ethnicity in the Nordic region*. Farnham: Ashgate.
van Walsum, S., & Spijkerboer, T. (2007). *Women and immigration law. New variations on classical feminist themes*. Cavendish: Routledge.
Yuval-Davis, N. (2008). Intersectionality, citizenship and contemporary politics of belonging. In B. Siim & J. Squires (Eds.), *Contesting citizenship*. London: Routledge.

4

Paid Domestic Work in Spain: Gendered Framings of Work and Care in Policies on Social Citizenship

Elin Peterson

Introduction

During the 1960s and 1970s, paid domestic work was disappearing in Spain. Since the 1990s, however, household employment has become increasingly important. While paid domestic work involves a wide range of household tasks, such as cleaning, ironing and cooking, the increase in employment in this sector is essentially related to Spanish families' externalisation of care for older dependent people and small children. The 'commodification' of care—that is, the transition of unpaid care work to paid work—has largely taken place through the employment of domestic workers, who are predominantly migrant women (Pérez Orozco & Gil, 2011; Vega Solís, 2009). The need for new forms of care provision is linked to social, economic and demographic changes, such as the growing importance of the adult worker model—with women as well as men

---

E. Peterson
Department of Social Work, Stockholm University, Stockholm, Sweden

© The Editor(s) (if applicable) and The Author(s) 2016
B. Gullikstad et al. (eds.), *Paid Migrant Domestic Labour in a Changing Europe*, DOI 10.1057/978-1-137-51742-5_4

in paid labour—and the ageing population. Today, within the European Union, Spain has the highest number of employees in paid domestic work. Over half a million people are working in the household sector, which includes both formal and informal employment (García Sainz, Santos Pérez, & Valencia Olivero, 2014; León, 2013). About half of these workers are in formal employment and, even in the context of the economic crisis, such employment has continued to increase (Ibañez & León, 2014). Today, domestic workers definitively contribute to (some) Spanish women and men's social citizenship by providing them with care services, relieving them from unpaid care work and facilitating their reconciliation of work and care. It is therefore highly relevant to ask if and how this shift is reflected in Spanish public policies on social citizenship. In connection to this, the social citizenship of paid domestic workers must also be explored.

This chapter focuses on new policy framings of paid domestic work and caring. I take a closer look at the public policies that constitute social citizenship in Spain in order to scrutinise paid domestic workers' social citizenship status and the role and value their care work is attributed. Three fundamental policy areas are analysed: the regulation of household employment, the dependent care policy and the policies facilitating the reconciliation of work and family life. I argue that these policies jointly shape the rights and positions of domestic workers and the social and economic valuation of paid work and care in private homes. Important reforms have been adopted in all three policy areas. The 2011 Household Employment Act has addressed and improved domestic workers' labour and social citizenship rights. The 2006 Dependent Care Act has made the care deficit in the field of eldercare a visible policy problem. This reform has constituted an important step in the development of social citizenship in Spain. Additionally, several policy reforms have been adopted to help working mothers and fathers reconcile work and family life. These policies have been articulated as particularly vital for promoting gender equality. The analysis looks into the framing of policy problems and solutions, the representations of paid domestic and care work and the articulation of gender and equality. While these policies have been guided by norms of equality and inclusion, the analysis shows that they have also (re)produced inequalities.

Gendered Social Citizenship and Care Work

Care work can be defined in terms of social reproduction: 'the array of activities and relationships involved in maintaining people on a daily basis and inter-generationally' (Glenn, 1992, p. 1). Care can also be more specifically connected to the notion of dependency.[1] In this vein, the core of care work is the dependency of another person, that she/he cannot manage activities in daily life by herself/himself (Wærness, 1984). Defined in these terms, care is closely related to questions of state responsibility, the welfare state and social citizenship.

Feminist social policy research has revealed gender differences in social citizenship and argued that welfare states effectively accord women second-class citizenship because of their involvement in unpaid care work (Knijn & Kremer, 1997; Lister, 1995; O'Connor, 1993; Orloff, 1993). Pointing at the centrality of care, feminist approaches to social citizenship have challenged the construction of the ideal citizen as the 'citizen worker'. An inclusive citizenship has been envisioned, based on the assumption that every citizen—male or female—at some time or another must take care of people they care about (Knijn & Kremer, 1997). Care must be recognised through the lens of the rights and entitlements of those providing and receiving care.

Who is available to carry out the labour of care and who receives the care required is contextual and contingent on political, economic and social organisation (Kittay, Jennings, & Wasunna, 2005). In the Southern European family care regime, social rights related to caregiving and care receiving are limited. Familialism prevails, meaning a permanent trust in the family, intergenerational solidarity and gender structures for the provision of help and support (Saraceno & Keck, 2010). However, while households with low incomes mainly rely on informal unpaid care, middle- and upper-class households increasingly use market-provided care services. The commodification of care largely occurs through the direct employment of domestic workers—predominantly women and migrants. Indeed, scholars have discerned a transition from the family care model

---

[1] For a critical discussion on the concept of 'dependency', see for instance Bacchi and Beasley (2005).

towards a 'migrant-in-the-family' model of care, focusing particularly on the deficit in eldercare (Agrela Romero, 2012; Bettio, Simonazzi, & Villa, 2006). Feminists have long demanded the recognition of women's unpaid caregiving as work, but paid care work is also economically and culturally undervalued work. Research reveals that migrant care work is often undervalued in terms of the worker's salary, social status and rights (Razavi & Staab, 2010). The intersection of care work with inequalities related to gender, class, race, ethnicity and migrant/citizen status has been explored in numerous studies (see Sainsbury, 2014).

Mignon Duffy (2005) argues that the analysis of care work should include 'domestic work' and embrace cleaning, cooking and other non-relational reproductive work. Defining care exclusively as nurturance and relational work excludes very low-paid workers and obscures the class and racial hierarchies of gendered care activities. I argue that it is also vital to stress the caring aspect of 'domestic work'—that is, the often invisible but indispensable care work that is performed for dependent older people and children under the notion of paid domestic work. In this chapter, I highlight the caring dimension of paid domestic work. This is to accentuate the care for dependent older people and small children performed by paid domestic workers in the Spanish context.

Debates Surrounding Social Citizenship: A Discursive Policy Analysis

This chapter examines public policies regarding household employment, dependent care and the reconciliation of work and family life. The material used for the analysis consists of key policy documents related to the major policy reforms in Spain. These are mainly acts and policy plans.

From a feminist perspective, getting care on the political agenda is vital, but the framing of the issue is just as important (Sainsbury, 2014). Centring upon the construction of meaning, the analysis uses a discursive approach to public policy. Drawing upon Carol Bacchi's approach to policy analysis (2009), the focus is the way in which problems are represented in policy. Every 'solution', policy measure and policy proposal involves a particular representation of a problem. The approach aims to capture the ways in which policy shapes the world through a framing of 'problems' and government 'solutions' and a construction of concepts, categories and subject positions (Goodwin, 2011). Problem representations are also subjected to critical scrutiny. This scrutiny involves an exploration of the normative assumptions that underpin the problem representations and a consideration of what is left unproblematic and a reflection on the silences and effects produced by framing a problem in a specific way (Bacchi, 2009). The analysis examines the forms of knowledge or discourses the policy problem relies upon. Discourses can be seen as systems of thoughts composed of ideas, beliefs and practices (Lessa, 2006). As such, they make visible certain issues and marginalise others.

Policy analysis is a central and critical tool for understanding social citizenship. Formal institutions, such as laws and regulations, attribute authority to discourses; they officially confirm particular categorisations and ascribe rights and duties to different social groups, creating hierarchies of needs, rights and obligations (Brodin, 2005). Nancy Fraser argues that recognition stems from social institutions such as law, governmental policies and practices, wherein some categories are constituted as normative and others as inferior, excluded or simply invisible (Fraser, 2000, 2007). The policy analysis presented in this chapter emphasises the extent to which paid domestic workers are visible and recognised as workers and carers. Within this vein, the valuation of paid domestic work and—particularly—care work is analysed.

Paid Domestic Work and Social Citizenship

Household Employment

This part explores the new Spanish regulation on household employment. This regulation is crucial for constituting the rights and social positions of domestic workers, their social citizenship status and the valuation of their work. I examine the way in which problems and solutions are framed in the policy and ask to what extent paid domestic workers are recognised as workers—and carers.

The policy background is important for understanding the recent legal reform. Paid domestic work was fundamentally informal and unregulated work until the Special Regime for Domestic Workers was created in 1969, under the Franco regime. In this first attempt to regulate domestic work in civil law, the 'atypical character' of work in the home justified the exclusion of domestic workers from labour law (León, 2013). With the Special Regime for Domestic Workers of 1985, domestic workers were included in labour law, but this regime provided far less social protection than the General Regime of the Social Security system. For instance, written employment contracts were not required, workers were excluded from unemployment benefits, professional illnesses and accidents were not recognised, sickness leave was covered only from day 29, up to 45 % of the salary could be paid in kind (food and housing) and unpaid presence time was accepted. The employer was required to pay Social Security contributions only if the number of working hours exceeded 20 hours per week. By appealing to the priority of the rights of private family life, domestic workers' rights were subordinated to employers' rights (León, 2010). The Special Regime was criticised and challenged by a variety of social and political actors, including domestic workers' associations, migrant associations, feminist organisations, trade unions and the European Commission (Peterson, 2011, 2015).

Rights can be framed as a matter of equality or a matter of difference—that is, the 'same rights' based on equality/sameness or 'special rights' based on difference (Lister et al., 2007). For paid domestic workers, rights have been represented as special rights and domestic work has been understood as essentially different from 'normal' work. Special rights have meant weaker rights; the framing of domestic work as different has legitimated weaker social and labour protection for domestic workers than for other categories of workers.

The current Household Employment Act of 2011 (Act on the Special Labour Relation of Household Service) addresses the labour and social citizenship rights of domestic workers. The Act frames the problem of household employment in terms of a lack of workers' rights. 'Dignifying the working conditions' is stated as the central objective of the new regulation. In this vein, the reform moves towards a notion of domestic work as 'normal', regular work; domestic workers are recognised as workers with rights and obligations similar to other workers. These rights are improved in various respects. The Act establishes that the rules on minimum wage must apply to household employment and that the salary and tasks to be performed must be agreed by both parties and specified in an employment contract. Weekly working hours cannot exceed 40 hours of 'actual work', and additional presence time must be paid. Domestic workers are granted the same rights as other workers in terms of the reconciliation of work and family life, such as the right to paid maternity leave and paternity leave, and other unpaid leaves. Sickness benefits are to be conceded after the fourth day of illness. As for the live-in modality, special rules apply. Also here, the rights are improved. For instance, 30 % of the salary can be paid in kind—not 45 %, as before the reform. Live-ins must have at least 2 hours off during the day for meals (not counting as working time). Finally, the requirement of live-in workers to spend the night in the home of the employer must be specified in the contract.

The reasons offered for this reform relate to 'social transformations' and the 'natural evolution of habits', although there is no closer explanation of these social changes. The Special Regime for Domestic Workers is claimed to have simply become 'outdated' and the legislation thus serves to 'adapt to the new circumstances'. The 'feminisation' of paid domestic work is mentioned as strengthening the need for reform:

> In this context the strong feminization of domestic employment is particularly relevant. The available data show a distribution that mainly comprises women in percentages close to 94 %, and the remaining 6 % men. (Act 1620/2011)

It is hence assumed that the reform will help women by improving domestic workers' rights as workers and their related social citizenship rights. However, contradictory to the initial recognition that domestic workers are (mainly) women workers, the entire legal text refers to domestic workers in the 'neutral'—that is, the masculine form of a worker (*el trabajador*). The reform frames paid domestic work as a 'women's issue' but without a feminist or social justice perspective. Equality is framed as equal workers' rights and not gender equality or gender justice. Migration policy and migrant status influence workers' rights, conditions and social citizenship status. The Household Employment Act is nevertheless silent on the issue of migration. Migrant workers are not mentioned at all, either as part of the problem (for example, a lack of rights) or as part of the solution (equal rights and dignified working conditions). This can be contrasted with studies that have shown that, apart from being a female-dominated job, domestic work is predominately performed by migrants. In 2009, 63 % of all domestic workers were non-nationals (León, 2013, p. 173). Hence, the law obscures the fact that many of the women working in this sector have a migrant background and their migrant status puts them in an especially vulnerable position.

The reform frames the solution in terms of equal rights. However, difference still matters. Special rules apply in domestic work, given the 'special labour relation'. The Act seeks a 'balance' between equality and difference:

> Changes in the legal framework of the special employment relationship of domestic service is approached from a perspective that seeks to balance the maintenance of differences, where these have an objective and reasonable justification, with the reduction or elimination of differences, when it becomes clear that their reason for being can no longer be motived. (Act 1620/2011)

Different rights are maintained when they are 'objectively' justified by the 'difference' in the character of the work. The definition of the work as special and different from other kinds of work hence continues to legitimise different, and weaker, rights. For instance, domestic workers continue to be excluded from the right to unemployment benefits and employers still have the right to dismiss a worker at any time, in the event that they 'lose confidence' in the worker.[2] The motivation for this special treatment of domestic workers is represented as common sense:

---

[2] The recent reform has already been revised, supposedly to improve the management and social protection in the Special System of Household Employees. While the 2011 reform made employers responsible for managing the social security affiliation and contributions of their workers, the subsequent Act 29/2012 made workers responsible for their own affiliation and contribution to social security when working fewer than 60 hours monthly in a household and when working in various households. The new rules make domestic workers responsible for any failure to register and contribute to Social Security.

4 Paid Domestic Work in Spain: Gendered Framings of Work ...

The particular conditions in which the activities of the people who work in domestic service are carried out, which justify a specific and differentiated regulation, are well known. In the first place, the sphere in which the service is provided, the family home, so closely related to personal and family intimacy and totally alien to and different from the common denominator of labour relations, which are carried out in environments of productive activity dominated by the principles of the market economy; and, secondly, and corollary of the previous, the personal link based on a special relation of confidence that, from its beginning, presides over the labour relation between the head of the household and the domestic worker [*el trabajador*], which does not necessarily exist in the other types of work relations. (Act 1620/2011)

The representation of paid domestic work as different is linked to assumptions about the home, intimacy, family and social reproduction. Domestic work in the home is contrasted with productive work in the public sphere. While productive work is associated with the market economy, paid reproductive work is assumed to follow a different logic. This logic draws on the logic assumed to apply to unpaid reproductive work, based on altruism and love, rather than economic interests. The hierarchy between reproductive and productive work is used in this policy reform to explain why paid domestic work must be connected with weaker rights. The productive–reproductive dichotomy is inherently linked with gender relations. Gender structures the division of labour between paid productive labour and unpaid reproductive labour, assigning women the primary responsibility in the latter. Gender also structures the division within paid labour, between higher paid male-dominated occupations and lower paid female-dominated occupations. In Nancy Fraser's terms (2007, p. 26), recognition is about institutionalised patterns of cultural value, as expressed in law, policy and practices. The Household Employment Act is inscribed in a discourse that privileges work associated with production, the public sphere and masculinity, attributing lower value to reproductive work, the private sphere and work coded as feminine. While striving for equality and inclusion, paid domestic work is still not recognised as equal to other forms of paid work. As such, paid domestic workers are not recognised as equal workers. The misrecognition of domestic work is legitimised in the policy by the connection that is drawn between paid domestic work and unpaid reproductive work.

While paid domestic work is associated with social reproduction and differentiated from productive work, the tasks included in household employment go beyond what is usually considered reproductive work. The activities included in the definition of this category of work are quite diverse, and they incorporate, for instance, gardening and driving:

> The objects of this special employment relation are the services and activities provided for the family home, which may take any form of housework, such as management and care for the home as a whole or some of its parts, care for and attention to family members or people who are part of the household, and other tasks that are developed as part of the household work as a whole, such as child care, gardening, driving and other similar tasks. (Act 1960/2011)

In this list of tasks, caregiving is just another activity among other activities and services performed in and around the household (see also Palenga-Möllenbeck, this volume).[3] While the provision of services for able adults is clearly part of this work, and care for dependents is explicitly included in the definition in terms of childcare, care for dependent older people is not mentioned specifically. Despite considering social changes as a motivation for the reform, the reform does not address the fact that the household employment sector increasingly involves care for older dependent people, often within the live-in modality, as the workers live with the older person for whom they care. This care work is regulated by the Household Employment Act. Nevertheless, by using the label domestic work, public policy conceals the widespread use of domestic workers for eldercare, particularly in the absence of publicly financed care services. Given the invisibility of care work for older people, the reform contributes specifically to the undervaluation of this work. The policy does not take into account the specific tasks, skills and characteristics of eldercare.

---

[3] Likewise, official statistics on employment and social security do not differentiate between the different types of domestic service in Spain.

The Household Employment reform has involved a shift towards recognition of domestic workers as workers, and this recognition is vital for both their labour-related rights and their social citizenship. However, the norms of inclusion and equality are only partially endorsed with this reform. As we have seen, domestic workers are still not represented as equal to other workers. Additionally, the caring dimension of paid domestic work is only weakly recognised and care for older dependent people is entirely invisible.

Dependent Care

This section explores the 2006 Dependent Care Act, a crucial policy for the development of social citizenship rights in Spain. I examine the way in which problems and solutions are represented in the policy on dependent care and explore the (in)visibility of paid domestic work. The analysis underlines the exclusionary effects of the definition of care in use.

Eldercare entered the national political agenda with the 2006 Personal Autonomy and Dependent Care Act. The policy was elaborated on the initiative of the Socialist government and the negotiations involved a range of different actors—the most influential being trade unions, employers' organisations and organisations representing older people and people with disabilities (Serrano, Artiaga, & Davila, 2013). The reform shifted away from the construction of care for older people and people with disability as an almost exclusively family matter. It constituted a significant change, as the care needs and citizenship rights of dependent people became a public concern and a visible policy problem:

> The care for dependent people and the promotion of their autonomy constitute one of the principal challenges of social policy in developed countries. The challenge is nothing else but attending to the needs of those who, because of their situation of special vulnerability, require support to carry out essential daily life activities, to achieve more personal autonomy and to be able to exercise their citizen rights. (Act 39/2006)

In the Act, 'dependency' is represented as an urgent problem that must be addressed. The demographic development in Spain, with a strongly ageing population, is used to explain the need for a reform. The Act establishes a universal right to support based on care needs—not related to labour market participation or nationality; the right can be conferred to any dependent person residing legally in Spain.[4] The Act also establishes a catalogue of social services and benefits. It encourages home-based care, with dependent people staying in their 'usual environment' for as long as possible. A care allowance is introduced for 'non-professional' care—that is, family care in the home.

The White Paper for Dependent Care from 2005 (IMSERSO, 2005) was used as a point of departure to discuss and negotiate the future law. The White Paper underlines the need for advances in 'social justice', making public institutions responsible for the work women have traditionally performed and guaranteeing adequate care for dependent persons. In contrast, the 2006 Act does not frame the issue in terms of justice. The focus falls on the deficit in informal care caused by social changes such as women's labour market participation.

> One should not forget that, until now, it has been the families, and especially women, who traditionally have taken care of dependent persons, which constitutes what has come to be called 'informal support'. The changes in the family model and the progressive incorporation of almost three million women, in the last decade, in the labour market introduce new factors in this situation which makes a reform of the traditional system of care essential in order to secure an adequate capacity of care provision for those who need it. (Act 39/2006)

State responsibility in dependent care is represented as necessary because women are no longer able to assume the entire burden on an informal (and unpaid) basis. Eldercare is represented as a women's issue, given that most family carers are women. Following from this, the reform is assumed to help women. Nevertheless, the Act does not consider the norm of gender equality. Indeed, an analysis of the policy debates preceding the Act has shown that the issues of gender equality and men's

---

[4] In the context of the economic crisis, austerity measures have been adopted and important cuts in social spending have been carried out. Universality as a norm is challenged, given that many older dependent people do not receive help (Ibañez & León, 2014).

participation in and responsibility for care for older dependent people were absent. The gendered division of labour in dependent care was taken for granted (Peterson, 2011). The reform is assumed to be women-friendly, however, because it relieves (mainly) women from unpaid care work and helps to reconcile work and family life.

The Dependent Care Act establishes that care for dependent people can be divided into different categories. The first category, 'professional care', is defined as care provided by a public institution or organisation, either for-profit or non-profit, or by a self-employed professional specialised in the provision of care services. The second category, 'non-professional care', is defined as help and support provided by the family. Two other categories of care are included: 'personal assistance' (related to care for younger people with disabilities) and care provided by the 'third sector' (characterised by non-profit solidarity work). This definition of care excludes the care provided by paid domestic workers; they do not fit into either of the established categories. Following from this, the conditions, rights and qualifications of domestic workers caring for older dependent people are not dealt with in this legal framework. The exclusion of the category of domestic workers has been criticised by feminist organisations and domestic workers' associations (Peterson, 2015).

The silence on the care provided by paid domestic workers can be contrasted with studies that have emphasised that domestic workers are filling the gaps in eldercare: 14.5 % of older people in need of care have domestic workers as primary caregivers (Martínez Buján, 2011, p. 102). In the context of the economic crisis, austerity measures have been adopted and important cuts in social spending have been carried out (Ibañez & León, 2014). The care allowance for home-based family care has become a widespread benefit in spite of the law's intention to make this an 'exception' (Rodríguez & Marbán, 2013). Studies have pointed out that the care allowance lets families to outsource caring tasks, as they may use the allowance to employ a domestic worker. This foments informal work, since the family carer officially takes responsibility for the provision of care (Martínez Buján, 2010).

Serrano et al. (2013) argue that the influential role played by geriatric professions and organisations representing older people in the negotiation of the Dependent Care Act marginalises feminist claims related to unpaid caregivers and paid care workers. In this vein, caregiving work—whether paid or unpaid—receives at best a secondary role. Hence, the silence on paid domestic workers and their role in eldercare can be understood in light of the invisibility and low valuation of both paid and unpaid care work.

Considering that domestic workers' care work for older people is invisible in both the Dependent Care Act and the Household Employment Act, it can be concluded that the role of domestic workers in Spanish eldercare is not acknowledged in public policy. Indeed, this silence can be seen as a misrecognition of the domestic workers who care for older dependent people in Spain.

The Reconciliation of Work and Family Life

This section explores Spanish policy reforms that have aimed to facilitate the reconciliation of work and family life. These reforms have been articulated as central to support the inclusion of women in the labour market and to promote gender equality. As such, the policies can be seen as an extension of social citizenship in Spain. The framing of problems and solutions related to gender equality and the combination of work and care is in focus. I analyse the representation of paid domestic work and workers in the policies and in a parliamentary debate.[5]

The 'reconciliation of work and family life' entered the Spanish agenda under the Conservative government in the late 1990s. At that time, making family and work responsibilities compatible for 'working mothers' became an important national goal. It was emphasised that mothers should be able to develop their professional careers and have as many children as they wanted. The 1999 Act to Promote Workers' Reconciliation of Family and Work Life therefore introduced new rights related to paid and unpaid leave for mothers in relation to childbirth and adoption. The working mother was put forward as the normative subject of reconciliation policies and, in extension, gender equality policies. Given that class, ethnicity and sexuality were absent issues, the working

---

[5] This section on the reconciliation of work and family life draws upon research presented in Peterson (2011).

mother was assumed to be a middle-to upper-class heterosexual Spanish woman belonging to the ethnic majority. While women's paid work was considered the requisite for gender equality, the unequal distribution of care and domestic work between women and men was not in focus. At the same time, the policies emphasised 'family responsibility', stressing individual responsibility over collective solutions and state responsibility in care.

Nearly a decade after the Reconciliation Act, and under a Socialist government, 'co-responsibility' between women and men emerged as an important policy problem. The Act for Effective Equality between Women and Men from 2007 emphasises the role of fathers in childcare, with an individual right to paternity leave that promotes 'greater co-responsibility between women and men in assuming family obligations'. Co-responsibility is considered vital in order to increase women's paid work and promote gender equality. At the same time, women's 'employability' is emphasised. The emphasis on employability reveals that women's adaptation to labour market requirements is central. Helping people solve their care dilemmas is treated as only secondary.

The gender equality discourse has stressed paid work as the key. As Drucilla Barker (2005) contends, paid work is crucially important for women, but the association of paid work with emancipation, self-realisation and choice reflects the experience of only relatively privileged women. The Spanish gender equality discourse can be said to reflect the situation of more privileged working women. Paid domestic work and other kinds of feminised, low-paid and undervalued work have been marginal in the policy discourse. The silence on domestic workers in policies on reconciliation and gender equality can be understood in this context. While the more recent policies accentuate the importance of 'co-responsibility' between women and men, the externalisation of domestic work and care work to paid domestic care workers is not problematised (rather similar to the Norwegian policy discourse. See Gullikstad and Annfelt, this volume). The reproduction of the gendered division of labour, along divisions of class, race, ethnicity and nationality, through the transfer of domestic care work to 'other' women has not been challenged. The gender inequalities involved in this process have not been up for debate.

In contrast, scholars have pointed to the problem that (some) women's emancipation has not gone hand in hand with a reorganisation of the gendered division of labour (Lister et al., 2007; Oso, 1998; Peterson, 2007; Tobío, 2005; Williams & Gavanas, 2008). Laura Oso (1998, p. 196) wrote, almost two decades ago, in her study on migrant women in Spain that 'the domestic worker replaces her professional employer in reproductive tasks that neither the state nor the partners share'. Studies have demonstrated that employment of domestic workers for childcare, cooking, cleaning, clothes washing and ironing is a common coping strategy among working mothers. It is particularly common among middle- and upper-class women, but even working-class women use this strategy to some extent in Spain. A survey on the coping strategies of working mothers has shown that more than 50 % of the women at a high socio-economic level, about 30 % of women at a middle level and over 10 % of women at a lower level count on the assistance of domestic workers (Fernández Cordón & Tobío Soler, 2005, p. 35).[6] In academic research, also, domestic work has been associated with women, but it should be remarked here that men and working fathers obviously benefit from paid domestic work, as well (see Kristensen; Palenga-Möllenbeck, both this volume).

While paid domestic work and workers are largely absent issues, the representation of paid domestic work as necessary work appears in the parliamentary debate on the Special Regime for Domestic Workers from 2005. The debate shows a concern about domestic work being 'feminized' and 'undervalued'. Additionally, it is acknowledged in the debate that domestic workers are mainly migrant women who do not work to earn a 'complement to the male breadwinner', but to 'maintain their families'. Interestingly, the debate shows that domestic workers are seen as providing solutions to Spanish families' care dilemmas. The issue at stake is, hence, not only domestic workers' rights and working conditions, but also the interests of Spanish families 'where both men and women work outside of the home'. Thus, the emphasis lies on families' access to domestic services: domestic services should not be 'too expensive for

---

[6] The employment of domestic workers among working mothers has most probably decreased with the crisis. However, there is a need of more research here.

the middle class'. The debate reveals the view that domestic services are expected to be even more 'necessary' in the future:

> We should be aware that domestic work or employment will become more demanded in Spain due to the increasing incorporation of women in the labour market, as occurs in our neighbouring countries. It is work that every day becomes more necessary in order to better reconcile work and family life. (MP Lourdes Méndez Monasterio, Conservative Party *Partido Popular*, parliamentary debate, 21 June 2005)

While domestic workers are generally positioned as marginal subjects, they are here framed as a 'necessary' resource for Spanish families. The idea that domestic workers are necessary for Spanish families to manage work and care is taken as common sense. This means an emphasis on individual solutions to care dilemmas can be seen as legitimising the limited state responsibility in care provision.

Conclusions

The policies explored in this chapter can all be seen as extending social citizenship in Spain: strengthening social- and labour-related rights for employees in the household service sector, announcing new social rights and support for dependent people and introducing improved rights for combining work and care for small children. However, the very policies that aim for a more inclusive citizenship also have exclusionary effects.

The policies I have analysed in this chapter together shape the rights and positions of domestic workers and the social and economic valuation of paid work and care in private homes. The new household employment regulation implies movement towards a notion of domestic work as 'equal' to other forms of work. Nonetheless, the policy also emphasises that domestic work is 'different' and linked to the private sphere and social reproduction; this legitimises weaker rights. Thus, the law connects the low valuation of women's unpaid care and paid domestic work. I have drawn special attention to the caring dimension of paid domestic work and the analysis has shown that domestic workers only receive weak recognition as caregivers and their care for older dependent people is invisible in public policy. Paid domestic work does not fit into the official definition of care, as articulated in the dependent care policy. Consequently, the specific working conditions of domestic workers caring for older dependent people are not considered and questions related to their qualifications are absent. This particularly affects migrant women, who currently dominate this profession. In the policy aiming at reconciling work and family life, women's participation in paid work is represented as leading to gender equality. Within this discourse, paid domestic care workers are only marginal subjects, along with other categories of workers who perform low-paid, feminised and undervalued work. The externalisation of domestic work to 'other' women has not been problematised. At the same time, it is assumed that Spanish families need access to the services of domestic workers to 'solve' their work and care dilemmas.

Given the current economic crisis and the influence of austerity measures, Spanish households will most likely continue to turn to domestic workers for caring tasks in the absence of social services. A future challenge will be to combine the recognition of domestic workers—as workers and carers—on the one hand, and a more just distribution of care between genders and within society as a whole, on the other.

References

Agrela Romero, B. (2012). Towards a model of externalisation and denationalisation of care? The role of female migrant care workers for dependent older people in Spain. *European Journal of Social Work, 15*(1), 45–61.
Bacchi, C. (2009). *Analysing policy: What's the problem represented to be?* Frenchs Forest: Pearson.
Bacchi, C., & Beasley, C. (2005). The limits of trust and respect: Rethinking dependency. *Social Alternatives, 24*(4), 55–59.
Barker, D. K. (2005). Beyond women and economics: Rereading "women's work". *Signs: Journal of Women in Culture and Society, 30*(4), 2189–2209.
Bettio, F., Simonazzi, A., & Villa, P. (2006). Change in care regimes and female migration: The "care drain" in the Mediterranean. *Journal of European Social Policy, 16*(3), 271–285.

Brodin, H. (2005). *Does anybody care? Public and private responsibilities in Swedish eldercare 1940–2000*. Doctoral thesis, Department of Economic History, Umeå University.

Duffy, M. (2005). Reproducing labor inequalities: Challenges for feminists conceptualizing care at the intersections of gender, race and class. *Gender and Society, 19*(1), 66–82.

Fernández Cordón, J. A., & Tobío Soler, C. (2005). Conciliar las responsabilidades familiares y laborales: Políticas y prácticas sociales. *Documento de trabajo, 79*. Madrid: Fundación Alternativas.

Fraser, N. (2000). Rethinking recognition. *New Left Review, 3*(May/June), 107–120.

Fraser, N. (2007). Feminist politics in the age of recognition: A two-dimensional approach to gender justice. *Studies in Social Justice, 1*(1), 23–35.

García Sainz, C., Santos Pérez, M. L., & Valencia Olivero, N. (2014). La construcción social del mercado laboral doméstico en España a comienzos del siglo XXI. *Cuadernos de Relaciones Laborales, 32*(1), 101–131.

Glenn, E. N. (1992). From servitude to service: Historical continuities in the racial division of paid reproduction work. *Signs, 18*(1), 1–43.

Goodwin, S. (2011). Analysing policy as discourse: Methodological advances in policy analysis. In L. Markauskaite, P. Freebody, & J. Irwin (Eds.), *Methodological choice and design: Scholarship, policy and practice in social and educational research*. New York: Springer.

Ibañez, Z., & León, M. (2014). Resisting crisis at what cost? Migrant care workers in private households. In B. Anderson & I. Shutes (Eds.), *Migration and care labour. Theory, policy and politics*. Houndmills: Palgrave Macmillan.

IMSERSO. (2005). *Libro Blanco de atención a personas en situación de dependencia en España*. Madrid: IMSERSO.

Kittay, E. F., Jennings, B., & Wasunna, A. A. (2005). Dependency, difference and the global ethic of longterm care. *Journal of Political Philosophy, 13*, 443–469.

Knijn, T., & Kremer, M. (1997). Gender and the caring dimensions of welfare states: Toward inclusive citizenship. *Social Politics, 4*(3), 328–361.

León, M. (2010). Migration and care work in Spain: The domestic sector revisited. *Social Policy & Society, 9*(3), 409–418.

León, M. (2013). A real job? Regulating household work: The case of Spain. *European Journal of Women's Studies, 2*(2), 170–188.

Lessa, I. (2006). Discursive struggles within social welfare: Restaging teen motherhood. *British Journal of Social Work, 36*(2), 283–298.

Lister, R. (1995). Dilemmas of engendering citizenship. *Economy & Society, 24*(1), 1–40.

Lister, R., Williams, F., Anttonen, A., Bussemaker, J., Gerhard, U., Heinen, J., et al. (2007) *Gendering citizenship in Western Europe: New challenges for citizenship research in a cross-national context.* Bristol: Policy Press.

Martínez Buján, R. (2010). Servicio doméstico y trabajo de cuidados. Hacia la privatización del cuidado familiar. *Alternativas: Cuadernos de trabajo social, 17*, 157–179.

Martínez Buján, R. (2011). La reorganización de los cuidados familiares en un contexto de migración internacional. *Cuadernos de Relaciones Laborales, 29*(1), 93–123.

O'Connor, J. (1993). Gender, class and citizenship in the comparative analysis of welfare state regimes: Theoretical and methodological issues. *The British Journal of Sociology, 44*(3), 501–518.

Orloff, A. S. (1993). Gender and the social rights of citizenship: The comparative analysis of gender relations and welfare states. *American Sociological Review, 58*(3), 303–328.

Oso, L. (1998). *La migración hacia España de mujeres jefas de hogar.* Madrid: National Women's Agency.

Pérez Orozco, A., & Gil, S. (2011). *Desigualdades a flor de piel. Cadenas globales de cuidados—Concreciones en el empleo de hogar y articulaciones políticas.* Madrid: ONU Mujeres.

Peterson, E. (2007). The invisible carers: Framing domestic work(ers) in gender equality policies in Spain. *European Journal of Women's Studies, 14*(3), 265–280.

Peterson, E. (2011). *Beyond the 'women-friendly' welfare state: Framing gender inequality as a policy problem in Spanish and Swedish politics of care.* Doctoral thesis, University Complutense of Madrid.

Peterson, E. (2015). License to care? Migrant domestic workers in Spanish employment and family policies. In M. Kontos & G. Bonifacio (Eds.), *Migrant domestic workers and family life: International perspectives.* Houndmills: Palgrave Macmillan.

Razavi, S., & Staab, S. (2010). Underpaid and overworked: A cross-national perspective on care workers. *International Labour Review, 149*(4), 407–422.

Rodríguez, G., & Marbán, V. (2013). Long-term care in Spain: Between family care tradition and the public recognition of social risk. In C. Ranci & E. Pavolini (Eds.), *Reforms in long term care policies in Europe.* New York: Springer.

Sainsbury, D. (2014). Gender, care, and welfare. In G. Waylen, K. Celis, J. Kantola, & S. L. Weldon (Eds.), *Oxford handbook of gender and politics*. Oxford: Oxford University Press.

Saraceno, C., & Keck, W. (2010). Can we identify intergenerational policy regimes in Europe? *European Societies, 12*(5), 675–696.

Serrano, A., Artiaga, A., & Davila, M. C. (2013). Crisis de cuidados, Ley de Dependencia y confusión semántica. *Revista Internacional de Sociología, 71*(3), 669–694.

Tobío, C. (2005). *Madres que trabajan. Dilemas y estrategias*. Madrid: Cátedra.

Vega Solís, C. (2009). *Culturas del cuidado en transición. Espacios, sujetos e imaginarios en una sociedad de migración*. Barcelona: Editorial UOC.

Wærness, K. (1984). The rationality of caring. *Economic and Industrial Democracy, 5*, 185–211.

Williams, F., & Gavanas, A. (2008). The intersection of child-care regimes and migration regimes: A three country study. In H. Lutz (Ed.), *Migration and domestic work*. Aldershot: Ashgate.

5

Gendered Work and Citizenship: Diverse Experiences of Au Pairing in the UK

Rosie Cox and Nicky Busch

Introduction[1]

Au pairs are an important source of domestic and childcare labour for UK families. While there are no reliable or official statistics on the number of au pairs in Britain, one estimate suggests there may be as many as 90,000 au pairs living with families in the UK (Smith, 2008). Unlike the Nordic countries, the USA or France, the UK does not import au pairs from low-income countries of the Global South; rather au pairs in the UK are expected to be European Union (EU) citizens, in theory at least, people who have equal citizenship rights to UK nationals.

In this chapter, we use the case of au pairs in the UK to examine how the operation of a particular migration regime has 'moulded'

---

[1] This research was made possible by ESRC Research Grant ES/J007528/1 'Au Pairing After the Au Pair Scheme'.

R. Cox (✉) • N. Busch
Department of Geography, Environment and Development Studies, Birkbeck College, University of London, London, UK

© The Editor(s) (if applicable) and The Author(s) 2016
B. Gullikstad et al. (eds.), *Paid Migrant Domestic Labour in a Changing Europe*, DOI 10.1057/978-1-137-51742-5_5

101

(Anderson, 2010) migrants from different countries, with different relationships to a labour market and produced different experiences of citizenship. We argue that deregulation of the au pair sector in 2008 has produced au pairs whose lived experience of citizenship does not match their formal rights and au pairs from different EU nations, who have the same formal citizenship rights, actually have very different experiences of citizenship in the UK. Without clear government guidelines or regulation, au pairs in contemporary Britain have to negotiate their own standing in the sector in a context which is far from equal. Employer preferences for au pairs of different nationalities and the very different situations in au pairs' home countries—in terms of employment opportunities and pay rates—work together to produce a gap between the putative equality of formal EU citizenship and the practical and lived experience of citizenship as migrants in the UK. In the UK some au pairs are more equal than others.

The chapter begins by setting out the research methods used and then moves to discuss the relationship between citizenship rights, gender and domestic work, to show how the negation of women's unpaid labour in the home is related to domestic workers' and au pairs' unequal access to citizenship. Women, particularly those involved in domestic labour, have struggled to be recognised as citizens because their work is not recognised as 'work' and participation in work is the basis for citizenship. The chapter then relates this gendered aspect of citizenship to au pairing in the UK to show how changes to the regulation of au pair migration in the later twentieth and early twenty-first centuries have produced au pairs whose lived experience of citizenship does not match their formal rights. This has been possible because au pairing is constructed as something other than work in official discourse and policy. Au pairs do not have the legal rights of workers because of the gendering of domestic labour which excludes it from imaginings of work. Without status as workers, au pairs' ability to exercise citizenship rights is also impaired. We then turn to the findings from our empirical research to show how au pairs experience lived citizenship. We highlight how au pairs from different European countries, with the same formal citizenship rights, actually have very different experiences of belonging and exercising their rights within the UK. We look first at the effects of host family preferences and prejudices for au pairs of particular nationalities and then at the effects of conditions in au pairs' home countries and their class position on their ability to secure fair treatment in the UK.

Researching Au Pairs in the UK

This chapter draws on research carried out between May 2012 and January 2014. We interviewed 40 au pairs and 15 host families, key informants in the sector (NGOs, au pair agencies and so on), and analysed 1000 advertisements from Gumtree.com, a website that is a very popular place to advertise for au pairs and au pair positions. This chapter draws particularly on findings from the interviews with au pairs and host parents. The au pairs interviewed came from 15 different countries, all in Europe. The most important countries numerically were the Czech Republic (six interviewees), Germany (six interviewees), Romania (six interviewees) and Spain (five interviewees). Between them these four countries were home to more than half (23 out of 40) the interviewees in our au pair sample. The hosts—twelve women and three men—had between them hosted 50 au pairs over the years. The au pairs who were interviewed were not hosted by the hosts who were interviewed, in order to ensure anonymity. We also found that the hosts who agreed to be interviewed appeared to be 'good' hosts, as perhaps would be expected. Their attitudes towards au pairs and the conditions they offered the au pairs they hosted were better than the average experienced by our au pair interviewees or seen in the analysis of Gumtree.com advertisements.

The interviews yielded extremely rich data about the daily lives of au pairs and hosts and the ways that being an au pair or hosting an au pair fitted in with longer term plans to make a different or better future for themselves and/or their families. In analysing the data, we were particularly interested to identify the effects of the deregulation of au pairing on au pairs, and in this chapter we take up two themes from the interviews which we analysed in detail: narratives around nationality/ethnicity by both hosts and au pairs and details of the tasks and daily routines of au pairs and their resulting remuneration. The first of these themes allowed us to examine how nationality affects lived experiences in a situation where all au pairs are, in theory, equal European citizens. For example, at the time the research was carried out, despite Romania and Bulgaria being EU members, Romanian and Bulgarian nationals needed a work permit to enter as au pairs and that permit tied them to a named host family whom they could not leave (Anderson, 2014). Bulgarians and Romanians have also been subject to extensive adverse media representation, reflecting (and encouraging) broader prejudice against them in the UK (see Migration Observatory, 2014) and we were interested to discover how this was discussed by those involved in au pairing. The second theme enabled us to explore what 'au pairing' is when it is not defined by official discourse and how this might be experienced by different groups of au pairs differently. For example, our analysis of advertisements revealed a very wide range of working hours and tasks being required of au pairs and very wide variation in levels of 'pocket money' and other rewards offered. We were interested to find out which au pairs ended up in which au pair posts and how they were 'sorted' into them. Together attention to these themes reveals the ways that au pairs from different countries are discursively placed within hierarchies and the material effects of difference in nationality on working conditions and remuneration.

In this chapter we use the term 'au pair' to refer to people caring for children and performing domestic work in private homes in the UK under conditions that can be seen to reflect varying interpretations by these individuals, by their 'hosts' and by au pair agencies of a now-defunct Home Office au pair visa scheme, that were subsequently adopted by the British Au Pair Agencies Association (see BAPAA, 2015). We use the term 'au pair' despite acknowledging that after 2008 the 'au pair scheme' no longer exists and the distinction between someone employed as an au pair and someone employed as a nanny is arbitrary and dependent on self-definition and/or categorization by agencies and by hosts/employers. We continue to use the term because, despite the legal and policy vacuum surrounding au pairing at the time of our research, the term remains in common use (Busch, 2015).

Citizenship, Gender and Domestic Work

Anupama Roy (2005) describes citizenship as an inherently paradoxical concept. It is an exclusive category epitomising the hegemonic force of those who are able to define who and what is a citizen, yet at the same time it has the potential to be emancipatory and at some moments in history the extension of citizenship has involved the dismantling of structures of oppression. When gender and race/ethnicity are considered, this paradoxical nature of citizenship comes even further to the fore. The domain of citizenship has been 'very much conditioned [...] by the way women, slaves, workers and subject peoples [both] as social categories and lived experiences were simultaneously incorporated within and omitted from national-cultural and juridico-political identities as citizens' (Roy, 2005, p. 2). It is possible, therefore, to simultaneously struggle for citizenship rights for marginalised groups and to critique the concept of citizenship itself.

Modern (liberal) notions of citizenship are based on the idea that citizenship is egalitarian and that it is universal. That is, that citizenship involves the full and equal membership of a political community (after Marshall, 1950) and that citizenship can be extended to various marginalised sections of the population, granting the same rights to all regardless of class, gender or creed. However, liberal definitions of citizenship mask differences in class, culture, gender and ethnicity and overlook their relevance for the exercise of citizenship rights (see amongst others Roy, 2005; Young, 1989).

Importantly feminists have criticised liberal citizenship as being based on forms of social organisation and events which specifically excluded women. They have shown how the association of women with the 'private' sphere of the home has been an effective means of limiting both formal citizenship for women and the ability to access citizenship rights (Walby, 1994). Feminists have also revealed that citizenship usually depends upon being recognised as a worker in order to fully access rights. This is most clear in the case of wives or female partners of men who have taken on the traditional role of carers for their families. In these cases women are financially dependent on men and often denied full access to social welfare benefits, which are distributed to those who are seen to 'work'. Financial dependence can curtail women's political engagement and lack of access to welfare benefits is clearly a limitation on their social citizenship. Thus, the imagining of caring as something other than 'work' is important in mediating women's enjoyment of citizenship rights (Walby, 1994).

An examination of paid domestic labour is a particularly potent site to challenge the public/private divide and with this to explore how citizenship rights are distributed. Domestic workers often find themselves denied access to full citizenship rights in similar ways to unpaid 'housewives'. Their labour is not recognised as work and migrant domestic workers are often discriminated against in immigration and employment law (Cox, 2012). It is easy to assume that unpaid labour in the home is rarely recognised as work because it is unpaid; housework is imagined as a 'labour of love' carried out, not for pecuniary reward, but because of emotional attachment to those for whom it is performed. It would seem logical then that when such labours are paid for, they would be recognised as work like any other. However, this is rarely the case and domestic workers' activities are routinely elided with those of unpaid wives, excluding them from citizenship in similar ways (Anderson, 2014). For migrant domestic workers and au pairs, one important way in which this happens is through the operation of migration regimes which create conditions that limit citizenship rights or the ability to practically access citizenship (Cox, 2012).

A large number of studies of paid domestic workers and au pairs have shown their poor treatment to be related to a lack of formal citizenship rights, particularly for undocumented workers or workers whose visa status ties them to an employer who they also live with (see for example Anderson, 1993; Mundlak & Shamir, 2008). Domestic workers and au pairs are often subject to specific and highly restrictive migration rules, which for the most part give domestic workers fewer rights, for example, to permanent settlement or family reunification, than other migrants and impose stricter controls on their behaviour (Ozyegin & Hondagneu-Sotelo, 2008; Gullikstad and Annfelt; Peterson, this volume). Most commonly this includes stipulations that domestic workers live in their employers' homes but there may also be regulations on personal relationships, or even appearance (Constable, 2003; Yeoh & Huang, 1999; Stubberud, this volume). Domestic workers and au pairs, therefore, often face limits on their formal citizenship rights because their work is constructed differently to other forms of labour and they live and work in conditions which make it particularly difficult for them to access the rights that they do have.

The (De)Regulation of Au Pairing and Citizenship in the UK

The UK has a long history as a destination for au pairs. Au pairing developed within the context of a 'servant crisis' in a country riven by class inequalities and antagonisms. Au pairs were seen as a solution to this as they were supposed to be 'on a par' with their hosts and, therefore, outside the class antipathies which made domestic service unattractive (Liarou, 2015). Over the course of the late twentieth and early twenty-first centuries, the UK government first introduced, and then amended, an au pair visa which allowed young women (until 1993 when men were also included) from certain European countries to enter the UK temporarily as au pairs.[2] As the EU expanded, nationals of the countries which had been entitled to apply for the au pair visa increasingly gained free access to the UK labour market and au pairing became less attractive to them as a way to enter the UK. When this happened, the UK government responded first, in 2002, by extending the visa scheme to include Bulgaria, Estonia, Latvia, Lithuania, Poland and Romania in order to ensure a continuous supply of au pairs (Cox, 2006) and then by abolishing the visa and deregulating au pairing entirely (see Busch, 2015 and Cox, 2012 for details on this).

When, in November 2008, the UK abolished its au pair visa, it abolished with it the only government definition of what an au pair is. The expectation was not that there would no longer be au pairs in the UK,

---

[2] In 2000, before the scheme was expanded, these countries were Andora, Bosnia-Herzegovina. Croatia, Cyprus. the Czech Republic, the Faeroes, Greenland, Hungary, Lichtenstein, Macedonia, Malta, Monaco, San Marino, Slovak Republic, Slovenia. Switzerland and Turkey.

in fact numbers are booming, rather that au pairs would now come exclusively from EU countries and would, therefore, not need visas. This change has made au pairs invisible to the UK authorities and the conditions that they live in are entirely unmonitored. Between November 2008 and June 2014 the UK government provided neither definition of au pairing nor guidance on how au pairs should be treated, yet it did (in other legislation) specifically exclude au pairs from the categories of 'worker' and 'employee' and explicitly deny them rights to the National Minimum Wage, to holiday entitlement, to protection under the European Working Time Directive and other labour protections (Cox, 2012).

This deregulation of a numerically important migration route, and the negation of the very real work that au pairs do, is possible because of the low status of reproductive labour and the enduring power of the public/private divide. Au pairs are not classified as workers because the work they do is 'women's work' (Cox, 2012). As Bridget Anderson argues:

> The tasks performed by au pairs were not work because they were performed as 'part of the family.' This was not 'work' because au pairs were 'equal.' 'Equality' signified not getting paid: wives and daughters don't get paid, only servants, who are not equal. Thus the invisibility of the economic basis of the household was maintained, even as non-family members were accommodated [...] The history of the au pair visa demonstrates the shifting but mutually dependent nature of citizenship, family, work and gender, and the attempts to accommodate this within liberal discourses of equality (Anderson, 2014, p. 9).

From the outset the work of au pairing was disguised behind a rhetoric of equality and cultural exchange (Liarou, 2015) in a way that was only possible because of the gendering of domestic labour. The denial of their work compromised the citizenship of au pairs whilst supporting British nation building by maintaining rhetorics of home, family and equality.

Different EU nationals have been absorbed into this new world of au pairing in different ways despite their theoretical equality within the UK labour market as EU citizens. This reflects the subtleties of the workings of migration regimes and the way that migration and employment networks have their own dynamics and may persist despite changes in legislation (Massey, 1990).

In the section below, we look in detail at how three groups of au pairs in the UK are able to enjoy (or not) their citizenship rights. The exclusion of domestic work from imaginings of work affects the rights and experiences of au pairs both male and female, but these experiences are also mediated by class and nationality, meaning that some au pairs are more able to enjoy the rights that they all theoretically have.

Some Au Pairs are More Equal than Others

We have tentatively identified three groups who have different motivations to enter au pairing and who experience different treatment as au pairs: Eastern Europeans (particularly Romanian and Bulgarians); North-West Europeans (mostly German in our sample) and Spanish au pairs, whose numbers appear to have grown significantly during the current financial crisis. These three groups have had differential access to au pairing in both formal (legal) terms and practically because of stereotyping and prejudice by hosts and agencies, which favour some nationalities over others. Despite their formal EU citizenship, these groups have different experiences of practical or 'lived' citizenship. A range of types of 'au pairs' is produced within the UK au pair labour market, ranging from the most exploitable who are least able to access their rights, to the most assured who are better able to access citizenship rights, protect themselves from exploitation and avoid the worst host families. It is not the case that 'good' and 'bad' treatment of au pairs maps neatly onto nationalities—there are au pairs from all countries who are treated well and badly—rather there is a tendency, because of their structural position within labour markets, for au pairs from different EU countries to be more or less well treated by hosts in the UK and to have different aims for their au pair placement. Here we look at how employer preferences for au pairs of different nationalities and very different situations in au pairs' home countries work together to produce a gap between formal and practical citizenship and to create a situation where some au pairs are more equal than others.

Doing Nationality in the UK Au Pair Labour Market

Migration policies work not only through formal immigration rules but also through less formal cultural practices and prejudices which together produce migrants with different relationships to labour markets and different experiences of citizenship. Research shows that employers of domestic workers and hosts of au pairs often have strong preferences for particular national or ethnic groups and attribute skills or predispositions to particular groups (see amongst others Anderson, 2000; Bakan & Stasiulis, 1995; Cox, 1999; Lutz, 2002; Stiell & England, 1999; Williams, 2012). The host families we interviewed were no exceptions and while there were no particular patterns amongst our host interviewees as to which nationalities were favoured as au pairs, there were preferences expressed by a number of hosts, and stereotypes of different nationalities were important in the selection of au pairs.

> I had somebody for a few weeks from Estonia and that was another strange experience. The language problem was enormous but also there's a cultural barrier that is much bigger. I think that might be the problem I've got—I know lots of Romanian, I think with that particular girl was quite hard and I wouldn't have had her stay on, really. Then I got a Spanish girl, we reacted so strongly to the previous Italian girl, we decided no Italians anymore (Lucy).[3]
>
> We loved our original child-minder. So we just thought, "Oh Bulgarians are lovely" (Laura).
>
> She was a very, very good example of how enterprising you are if you're from Eastern Europe and you want to get ahead. She just made it all work. [...] I remember one of the children wrote an essay, a school project about his au pair being from Bulgaria and not from France or Sweden or whatever it was, and why she was better than everybody else's au pair which was very sweet. She kept a copy of that (Jack).

As these quotes show, stereotyping can be positive—in this case of Bulgarians—as well as negative (of Italians) but the characteristics of au

---

[3] All names are pseudonyms. Pseudonyms were attributed to participants from a list generated by the researchers. The first person interviewed has the first name in alphabetical order and the second the second and so on. The names do not in any way reflect the place of origin of the interviewees nor any other characteristic such as social class or age. Only gender has been accounted for.

pairs are seen to be national as well as personal and will be taken into account when host families search for an au pair. In our analysis of ads for au pairs on Gumtree.com, we found that 10 % specified the nationality of the au pair they wanted. Au pair agency representatives who were interviewed were also able to describe a broad hierarchy of preferences amongst host families whereby Eastern European and Spanish au pairs were favoured by families looking for someone who was mature, capable and wanting to work long hours. German, French or Nordic au pairs were looked to by host families wanting an au pair who would be working shorter hours and spending more time involved in cultural exchange, for example, studying English formally. Such preferences have a substantial effect on au pairs, shaping who can access which sorts of host families and the conditions that they will live and work in as au pairs.

Formal citizenship rights as equal EU citizens are not enough to ensure equal treatment within the same sector. Our au pair interviewees reported that preferences and prejudices held by hosts affected them in practical ways, revealing one of the ways in which formal citizenship rights do not automatically translate into equal experiences of citizenship in practical terms. Romanian and Bulgarian au pairs reported that they thought their hours, duties and wages were worse than those of au pairs from other nations. Lisa, a 20-year-old au pair from Bulgaria, exemplified this and was able to articulate her lived experience of being part of the hierarchy of national preferences. She was the sole helper in a household of two parents and five children who ranged in age from 6 to 21. She said she worked four days a week from 8 am to 8 pm and was paid £150 a week. Although Lisa was officially being hosted as an au pair, she said of the reality of her situation:

> I actually don't look after the kids, I just [do the] cooking for them and all the work I do is cleaning, ironing and washing. It is very much—it's every day. Actually, I came here to care for kids but then I'm actually cleaner or housekeeper.

We asked Lisa what she had known about the au pair scheme before she became an au pair and whether she felt that there was any aspect of cultural exchange in her arrangement and she replied:

Yes, I know. That's why I came, because I knew the idea and I wanted to be like that, but actually, it's not. Well, I know one German girl and the English family treat the Germans much better than us because we are so little country and—I don't know. I think [it] depends on the family what they are looking for. Most of the families are looking for au pair because they need someone to clean and help with the housework and with the kids.

While Lisa made clear that she did not want to generalise about all host families, she clearly saw a link between her nationality and the poor working conditions she was subject to as an au pair and she was not alone in expressing the feeling that Western European au pairs were treated better than those from the East.

Maria, a 23-year-old au pair from Bulgaria, told us that in her first placement in the UK she was paid £100 per week to work up to 60 hours. She was asked to do heavy cleaning tasks such as cleaning the oven and windows and was not provided with adequate food. When asked why she thought her hosts had treated her this way, she said:

She [host] doesn't look at me as if I am a human person. She looks at me like I am a slave, that I don't deserve anything. [...] She told me, "oh, from Bulgaria, you came here; you're very dirty, you're so..."—No, excuse me, I am a student; I have a diploma. Maybe I'm smarter than you. Okay, it wasn't my luck that I was born in Bulgaria; I'm not born in England. But I am not as stupid as you think.

This quote suggests that Maria experienced her poor working conditions as being a result of her nationality. Without having spoken to her host family, it is impossible to say if they really did think a Bulgarian au pair did not deserve fair treatment, but it is clear that Maria understands her nationality as a key factor in the way that she was treated and she exerts her self-respect by reference to her qualifications and her life outside au pairing. As Zuzana Búriková (2015) has argued, many au pairs take any opportunity available to find out about the pocket money and working conditions of other au pairs in order to see how their own situation compares. They may well have quite a lot of information about how others are treated and their own place in au pair hierarchies.

Lisa's comment above, that host families are looking for an au pair because they need someone to help with housework and to look after the kids, mirrors Jack's comment that his Bulgarian au pair was a 'very good example of how enterprising you are if you're from Eastern Europe and you want to get ahead.' As Anderson (2010) argues the migration regime moulds migrant workers to make them appropriate to the needs of British employers. Hosts can identify those au pairs who are in the weakest position in the labour market and see that this may mean that they are 'very enterprising' and so make efficient au pairs. At the time of the research, Romanian and Bulgarian people had the most limited rights amongst European au pairs. Unlike other EU nationals who were entitled to travel to and work in the UK freely, Bulgarians and Romanians needed a work permit to become an au pair in the UK and had extremely limited opportunities to enter the work force in any other role. The work permit tied them to a named host, so it was difficult for them to swap families or to leave au pairing. Lisa told us about a Bulgarian au pair friend of hers who worked up to 80 hours a week for just £75. When asked why her friend did not leave her host family, Lisa replied:

> Because for Bulgarian[s] here is very difficult to start a new job here because we have to wait for documents. Now I am with this family and I will receive one card, it's like permission card to stay with this family and it's only about this family. It's not for anyone else. You have to stay with this family one year after the issue of this card and you will get the documents, the rights to go and work somewhere else.

This experience echoes that of domestic workers who are tied to a named family by their visa (Anderson, 1993; Mundlak & Shamir, 2008); workers in such situations are known to be extremely vulnerable to abuse and exploitation. Some host families have discovered that the people from Bulgaria and Romania who are able to deal with the hurdles put before them are likely to be very able and prove to be capable au pairs; the immigration rules also make them pliable. Rather than being seen as good and efficient au pairs and this being a basis on which they are recognised and ensured citizenship rights, the opposite is true and their rights are limited in order to ensure that they are docile workers.

Host families have personal preferences for au pairs of different nationalities which may be based on their own experiences, prejudices or advice from agencies and others. While some of these preferences may be entirely personal and perhaps largely baseless, conditions within the au pair sector also produce a situation where au pairs of different nationalities will be 'moulded' (Anderson, 2010) to be suitable to different host families. Tougher entry requirements and a higher degree of prejudice weaken the position of Eastern European au pairs, making them more likely to take au pair posts which involve long hours and relatively little cultural exchange compared to the posts Western European au pairs take, and so a gap between formal citizenship rights and lived experiences of citizenship develops. This situation is also supported by differences in the alternative opportunities available to different groups of au pairs, particularly the conditions in their home countries.

Differences in Home Countries: Opening Already Open Doors?

Au pairs from different countries are differently placed in the UK au pair sector because their reasons for au pairing and the alternative opportunities available to them vary substantially. Within the EU there are very different rates of pay and different levels of youth unemployment and underemployment. An au pair from a country with relatively high wages and low unemployment is unlikely to become an au pair as a way of working to support himself or herself and is more likely to be motivated by the desire to travel, improve their English and engage in cultural exchange. Au pairs from lower-wage economies and countries with high unemployment are more likely to be looking to au pair posts in the UK as a way to earn money. Within these national differences there are also class differences between au pairs with those from better off families able to look for au pair posts that were for short hours and allowed time for language study even if they were not well paid. Au pairs who could not fall back on help from their own families would be more likely to look for posts which paid more even if this meant they would not have time to study. This external context combines with the UK migration regime to increase the differences between au pairs in terms of how they are treated by host families (in terms of pocket money rates, hours worked and opportunities for cultural exchange). We found that only au pairs from North-West Europe are able to consistently participate in the scheme as a form of cultural exchange and language learning.

The legal status of Bulgarian and Romanian au pairs is combined with economic circumstances in their home countries that make them more likely to accept exploitative working conditions with few opportunities for cultural exchange. The average net monthly salary in Bulgaria in 2013 was US$442, Romania US$485 compared to US$2722 in the UK (Wikipedia, 2014). This means that for Bulgarian and Romanian migrants even the meagre pocket money of an au pair, US$500–$800 per month, compared favourably with the pay of a professional at home, as Oscar from Romania explains:

> I can be a teacher in Romania and every salary for a beginner, a teacher who is a beginner is like £180 whereas I earn £320 here as an au pair and I work as many hours as a teacher. So for me it's still a good thing, but it's exploitation.

Oscar explained that he had a postgraduate degree in history from a university in Romania and had come to the UK with the intention of improving his English, before looking for work as a history teacher. At the time of our interview with him he had been an au pair for 5 years, but he had not yet given up on his aspirations to settle in the UK and eventually move from au pairing into professional employment. He had remained as an au pair for this extended period of time despite regarding the pay and working conditions he experienced as exploitative.

Freya, also from Romania, explained why she would take an au pair post that would probably not be attractive to a person from France, who she saw as having more opportunities at home and less need to move abroad to earn money:

> I'm seeing this from my Romanian perspective. I don't know, for a French—I mean you know for a French person, why would a French person accept this for the money? I would not accept it. You know I accept it

because for me it was a way to get out of Romania and because I wanted to get out of there. I wanted to learn English for me it was the driving force. I would accept a lot of things just to get out of there, you know?

Comparing the pay available at home with that in the UK tends to lead migrants into accepting poor working conditions, particularly working long hours, as the calculation of the value of that work is being made in terms of the value of labour at home, not in the place where the money is being earned.

For our interviewees from Bulgaria and Romania, au pairing was part of a well-thought-through project for long-term migration, rather than a 'gap year' or opportunity for cultural exchange. All of the au pairs from these countries that we have met are working long hours and are basically treated like domestic workers. Through the combination of visa rules, imaginings by British hosts of Bulgaria and Romania as 'poor' countries whose inhabitants will accept low pay and the economic circumstances of home which make this group more likely to accept poor conditions, the UK migration regime has moulded a group of 'au pairs' who are more like paid domestic workers and not treated as 'equals' as au pairs should be.

Au pairs from Spain have also emerged as a distinct group in our research and have also been noted in the UK press (see Murray-West, 2012). They tend to be older than the average au pair, highly educated and express their motivation for au pairing in terms of escaping the high rates of unemployment in Spain. While A2 nationals (from Bulgaria and Romania) seem to be motivated by low pay and lack of broader opportunities at home, Spanish au pairs are motivated to migrate by a stark lack of jobs.

Following the 2008 Global Financial Crisis, unemployment rates in the EU, and particularly the Eurozone countries, increased significantly. Spain was one of the hardest hit countries with youth unemployment (people 18–25 years old) running at 53.2 % (Eurostat, 2014). This persistent level of unemployment has encouraged, or forced, many young Spanish people to migrate abroad, both to find jobs and to augment skills so as to improve their place in the labour market at home, if they ever return (Duarte, 2012).

Isobel and Esther, both in their mid-20s, are friends from Spain who we interviewed together. Throughout the interview they both returned to the effect the economic crisis had on the employment opportunities of their generation in particular, and the specific effect it had had on their parallel decisions to leave Spain and come to the UK as au pairs. Isobel said:

> Spain now is horrible; I think we both work [as au pairs] for the same thing because of the crisis. I have a master's degree and I was working in a pizza shop, in Domino's Pizza. I decided that I had to do something else. I couldn't find a job in my area so I moved.

Au pairing in the UK is one of the migration routes available. It offers a source of income and accommodation in a single package and the opportunity to boost English skills which might be useful in the search for better paid work either at home or abroad.

Estelle was 26 years old when we interviewed her. She had qualified as a secondary school teacher in Spain and had been living in Madrid with her boyfriend before the lack of jobs and the pressing need to speak fluent English to compete in an enormously competitive job market in Spain had persuaded her to relocate to the UK as an au pair. Her succinct explanation of her decision was:

> Why [did I become an au pair]? It's for the situation—in Spain I don't have any job or anything… I'm a teacher and I don't have a job, so I need English.

In contrast to A2 nationals, Spanish au pairs are not discriminated against by migration rules, they have full access to the UK labour market. This gives them a stronger position to choose hosts and to negotiate working hours, meaning that they should be able to avoid the most exploitative situations. However, the conditions under which they have moved to the UK mean that many Spanish au pairs are experiencing substantial downgrading in terms of their skills and are having to delay living fully adult, independent lives.

During our research we also met au pairs from Germany and the Nordic countries. These au pairs tend to be young, middle class and have clear finite timeframes for their time in the UK—a year between school and university or a year after university. Generally speaking they are motivated by a desire to improve their English and to travel rather than to earn money or escape unemployment.

Tina from Bremen in Germany was 19 when we interviewed her. Tina had decided to come to the UK as an au pair both to improve her English and because she wanted to spend time in the UK as a kind of extended holiday between school and university. Tina's account of her motivation for becoming an au pair, and her treatment by the family with whom she was staying, were very much in line with the original intentions of the scheme and the rather idealised vision of host family motivations and au pair experiences presented by many au pair agencies. Tina attended language school three times a week (her parents paid for her English lessons), was included in her host family's evening and weekend plans, had very light childcare and household duties and was paid £100 a week in pocket money. She said:

> You really get [to be] part of the family here and yeah, I have a really nice job because my children are quite old. So I have a lot of time for myself and I can go to the gym every day, so yeah, but other au pairs are quite more stressful jobs…[in my host family] I think for my host mother she has a, I think, a really easy life. She can go out for lunch and this and that and yeah for them it is quite easy.

This group are also the only au pairs that we have met who were sent money from their families while in the UK (often to pay for English classes). In contrast, A2 nationals may be remitting money to their families.

Some German and Nordic au pairs come from families that are financially as well off, or even better off, than the hosts that they have in Britain and this can come as a surprise to their hosts. This negotiation of class and status in the home between host (employer) and au pair (staff) was discussed by Rachel, another German au pair we interviewed. Rachel said:

> My mum came over and I went shopping and I bought myself a DKNY jacket…and I was the au pair, you know? She [the teenage daughter of her host parents] was just like 'Oh… this is a really nice jacket…'. Then I was thinking why is she looking at me like that and she didn't say anything. She always said 'that looks really pretty' and the oldest one was like 'Oh, I've got that dress as well'. I was just, like, that's weird! I was just, like, why are you looking at me like this? She was just, like, 'Well the other au pairs we had before they couldn't afford that'. Then they were, like, the other au pairs came to become London citizens or something like that, to become English and didn't have any money or came from villages and stuff like

that…So this girl coming from Germany, from the city, my parents are not rich but they have enough money.

Hosting an au pair who really is 'on a par' with the family reveals the depths of inequality and assumption of servitude which are silenced within the official rhetoric of au pairing. Meeting au pairs who were able to, at least some extent, experience au pairing as a form of cultural exchange among equals, threw the experience of other au pairs into stark relief. Au pairs from well off families in Northern Europe have little invested in au pairing and this gives them power to secure good positions with relatively little work and lots of opportunity for cultural exchange. Their objective is to improve an already good education and enhance already good future opportunities, rather than to protect themselves from unemployment or poverty wages in the present. While it may seem that the 'best' au pair positions go to those who are already most privileged, it also needs to be noted that au pairs who want to earn money often seek host families who will offer them extra hours and conditions which are more like work than cultural exchange. Legal rights and economic conditions shape a diverse labour force made up of people who both desire and are able to access very different working conditions.

Ostensibly au pairs from Northern Europe have the same legal rights as those from Spain, and very similar rights to citizenship as au pairs from the new EU member states of Bulgaria and Romania. However, the abilities of the three different groups to access those rights and to live as is expected of an au pair are very different. The different situations and motivations of individuals and national groups work to make some au pairs more equal than others.

Conclusion

Following the abolition of the au pair visa in 2008, the UK government provided neither definition of au pairing nor guidance on how au pairs should be treated, yet it specifically excluded au pairs from the categories of 'worker' and 'employee' and explicitly denied them rights to the National Minimum Wage, to holiday entitlement and to protection under the European Working Time Directive. In this way the UK migration regime has produced a deregulated form of au pairing which covers a wide range of living and working conditions. Some au pair posts resemble the original intentions of the au pair scheme to provide cultural exchange between equals, and others resemble low paid, highly exploited domestic work. Our research suggests that nationals from different EU states form a hierarchy of au pairs with only those from the most prosperous states able to access the most 'au pair-like' conditions. Nationals of new EU member states, and those who face low pay or high unemployment at home, are more likely to accept 'work-like' conditions without opportunities for cultural exchange. Between them the prejudices and preferences of host families, UK migration rules and the very different opportunities available to au pairs in their home countries work to produce a gap between the putative equality of formal EU citizenship, which is shared by all, and the practical and lived experience of citizenship as migrants in the UK.

Through this highly differentiated labour market, the UK migration regime has delivered diverse, low-cost, flexible childcare to UK families and this labour is specifically excluded from definitions of 'work'. This means that host families are not burdened by having to worry about employment regulations or other formalities of employing someone and au pairs find it difficult to enjoy full rights to citizenship. The gendered construction of au pairing as something other than 'work' is at the heart of au pairs' poor treatment in terms of access to fair pay and labour protections—affecting both male and female au pairs. By examining how this affects au pairs of different nationalities, this chapter has shown how legal rights are not enough to ensure that people are able to access their rights as citizens; rather people are located in economic and social circumstances which also limit or expand their ability to enjoy their rights.

References

Anderson, B. (1993). *Britain's secret slaves: An investigation into the plight of overseas domestic workers*. London: Anti-Slavery International and Kalayaan.
Anderson, B. (2000). *Doing the dirty work: The global politics of domestic labour*. London: Zed Books.

Anderson, B. (2010). Migration, immigration controls and the fashioning of precarious workers. *Work, Employment & Society, 24*(2), 300–317.
Anderson, B. (2014). Nations, migration and domestic labour: The case of the UK. *Women's Studies International Forum, 46*, 5–12.
Bakan, A., & Stasiulis, D. K. (1995). Making the match: Domestic placement agencies and the racialization of women's household work. *Signs, 20*(2), 303–335.
BAPAA (British Au Pairs Agencies Association). (2015). What is an Au pair? Retrieved May 21, 2015, from http://www.bapaa.org.uk/displaypage.asp?page=31
Búriková, Z. (2015). 'Good families' and the shadows of servitude: Au pair gossip and norms of Au pair employment. In R. Cox (Ed.), *Au pairs' lives in global context: Sisters or servants?* (pp. 36–52). Basingstoke: Palgrave Macmillian.
Busch, N. (2015). When work doesn't pay: Outcomes of a deregulated childcare market and Au pair policy vacuum in the UK. In R. Cox (Ed.), *Au pairs' lives in global context sisters or servants?* (pp. 53–69). Basingstoke: Palgrave Macmillian.
Constable, N. (2003). Filipina workers in Hong Kong homes: Household rules and relations. In B. Ehrenreich & A. R. Hochschild (Eds.), *Global woman: Nannies, maids and sex workers in the new economy* (pp. 115–141). London: Granta Books.
Cox, R. (1999). The role of ethnicity in shaping the domestic employment sector in Britain. In J. Momsen (Ed.), *Gender, migration and domestic service* (pp. 134–147). London: Routledge.
Cox, R. (2006). *The servant problem: Domestic employment in a global economy*. London: I.B. Tauris.
Cox, R. (2012). Gendered work and migration regimes. In R. Sollund (Ed.), *Transnational migration, gender and rights* (Vol. 10, pp. 33–52). Advances in Ecopolitics. Bingley: Emerald.
Cox, R. (2015). Introduction. In R. Cox (Ed.), *Au pairs' lives in global context: Sisters or servants?* (pp. 1–18). Basingstoke: Palgrave Macmillian.
Duarte, C. M. (2012). Yesterday my daughter emigrated. *Huffington Post*, August 10, 2012. Retrieved January 29, 2014, from http://www.huffingtonpost.com/carlos-m-duarte/yesterday-my-daughter-emigrated_b_1948533.html
Eurostat. (2014). Unemployment rates. Retrieved January 29, 2014, from http://epp.eurostat.ec.europa.eu/statistics_explained/index.php/Unemployment_statistics

Liarou, E. (2015). 'Pink slave' or 'modern young woman'? A history of the Au pair in Britain. In R. Cox (Ed.), *Au pairs' lives in global context: Sisters or servants?* (pp. 19–35). Basingstoke: Palgrave Macmillian.

Lutz, H. (2002). At your service madam! The globalization of domestic service. *Feminist Review, 70*, 89–104.

Marshall, T. H. (1950). *Citizenship and social class*. London: Pluto Press.

Massey, D. S. (1990). Social structure, household strategies, and the cumulative causation of migration. *Population Index, 56*(1), 3–26.

Migration Observatory. (2014). *Bulgarians and Romanians in the British National Press*. December 1, 2012–December 1, 2013. Retrieved from http://www.migrationobservatory.ox.ac.uk/sites/files /migobs/Report-Bulgarians_Romanians_Press_0.pdf

Mundlak, G., & Shamir, H. (2008). Between intimacy and alienage: The legal construction of domestic and carework in the welfare state. In H. Lutz (Ed.), *Migration and domestic work: A European perspective on a global theme* (pp. 161–176). Aldershot: Ashgate.

Murray-West, R. (2012). Wanted: One Au pair. Result: 2,000 applications. *The Telegraph*, October 1, 2012. Retrieved from http://www.telegraph.co.uk/lifestyle/9579502/Wanted-one-au-pair.-Result-2000-applications.html

Ozyegin, G., & Hondagneu-Sotelo, P. (2008). Conclusion: Domestic work, migration and the new gender order in contemporary Europe. In H. Lutz (Ed.), *Migration and domestic work: A European perspective on a global theme* (pp. 195–208). Aldershot: Ashgate.

Roy, A. (2005). *Gendered citizenship: Historical and conceptual explorations*. Hyderabad, India: Orient Blackswan.

Smith, J. L. (2008). The silent abuse suffered by nannies and Au pairs. *The Telegraph*, September 6, 2008. Retrieved from http://www.telegraph.co.uk/news/uknews/2695891/The-silent-abuse-suffered-by-nannies-and-au-pairs.html

Stiell, B., & England, K. (1999). Jamaican domestics, Filipina housekeepers and English nannies: Representations of Toronto's domestic workers. In J. Momsen (Ed.), *Gender, migration and domestic service* (pp. 43–61). London: Routledge.

Walby, S. (1994). Is citizenship gendered? *Sociology, 28*(2), 379–395.

Wikipedia. (2014). List of countries in Europe by monthly average wage. Retrieved from http://en.wikipedia.org/wiki/List_of_countries_in_Europe_by_monthly_average_wage

Williams, F. (2012). Converging variations in migrant care work in Europe. *Journal of European Social Policy, 22*(4), 363–376.

Yeoh, B., & Huang, S. (1999). Spaces at the margins: Migrant domestic workers and the development of civil society in Singapore. *Environment and Planning A, 31*, 1149–1167.

Young, I. M. (1989). Polity and group difference: A critique of the ideal of universal citizenship. *Ethics, 99*(2), 250–274.

6

From Intimate Relations to Citizenship? Au Pairing and the Potential for Citizenship in Norway

Elisabeth Stubberud

This chapter explores au pairs' intimate relations and their potential to facilitate access to formal and informal citizenship. The issue of citizenship in au pairs' host nations is complex. Au pairs' visas are tied to specific host families for the duration of their stay. And the au pair scheme is not designed for migration, yet two years—the maximum length of an au pair visa—is ample time to get acquainted with the country and the language and many au pairs consider the possibility of staying on after their contract runs out.[1] This indicates that the au pair scheme to some extent is used as a migration route, making it an interesting case study for exploring questions of formal and informal citizenship. Yet, au pairs have to approach the issue of formal citizenship in indirect ways. In this chapter, I look at the possibilities which intimate relationships open up for accessing formal and informal citizenship, both within the au pair

[1] In 2012, 54 % of the 810 former au pairs who returned to Norway received student visas; 6 % received working visas; and 40 % returned on a family reunification visa (statistics from the Norwegian Directorate of Immigration, retrieved via personal communication 15.11.2013).

E. Stubberud
KUN, Centre for Gender Equality, Norfold, Norway

© The Editor(s) (if applicable) and The Author(s) 2016
B. Gullikstad et al. (eds.), *Paid Migrant Domestic Labour in a Changing Europe*, DOI 10.1057/978-1-137-51742-5_6

scheme and after au pairing, using narratives from in-depth interviews with 15 current or former au pairs in Norway.[2] Of these au pairs, only three stated that they wanted to return home after the end of their contract. All of the others were considering options for staying on or had already done so. When discussing my informants' decision or ambition to stay in Norway in the interviews, it became clear that their options for staying were closely intertwined with their personal and intimate relationships, not only with current and future employers, but also with partners or potential partners.

The narratives around these intimate relationships had a gendered form where au pairs' heterosexuality appeared to be a condition for the narrative. In the analysis that follows, I explore heterosexuality as a way of gendering citizenship in practice. I use the concept of *intimate citizenship* (Plummer, 2003) to capture relational routes to formal and informal citizenship rights in the imagined community of the nation (Anderson, 2006). I understand the *nation* as a stand-in for a particular physical location where a future is imagined, and focus specifically on the way in which au pairs' narratives often rely implicitly on the 'heterosexual contract' (Butler, 1999; Wittig, 1989). This seems to produce heterosexuality as a precondition for some fantasies of formal and informal citizenship, which, in the case of au pairs, takes the form of replacing the host family as providers of citizenship with husbands as the imaginable route to formal rights and informal belonging. The 'family',[3] in either of these forms, is thus a key symbolic structure as well as a material condition for au pairs' negotiation of potential formal and informal citizenship. Heredity and family lines are crucial components of everyday conceptions of national belonging, and becoming 'part of the family' in a literal sense through marriage is a way for au pairs to acquire both legal and affective citizenship rights in the nation (Fortier, 2008). This

---

[2] The empirical material was produced as part of the research project 'Buying and Selling Gender Equality. Feminised Migration and (Gender) Equality in Contemporary Norway', financed by the Research Council of Norway.

[3] In the analysis, I discuss 'au pairs', 'host families', 'host mums', and 'host dads'. My use of these terms does not imply that I believe their description of the relationships they refer to is in any way unambiguous. Rather, they attempt to create what they describe, as pointed out by Gulliksen and Annfelt (this volume).

suggests that the relationship between formal and informal citizenship and the significance of intimate relations for these forms of citizenship are crucial for my analysis of the au pairs' narratives. In the following section, I discuss key concepts of citizenship with a special emphasis on formal, informal, and intimate citizenship, and with au pairing as the starting point.

Formal, Informal, and Intimate (Heterosexual) Citizenship

Those who come to Norway on au pair visas have limited and time-restricted citizenship rights. Au pairing is intended as cultural exchange for foreign nationals between the ages of 18 and 30, who work for Norwegian families doing 'light housework' for a maximum of 30 hours a week, for up to 2 years. In return, au pairs receive free board and lodging, Norwegian classes, and monthly 'pocket money' of around 600 euros (before tax). The rules do not formally apply to au pairs from the European Union (EU)/Schengen Area.[4] In 2010, around 1500 third-country nationals acquired au pair visas, and almost 400 of these re-applied for a working, student, or family reunification visa in 2012.[5] Au pairs have to negotiate the roles of both 'family member' and 'employee' in their host families, and this often creates problems (Stubberud, 2015). At its best, however, the 2-year stay with the host family supplies au pairs with language skills, a social network, and the chance to set aside money while they consider options for remaining in the country and extending formal and informal citizenship rights.

Citizenship can be understood as formal rights and obligations connected to temporary or permanent residence in a particular place, as captured in modes of governance, rights, and duties, but citizenship

---

[4] People from the EU/Schengen Area are not formally part of the au pair scheme because of current migration regulations. They have to register upon arrival in Norway, but are not obliged to use the Norwegian Directorate of Immigration's formal au pair contract. My informants who came from EU/Schengen countries nevertheless self-identified as au pairs, used the formal contract, or travelled through an agency that used a version of this contract.

[5] Personal communication with the UDI, 15.11.2013.

also entails informal elements connected to lived experiences, cultural knowledge, participation, and belonging (Bosniak, 2001; Eggebø, 2012; Halsaa, Roseneil, & Sümer, 2012; Lister et al., 2007). Au pairs are a highly diverse group of people who have different formal and temporal citizenship rights upon entering Norway, depending on their home country, as well as their different resources to negotiate informal and relational citizenship. Furthermore, no contemporary exploration of citizenship, Nira Yuval-Davis argues, can be complete without looking at the changing ways in which people's intimate relations, family relations, and networks of friends and acquaintances, as well as their gender, affect the way in which they *do* citizenship (2010, p. 123). Yet, in addition to this, the material analysed here requires attention to not only the fluctuating meanings of citizenship, but also to complementary concepts of formal and informal citizenship (Bauder, 2008).

Formal citizenship denotes the right to legally reside in a nation, either temporarily or permanently. Yet, as argued by Lucy Williams, 'laws regulating migration are often highly gendered.... Gender ... shapes the social meaning migration has for the individual as a member of their specific social group and it shapes the perceptions of the migrant by outsiders' (2010, p. 21). The gendered nature of the au pair scheme is reflected in terms of both visa applicants—98 % of all applicants to Norway are women (Øien, 2009, p. 22)—and the gendered housework and carework au pairs are supposed to carry out. The fact that au pairs are conceptualised as a 'members of the family' on 'cultural exchange' is also highly relevant to the way in which the scheme is understood in the public sphere, and important to the intimate relations between au pairs and their host families (see Gullikstad and Annfelt, this volume). Williams further points out that the right to reside for those not born as residents is calculated based on the 'worth' of an applicant, and this 'worth' must be demonstrated and earned 'through attachment to an existing member ... of the state, or through prior [labour] experiences' (Williams, 2010, p. 76).

With regards to *informal citizenship*, I draw on Harald Bauder's definition of *citizenship* as a form of capital in Pierre Bourdieu's sense, and informal citizenship as a dimension of cultural membership in a national community connected to practices of identity and belonging

(Bauder, 2008). Au pairs and other migrants thus have to gain 'access to territorially defined cultural codes and conventions and [be] able to enact place-particular habitual performances'—in addition to learning the language—in order to have full access to informal citizenship (Bauder, 2008, p. 324).

While the concepts of formal and informal citizenship are useful for addressing access or lack of access to residence or work in a particular nation/place through, for example, knowledge of local codes and conventions in job applications, they do not help us theorise or conceptualise the processes that are involved in giving, taking, or acting out citizenship. Formal/informal citizenship does not take into account gendered, intimate, and relational aspects of citizenship, nor is it particularly useful for addressing the intersection between the private and the public realm of individual life or the social relations between people that often mediate the individual's relationship to the state—which has been a concern in feminist perspectives on citizenship (Eggebø, 2012, p. 51).

One way of conceptualising these relationships is to combine the notion of formal/informal citizenship with the concept of *intimate citizenship*. The term 'intimate citizenship', coined by Ken Plummer (2003), refers to the array of possible bodily and intimate practices and choices; it is a sensitising concept that 'describes how our private decisions and practices have become intertwined with public institutions and state policies' (Oleksy, 2009, p. 4). Both personal and intimate relationships are pivotal in au pairs' narratives of formal and informal citizenship, and attention to the intersection of the public and the private sphere allows for a gender-sensitive analysis of citizenship. However, Helga Eggebø (2012) points to the risk of discussing already presumed members of the nation when addressing forms of intimate citizenship. In her thesis on marriage migration, Eggebø merges the insights conceptualised in the concept of intimate citizenship, with attention to the inside and the outside of the nation. She argues that:

> The citizenship literature includes contributions questioning both the distinction between the inside and the outside of the nation state, and the public/private distinction. Nevertheless, hardly any contributions have sought to make a clear conceptualisation of citizenship bridging both these

distinctions.... Combining perspectives from these two sections of citizenship scholarship exposes the fundamental and inextricable link between public and private concerns and the porousness of the borders that separate the inside and outside of the nation-state. (Eggebø, 2012, p. 53)

Studying au pairs with attention to citizenship requires a conceptualisation of both those who lack formal citizenship rights (or will lack such rights in the future) and those who are legally permitted to reside in Norway but may lack informal citizenship through social and cultural belonging. By combining the concepts of formal/informal citizenship and intimate citizenship, my aim is to draw attention to a public/private distinction *and* the inside/outside of the nation state. Au pairs have a wide range of personal and cultural resources, different migrant statuses, and different material resources. This makes the au pair scheme an interesting case for studying the intersection between formal rights and obligations and informal belongings, the private and the public sphere, and the intimate, personal, and relational—which is where au pairs seem to have the greatest amount of agency and where they are most likely to gain formal and informal citizenship.

Here, heterosexuality plays a central role. I have already noted that heterosexuality appears as an unspoken condition in the au pairs' considerations of future formal and informal citizenship. This condition should not be read as an effect of national regulations; homosexual marriages are equally effective for securing formal citizenship in Norway. Nor should it be read as a mere effect of the informants' self-presentation as heterosexual women. Rather, it is constitutive of a cultural order in which heteronormative family arrangements structure citizenship symbolically (Ahmed, 2006; Nagel, 2000). When birthrights are out of the question, sex is a site that one can invest with optimistic attachment to the nation through the hopes of becoming someone else's family—granted that the sexual relation imagined takes a socially celebrated form, most often heterosexual marriage (Berlant & Edelman, 2014). In such cases, sex is invested with optimism that both confirms the structures of power and salvages desire from the ever-present threat of becoming subversive (Berlant & Edelman, 2014). This mode of regulation is intrinsic to 'sexual freedom' in Western countries and should be understood as a specific form of sexual regulation, to the extent that it is built into state policies through, for example, migration regulations and the privileged status of marriage (Mühleisen, Røthing, & Svendsen, 2012).

Analysing Cultural Narratives of Intimacy

The different ways in which au pairs engage with the possibilities of accessing formal and informal citizenship are explored through the analysis of 15 in-depth interviews with 18- to 32-year-old current or former au pairs from Asia, Africa, Latin America, and Europe, living in Norway. In the interviews, I was interested in the informants' plans for the future; when I asked about this, issues of rights and belonging surfaced, most notably through stories of (potential) partners. The narratives analysed below shed light on questions of formal and informal citizenship through intimate relations: Marian 'queers' her relationship to her boyfriend in protest to her host mum's invasive involvement and acquires informal and temporary formal citizenship on her own terms. Imelda's story shows how the host father can become an imaginable spouse through the heterosexual contract and the struggle to bring together various plans and desires. Sonya's story illustrates the limits of national belonging as excluding Muslims, making her work hard to signal informal citizenship through cultural belonging and being a 'family member'. Finally, Paulina's story of becoming independent from her host family illustrates how boyfriends, rather than host families, can meet unfulfilled expectations of informal citizenship.

When analysing their stories, I tried to keep the 'whole' of their narratives in mind (Hollway & Jefferson, 2000). I perceive the stories of my informants less as individual tales and more as living, collective narratives that appear as legitimate ways of framing life events (Johansson, 2005). These narratives are circulated socially, and the act of framing events through culturally familiar narratives might—in some cases—allow the storyteller to create or imagine agency. The stories below thus touch upon broader issues of migration, domestic work, intimate relations, citizenship rights, belonging, and agency. At the same time, a narrative of citizenship through heterosexual intimacy runs through the stories. I now turn to the informants' stories to explore this further.

Queering Independence

At the time of the interview, Marian (32) had a student visa and was working part-time while living with her fiancé, a Norwegian man she had met whilst au pairing. She had migrated from a country in South-East Asia[6] in order to provide for her children. She had worked as an au pair for 2 years, and her host mum had encouraged her to start dating. Yet, according to Marian, she had become a little too involved in her dating projects. Marian explained:

> [Host mum] knows all about my dates (laughs). I was out dating, and she was the one who set up my account at [dating website] (laughs). I couldn't do it myself, because it was in Norwegian! 'No, I'll set up an account for you, Marian, here's your username and password, and I want to know who this man you're dating is!' (laughs).... The first time I exchanged text messages with a man in a different town ... the whole [family] went, and I met the Norwegian man, and [host mum] said 'If something happens, call the police and call me, and I'll come pick you up'.

Marian told me that the host mum had bought train and bus tickets for Marian to go on dates, and insisted on knowing everything. She had also set up a date with one of her own colleagues, and invited Marian's dates home to the family. Marian said:

> It was like she wanted to interview the men I dated, because she wants me to be happy. She wants me to have a proper Norwegian, kind man.

Marian still found a man on her own, a pensioner who was around twice her age. She described a loving relationship, and spoke humorously about him as 'my au pair', stating that he did most of the housework and cooking. According to Marian, the host mum was annoyed because the fiancé did not fulfil her requirements:

> She wants me to find a man in his forties, and rich (laughs)! A steady job and rich, with his own house and.... But no. Once she told me that 'You're old enough to choose. Just make sure that he's kind'.

---

[6] To protect my informants' identities I have chosen not to specify the countries they travelled from.

Several other informants also spoke of host parents' involvement and encouragement regarding their dating.[7] This might be unusual for au pairs; the host families of Zuzana Búriková and Daniel Miller's (2010) au pair informants in London outlawed dating. What does the host parents' active involvement and encouragement here mean? It might be that the host parents were micro-resisting strict migration policies (while, at the same time, micro-managing their au pairs' love life). Or it might be a sign of respect on behalf of the host parents, who acknowledge the au pairs' desire to have a social life outside the family that might include a partner. Another possible interpretation is a form of nationalism; host parents want au pairs to become Norwegian because they deem it beyond question that the particular category of au pairs that Marian belonged to—the ones who have travelled from a less affluent background in order to provide financially for their families—should want to live in Norway. A partner may have been thought to help Marian 'affectively assimilate' (Myong & Bissenbakker, 2014) and become part of (the right type of) 'kind' and 'rich') Norwegian culture through love.

When talking about her partner, Marian made a point out of mentioning that the reason they were together was love. 'Love', Eileen Muller Myrdahl argues, is 'a requirement for the recognition as a national: it is the acceptable basis on which liberal subjects of the modern nation create new families' (Myrdahl, 2010, p. 113; see also Eggebø, 2012; Flemmen, 2008; Fredriksen & Myong, 2012). If love is the idealised reason for marriage, legitimacy (as opposed to pro forma or arranged marriages) and parity between spouses through a common language, knowledge of each other, and similar ages are imagined to be of equal importance (Flemmen, 2008), and marriages that break from these ideals are often rendered suspicious. Marian's emphasis on love might have been a response to the host mum's suggestion that she should find a 'proper Norwegian kind man who is also rich'. In this statement, the host mum tapped into the question of how Marian should acquire formal citizenship in Norway as well as financial security. Yet, this type of arrangement does not always work out; the husband may refuse to participate in remittances or the couple may divorce (Dahl & Spanger, 2010). Furthermore, the host mum's

---

[7] See Marchetti (this volume) for a discussion of different forms of maternalism in female employers' relationships with their domestic workers.

suggestion that the man should be rich could be read as an Orientalist (Said, 2001) assumption that inscribes Marian as a woman who is willing to trade sex for other goods (money, citizenship) in the heteronormative exchange, wherein younger, foreign women are imagined to be willing to make this exchange (Mühleisen et al., 2012).

During the interview, Marian described the host mum's involvement in her dating with a sense of humour and intensity. Although she was laughing while telling the story, the way she contrasted the host mum's requirements with her life with her partner suggests that she perhaps did not deem the host mum's involvement as altogether appropriate. Yet she seemed to have some strategies for dealing with this behaviour, which involved a form of queering of her relationship with the older man. By queering, I mean that she described her relationship in ways that explicitly departed from heteronormative ideals, and seemed conscious of the fact that she was disturbing these norms through exposing them. The humorous comment that Marian's partner was her own 'au pair' could be interpreted as a reaction to the unequal distribution of power between Marian and the host mum, which was now reversed. Also, if Marian's presence in the former host family produced a situation in which traditional gender roles were reinforced through her cooking and cleaning, the comment also served to reverse these gender roles in her own household, in which Marian was providing financially for herself and her family back home while her partner was cooking and cleaning. She also emphasised her ability to adjust to a new and difficult situation and to secure a happy life for herself without the host mum's involvement; she had learnt the language, made friends, worked voluntarily to enhance her career options, found a partner on her own, and started studying. All of this involved the acquisition of informal citizenship, as well as temporary formal citizenship through her student visa.

Marrying 'Dad'

The heterosexual contract also played into Imelda's story. Imelda (27) had recently migrated from a country in South-East Asia and was working for a single father with two children whom he had the responsibility for every other week. Imelda had a boyfriend at home whom she planned to marry, yet they seemed to disagree about the timing as she wanted to stay abroad for another few years to work, while the boyfriend wanted to get married soon.

> I told him to wait, because ... I want to pursue all my dreams. I want to set myself first before I get married.

Imelda talked about her ambition to start a business after working abroad—yet she also wanted to be a stay-at-home mum. Her dreams for the future were, in other words, pulling her in two different directions. Nevertheless, she was clear about her ambition regarding her relationship with her boyfriend:

> I promised to my boyfriend that I would come back, because I love him and I know that he also love me... You know what, long-term relationships are hard.... Trust is really important, not only love... You really need to fight against the temptation. If someone would court me I'd just fix in my mind that I will not entertain him, I'll just focus my mind and my heart for my boyfriend.

This comment suggests that staying faithful was something Imelda had thought through, perhaps because she did not find it altogether easy. At several points through the interview, she mentioned women she knew from her own country who had married Scandinavian men, or she spoke in more general terms about this. The fact that this surfaced in the interview could mean that Imelda had experienced a real desire and need to 'fight against temptation' in her present life.

During the interview, she also spoke a lot about the host father. She admired him for his business skills and argued that he might have chosen her as an au pair because they had a shared interest in business. At a later point in the interview, we talked about discrimination, and Imelda firmly stated that she had never experienced this in Norway. She illustrated with an example of how she thought equality played out in practical terms:

> There is no discrimination here in Norway, right.... I'll just give you an example. Because this is related to the au pair who got married to her host.

Sometimes the au pair gets married with her host… Here in Norway, even if you are rich or poor, you can marry each other.

This quotation can be interpreted in several ways. Imelda's life was fraught with tension and she seemed to be struggling to bring together various plans and ambitions. Given that she appeared happy with her present life, which provided her with work, a sense of adventure, and a stable family constellation, this statement could also be taken to mean that she was open to fantasising about remaining exactly where she was. In this fantasy, the host dad would become a stand-in for the possibility of a life Imelda desired. She pointed out how she and the host dad had things in common, followed by an argument of how the society she was currently a part of did not judge people who married 'up' or 'down' in a class hierarchy, as illustrated by the example of the relationship between an au pair and her host dad. I interpret this as suggesting that Imelda would be open to considering the host dad as a potential spouse.

Imelda already had a kind of intimate relationship with the host dad through looking after his children, living in the same house, and cleaning and cooking for the family. Every other week, the two of them were also, at least in principle, alone in the house. And although she spoke about him as the 'host dad', she seemed open to reinterpreting their relationship. This suggests that when citizenship is at stake, intimate relations slide. In this case, the relationship between Imelda and the host dad, which is both an employer/employee relation and a quasi-familial one, has the potential to become conflated with the fantasy of another kind of intimate relation. The relation between the older, more experienced and privileged man and the younger woman who is dependent on him is a readily available cultural fantasy that contributes to constructing the heterosexual contract (Chow, 2002). In this fantasy, women achieve rights, possessions, skills, or indeed citizenship via men (Mühleisen et al., 2012). Imelda, along with a few other informants who spoke of the host dad in similar terms, internalises the widely circulated fantasy in Western culture, whereby heterosexual capacity is a legitimate route to citizenship.

The Limits of Belonging

Sonya (26) arrived as an au pair as a third-country national from Europe. She was a Muslim, and this background became relevant in the interview as she described her initially cautious self-presentation and her reluctance to 'come out' as a Muslim. In my analysis, I connect this to Sonya's ability to perform informal citizenship in the intimate sphere and, by extension, to gain formal citizenship in the nation, where she imagined herself as undesirable.

Sonya was highly motivated to stay in Norway after the end of her contract and wanted to continue her university studies. She was, however, also open to the prospect of settling down with a Norwegian partner in the future. She explained that she had migrated to Norway as an au pair because:

> I like skiing and biathlon, to watch it on TV. My favourite sportsmen are … Liv Grete Poiree and Petter Northug [famous Norwegian skiers], and I… the reason why I wanted to visit Norway was not to go on holiday but maybe live and learn to get to know this country.

When discussing her motivation to stay, Sonya expressed her desire for Norwegian culture, and as such performed a kind of informal citizenship, culturally. Winter sports, and the mentioned skiers, are extremely popular in Norway, and Sonya's mention of these aspects of life in Norway as part of her motivation to stay in the country could be interpreted as a way of signalling informal belonging.

At the time of the interview, Sonya was working for a couple in which the host mum had a highly demanding job. As a result, contrary to most of my other informants, she described a closer relationship to the host dad. She categorised him 'not as a friend, but as an older family member, I think'. She gave an example to illustrate this:

> When I had a date, for example, he asked me 'Who is he and where are you going?' (smiles), but not seriously of course. But once he said 'Now I am your dad and I need to ask whom you are going out with' (smiles).

There are some gendered power dynamics at play here, evoked through notions of family, when the host dad described Sonya as his daughter. Sonya equated the host dad's policing of her dating activities with her expectations of an older family member confronted with a daughter's romantic explorations. Her motivation for telling this story in the interview may have been to communicate that the host dad was discursively producing her as a family member. Since her current visa depended on her relationship with the host family, this assumption would be a reassuring confirmation of her role in the family.

Later in the interview, I asked her if there was anything she could not speak to the host family about. She stated that:

> I don't keep secrets. But on my [au pair] profile, at first, I wrote that I'm an atheist, because I think that maybe, um, I was going to Norway when it happened with Anders Behring Breivik,[8] and I think that maybe the host family was a little afraid because there are many types of Muslims in the world, but when I came here, I told them that I was a Muslim, and now I tell it to everybody... We are not like Arab Muslims, we don't pray a lot and don't wear hijab, and we're like European people... In the beginning I didn't speak a lot about my future because I was not sure that they like people who want to stay in Norway. But now I think it's ok, I speak about that too.

In this quote, Sonya's Muslim background is portrayed as a disqualifier for finding a host family, friends, and a partner—all of which have the potential of providing ways to achieve temporary or permanent formal citizenship. Sonya appears well aware of the racism, prejudice, and marginalisation that disproportionately affects Muslims in Norway, and her mention of the terror attack on 22 July 2011 is an implicit reference not to the terrorist, but to the violence Norwegian Muslims were subject to before it was known that the terrorist was a white, ethnic Norwegian man (Auestad, 2013). The quote points to Sonya's worries that people might not want her to stay because she is a Muslim, and I interpret her cautious self-presentation as a strategy for bettering her chances for formal and informal intimate citizenship. This strategy also seems to have involved

---

[8] Sonya was referring to the terrorist who attacked the Workers' Youth League camp at Utøya and the government quarters in Oslo on the 22 July 2011.

(re)constructing an image of the 'stereotypical Arab Muslims' who wear the hijab and pray a lot, and then distancing herself from this image by describing herself as rather 'like European people'. This could be interpreted as drawing a strategic border around a nation that she wished to be a part of, by constructing others as outcasts. Sonya's worries and her desire to cast herself as different show how racism feeds directly into the way in which people imagine themselves as (potential) parts of a community or not (Fortier, 2008).

It is interesting that Sonya was so cautious about exposing her background when creating her au pair profile, and simultaneously so concerned with expressing belonging to a very particular form of Norwegian culture, namely winter sports. Her narrative suggests that informal citizenship must be carefully managed, especially by those who perceive themselves formally and culturally at the borders of the nation, and whose formal citizenship status depends on relationships with others. Sonya was hoping to access a more permanent form of formal citizenship through studies, work, or marriage, and her religion, culture, and interests all played a part—along with her heterosexuality, which provided one clear, imaginable way for her to remain in Norway. Walking a tightrope between cultural similarity and difference led to this careful management of informal citizenship and expressions of belonging. In order to be perceived as an imaginable part of the nation to others—both her host family and potential friends or partners—she underplayed her background in order to 'pass' as a family member in the broader sense of the word.

Agency in Informal Citizenship

Paulina (24) came to Norway from an EU country, meaning that her formal right to reside was not dependent on the host family. In fact, had this been the case the interview could not have taken place as Paulina had been fired at the time of the interview, yet she had remained in Norway with her partner. Her story highlights the significance of the transition from intimate relations with the host family to intimate relations with a partner, and how, even with formal citizenship rights, informal citizenship might be both desirable and necessary for securing a good life.

Paulina started au pairing for a family in a small town because she wanted a gap year between jobs, and explained that:

> I had been in Norway before and I thought it's a beautiful country and it's interesting to go here ... and I had also done some babysitting so I knew how to do it, and I think it's a good experience anyway to live in a family... Maybe learn the language.

She argued that her interest in Norwegian culture and language was the reason she migrated, and travelling as an au pair provided an easy and convenient way for her to do so. Her emphasis on her babysitting experience suggests that she initially expected this to be her main task in the family. Thus, whilst she was not formally dependent on the host family, she argued that it would be a 'good experience' for her to learn the language. This indicates that Paulina expected the host family to provide informal citizenship; through her relationship with them, she believed she would gain access to Norwegian culture and language more easily and affordably than by settling down on her own.

However, au pairing did not turn out quite the way Paulina had expected; her own mother tongue was spoken in the household instead of Norwegian, and Paulina was unable to attend Norwegian classes because her host mum needed her in the house. Her description of the workload indicated that her expectations outlined in the first quote were far from her experiences upon arriving in the family:

> I was pretty much always the one cleaning the house, doing the laundry and making dinner. The other kids were in kindergarten, so… yeah. I was taking care of the baby girl all day, and everything with housework.

Paulina seemed to expect the host family to provide her with a sense of informal citizenship, whilst the host family expected a degree of help in the house that Paulina was not prepared for. Yet she described that she did try to fulfil her host family's expectations in the beginning of her stay. Mainly, she explained, she did so because she had nowhere else to go, and no one to spend her spare time with. This changed when she met her boyfriend:

I started my independent life (laughs).... I got to go out and go skiing, and ice fishing and everything. You know, do something that I expected to do with the family.... So then it got a bit tense [with the family] because ... I wasn't at home all the time [to] watch the kids whenever they wanted, so it became a bit... they didn't like it.

There seems to be significant discrepancy between Paulina's description of her expectations of 'cultural exchange' and the host family's expectation of a worker. Paulina attributes her being fired to her 'independent life', which started when she met her boyfriend. This suggests a sense of dependency on the host family, despite having formal citizenship rights that were independent of her au pair job. Paulina was, after all, living in a relatively remote place in a foreign country, with no social network. Through her boyfriend, she gained other options when she was fired; she moved in with him and found other work with his help. Yet, job applications are full of cultural conventions. Would Paulina have got her next job had she not known who to get in touch with or how to write the application in the 'proper Norwegian way'? She did not specify her boyfriend's role in her decision to remain in Norway, but it seems likely that an intimate relation might have served as a shortcut for her to become acquainted with what Bauder (2008) calls 'the commitment to imagined national behavioural norms, attitudes, and cultural conventions [that] distinguishes citizens from those migrants who are unable to express belonging' (Bauder, 2008, p. 325).

Paulina's relationships with her partner and her extended social network in Norway might have provided some shortcuts to informal citizenship, which she needed in order to remain in the country. What is interesting in Paulina's story is the transition from informal citizenship based on a 'family' relation with a limited amount of agency to another kind of more intimate informal citizenship with a greater degree of agency. When Paulina described her 'independent life', she could have been talking about a more age-appropriate form of relationality. In the relationship with her boyfriend, she had a greater amount of agency and equality than she had achieved in her relationship with the host family. Needless to say, however, this kind of informal citizenship with agency is only available to EU/Schengen citizens.

Promising Intimacy?

In the stories presented, the paradoxical nature of citizenship in the au pair scheme becomes visible; the scheme is not intended as a migration route, but often becomes precisely this for au pairs. As the au pair scheme only allows for a limited type of citizenship, my informants used strategies such as looking for work, enrolling in further education, and dating in order to gain formal and informal citizenship. Au pairing could thus serve as a springboard to a more permanent life in Norway. However, au pairs are always dependent on others, be these host families or partners. My informants' stories underline that it is difficult for au pairs to succeed on their own, even with formal citizenship rights. The state of in-betweenness—between the state of citizen and alien, family member, and employee—is a confusing space within which au pairs must manoeuvre rights and duties with limited amounts of agency.

This consequence of the au pair scheme is highly gendered; au pairs' relationships with host families are often fraught with tension and lacking in agency, with au pairs not necessarily fitting either the scheme's image of a 'family member' or the host family's expectation of a domestic worker. One way to interpret the au pairs' relatively enthusiastic stories of dating could be that dating provided them a familiar space, wherein a more age-appropriate sense of agency was available as they were more likely to be *on par* with a partner than with a host family. Intimate relationships also held the promise of solving issues of formal and informal citizenship as the narratives of Marian, Imelda, and Paulina suggest, given that they were able to gain the right amount of informal citizenship through expressions of cultural belonging, as Sonya's story shows. By implication, informal citizenship was something that could be gained, but also something that could be performed relationally.

Au pairing provides an interesting case for thinking about citizenship because of the compulsory gendered relationality involved. It relies on a family-based rhetoric in which au pairs lack agency by being constructed as 'family members' who perform live-in domestic work while their visas depend on their relationship with the host family/employers. The au pairs' stories of dating not only highlight the intimate and relational aspects of citizenship in the au pair scheme, but also reveal an apparent gradual symbolic transition from 'daughter' to 'wife' through a cultural kinning process that has its natural conclusion in family reunification. The discourse of the scheme places the au pair in a symbolic family structure in which she is figured as a 'big sister'. This allows for her factual adulthood and labour capacities, while, at the same time, constitutes her as a child in relation to the host 'mum' and 'dad'. The symbolic position of a child functions as a de-sexualisation of the adult woman within the walls of the household. Yet the au pair is not supposed to be a child. Rather, au pairs perform adult women's tasks in the household—tasks that are normally administered by the woman of the household and that are generally (still) constituted as primarily women's responsibilities in the heterosexual household contract. It seems, then, that the au pair is not a symbolic 'big sister' but an auxiliary wife. In this light, the 'big sister' label can be seen as an attempt to recruit the incest taboo to prevent the possibility of sexual relations between the au pair and the host dad (Phillips, 2006). It is quite evident that there is a high degree of concern for the ever-present possibility of this particular sexual relation (Cox, 2007). Many, if not most, au pairs report having minimal interaction with the host dad (Hess & Puckhaber, 2004). At the same time, reports of host dads' sexual abuse of au pairs circulate (Sunde & Isungset, 2013). The tension that this particular symbolic and practical relationship produces needs to be taken seriously. This is of political, as well as analytic, importance. The practice of denying exactly how desirable this coupling can seem to both the man in the household and the au pair is likely to contribute to the current inability to address the problem of the sexual abuse of au pairs.

In this chapter, I have analysed au pairs' narratives. I will end by addressing the question behind the subheading above: 'Promising intimacy?'. While the tales of boyfriends and dating seem to have implied that these relationships provided the au pairs with a greater degree of agency than their relationships with host families did, family reunification through marriage also involves a form of intimate relational citizenship characterised by a potentially unequal situation of dependency. Thus, au pairing as a migration route remains an inherently individualistic project where it is up to each au pair (or woman in an au pair–like situation) to carve out a life for herself, in Norway or elsewhere. It becomes an individualistic project because it is not, in fact, regulated as a migration route. There is a sense of cruel optimism (Berlant, 2011) in this tale, because formal citizenship is, in the end, always governed from above. And regarding informal citizenship, host families still have the upper hand, as there is no control mechanism or formalised punishment for denying au pairs access to informal citizenship—for example, by making them work rather than attend Norwegian classes. Thus, despite the (sometimes) promising tale of agency and increased access to informal and (perhaps eventually) formal citizenship through intimate relations, au pairs' narratives are still shaped by immigration policies, conceptualisations of domestic work, racialisation, and othering, all interwoven in the nitty-gritty fabric of the intimate sphere and loaded with the weight of 'family'.

References

Ahmed, S. (2006). *Queer phenomenology: Orientations, objects, others*. Durham, NC: Duke University Press.
Anderson, B. (2006). *Imagined communities: Reflections on the origin and spread of nationalism*. London: Verso.
Auestad, L. (2013). Idealised sameness and orchestrated hatred: Extreme and mainstream nationalism in Norway. In L. Auestad (Ed.), *Nationalism and the body politic. Psychoanalysis and the rise of ethnocentrism and xenophobia* (Kindle ed., pp. 41–60). London: Karnac Books.
Bauder, H. (2008). Citizenship as capital: The distinction of migrant labor. *Alternatives: Global, Local, Political, 33*(3), 315–333.
Berlant, L. (2011). *Cruel optimism*. Durham, NC and London: Duke University Press.
Berlant, L., & Edelman, L. (2014). *Sex, or the unbearable*. Durham, NC and London: Duke University Press.
Bosniak, L. (2001). Denationalizing citizenship. In T. A. Aleinikoff & D. B. Klusmeyer (Eds.), *Citizenship today: Global perspectives and practices* (Kindle ed.). Washington, DC: Carnegie Endowment for International Peace.
Búriková, Z., & Miller, D. (2010). *Au pair*. Cambridge and Malden: Polity Press.
Butler, J. (1999). *Gender trouble: Feminism and the subversion of identity*. New York: Routledge.

Chow, R. (2002). The dream of a butterfly. In Y. J. Hwa (Ed.), *Comparative political culture in the age of globalization* (pp. 109–136). Lanham: Lexington Books.

Cox, R. (2007). The Au pair body: Sex object, sister or student? *European Journal of Women's Studies, 14*(3), 281–296.

Dahl, H. M., and Spanger, M. (2010) Sex workers' transnational and local motherhood: Presence and/or absence. In Isaksen, L. W. (Ed.), *Global care work* (pp. 117–136). (Lund: Nordic Academic Press).

Eggebø, H. (2012). *The regulation of marriage migration to Norway*. Doctoral dissertation, University of Bergen, Bergen.

Flemmen, A. B. (2008). Transnational marriages—Empirical complexities and theoretical challenges. *NORA, 16*(2), 114–129.

Fortier, A.-M. (2008). *Multicultural horizons. Diversity and the limits of the civil nation*. Oxon and New York: Routledge.

Fredriksen, M. M. B., & Myong, L. (2012). Love will keep us together: Kærlighed og hvid transracialitet i protester mod danske familiesammenføringsregler. Tidsskrift for kjønnsforskning, 35(3–4), 188–203.

Halsaa, B., Roseneil, S., & Sümer, S. (Eds.) (2012). *Remaking citizenship in multicultural Europe: Women's movements, gender and diversity*. Basingstoke: Palgrave Macmillan.

Hess, S., & Puckhaber, A. (2004). 'Big sisters' are better domestic servants? Comments on the booming Au pair business. *Feminist Review, 77*, 65–78.

Hollway, W., & Jefferson, T. (2000). *Doing qualitative research differently*. London: Sage.

Johansson, A. (2005). *Narrativ teori och metod*. Lund: Studentlitteratur.

Lister, R., Williams, F., Antonette, A., Bussmaker, J., Gerhard, U., Heinen, J., et al. (2007). *Gendering citizenship in Western Europe: New challenges for citizenship research in a cross-national context*. Bristol: Policy Press.

Mühleisen, W., Røthing, Å., & Svendsen, S. H. B. (2012). Norwegian sexualities: Assimilation and exclusion in Norwegian immigration policy. *Sexualities, 15*(2), 139–155.

Myong, L., & Bissenbakker, M. (2014). Forstyrret kærlighed: Affektiv assimilation som nyt ideal for transnational adoption. *Social Kritik, 137*, 56–67.

Myrdahl, E. M. (2010). Legislating love: Norwegian family reunification law as a racial project. *Social and Cultural Geography, 11*(2), 103–116.

Nagel, J. (2000). Ethnicity and sexuality. *Annual Review of Sociology, 26*, 107–133.

Øien, C. (2009). *On equal terms? An evaluation of the Norwegian Au pair scheme*. Oslo: Fafo.

Oleksy, E. H. (Ed.) (2009). *Intimate citizenships*. New York: Routledge.
Phillips, A. (Ed.) (2006). *The penguin Freud reader*. London: Penguin.
Plummer, K. (2003). *Intimate citizenship*. Seattle, WA and London: University of Washington Press.
Said, E. W. (2001). *Orientalismen: Vestlige oppfatninger av Orienten*. Oslo: De norske bokklubbene.
Stubberud, E. (2015). 'It's not much': Affective (boundary) work in the Au pair scheme. In R. Cox (Ed.), *Au pairs' lives in global context* (pp. 121–135). Hampshire: Palgrave.
Sunde, I., & Isungset, O. (Writers). (2013). Herskap og tenarar [Television series] *Brennpunkt*. Oslo: NRK.
Williams, L. (2010). *Global marriage. Cross-border marriage migration in global context*. New York: Palgrave Macmillan.
Wittig, M. (1989). On the social contract. *Feminist Issues, 9*(1), 3–12.
Yuval-Davis, N. (2010). The 'multi-layered citizen'. *International Feminist Journal of Politics, 1*(1), 119–136.

7

Citizenship and Maternalism in Migrant Domestic Labour: Filipina Workers and Their Employers in Amsterdam and Rome

Sabrina Marchetti

Introduction

Frequent references to family ties on the part of paid domestic workers and employers when describing their relationship have aroused significant scholarly interest. For instance, the use of expressions such as 'being part of the family'—interchangeably used by employers and employees alike—is a recurrent topic of analysis in studies on paid domestic work in different contexts (Lan, 2006; Locher-Scholten, 2000; Parreñas, 2001; Ray & Qayum, 2009; Rothenberg, 2000). In this chapter, I contribute to this debate on family-like relationships in paid domestic work by drawing attention to the issue of the 'maternalistic' attitudes that are at play in relationships between migrant employees and non-migrant employers. In particular, the aim of this chapter is to examine the ways in which a

---

S. Marchetti
Department of Philosophy and Cultural Heritage, Ca' Foscari University of Venice, Venice, Italy

© The Editor(s) (if applicable) and The Author(s) 2016
B. Gullikstad et al. (eds.), *Paid Migrant Domestic Labour in a Changing Europe*, DOI 10.1057/978-1-137-51742-5_7

lack of citizenship rights on the part of migrant workers, resulting from being either temporary or undocumented migrants in Europe, influences their relationship with female employers. With this purpose, I will analyse the case of Filipina women employed as domestic workers in Amsterdam and Rome and discuss the way in which their citizenship status reinforces maternalistic relationships with their employers.

In doing this, I articulate the expression of maternalistic attitudes around the analysis of two separate issues: (1) the recurrent use, by both sides, of sentiments of pity and gratitude as a way of expressing their attitudes towards each other and (2) the workers' dependency on help from their employers, which is often necessary, given the limitations imposed on these workers by migration and citizenship legislation. I argue, however, that maternalism between migrant employees and their non-migrant employers, although it might bring workers some immediate benefits, is ultimately detrimental to the workers. This is due to the fact that this maternalism brings with it a series of stereotypical representations, such as that of migrant women as victims of their own decisions to migrate or transnational mothers as suffering figures, which promotes an image of migrant domestic workers as vulnerable and needy subjects, dependent on the goodwill of helpful employers.

This argument is based on the analysis of in-depth interviews that I conducted in 2005 for a small research project that I carried out to examine the way in which gender, citizenship and ethnicity affect the relationship between employers and employees in migrant domestic work. For this project, I interviewed four women from the Philippines (Nelly and Fanny in Amsterdam; Minda and Dona in Rome) who were either undocumented or temporary migrants. I also interviewed six employers (Hanneke, Ilse and Sophie in Amsterdam; Lorenza, Valeria and Paola in Rome). Participants were recruited through my personal channels and the snowballing technique. More details on the individual profiles of the interviewees will be given together with the analysis of the interviews.

In the next pages, I will first elaborate on the importance of the notion of maternalism to paid domestic work. I will then introduce a citizenship-based perspective and move on to an analysis of the interview material, which is organised in two main sections—one based on my interviews with employers and the other on those with employees.

Maternalism and the 'Family Analogy' in Paid Domestic Work

Reference to 'being part of the family', as applied to people who are *not* family members, has been called the 'family analogy'. The frequent use of this analogy on the part of both employers and employees has animated a large part of the scholarly debate on paid domestic work. Not only scholarly writings, but also personal memories, novels and films on the topic of paid domestic work question whether or not domestic workers can be equated to members of the families for whom they work. Accounts of this issue vary greatly. Some scholars find the use of the family analogy to be one of the most pervasive forms of control and exploitation operating in this labour sector (Lan, 2006; Ray & Qayum, 2009), especially in the context of nationalist and colonialist discourses (Anderson, 2014; Kofman, 2005; Locher-Scholten, 2000). Other scholars instead see the use of the family analogy as a positive element that offers workers an opportunity to express intimacy with and closeness to their employers (Näre, 2011; Parreñas, 2001).

Within this larger debate on family-based narratives of paid domestic work, the question of maternalism has attracted the attention of those who are specifically interested in employer–employee interactions as examples of negotiations between women across racial and/or socio-economic hierarchies (see also Cox and Busch, this volume; Kristensen, this volume; Stubberud, this volume). In her pioneering book on African-American domestic workers in Boston, Judith Rollins (1985) devotes a chapter to 'deference and maternalism'. Her focus is the legacy of ancient forms of servitude in contemporary paid domestic work.

Rollins says that in ancient Rome, servants were depicted as childlike, irresponsible and lacking autonomy; they lived under the responsibility of their master, the 'father of the house' (*pater familias*), who was accountable for them, extracting service and loyalty in exchange for protection. In her view, a similar pattern applies today to the employment of paid domestic workers, wherein women are typically hired, instructed and controlled by other women. For Rollins, maternalistic attitudes between employers and employees come up in the tendency of employers, who are women in positions constructed as racially and socio-economically superior, to seek 'deference and gratitude' on the part of domestic workers. Their generous and charitable gestures provide a confirmation of their higher status. For this reason, 'maternalism may protect and nurture, [but] it also degrades and insults' (Rollins, 1985, p. 186). In other words, 'maternalistic employers' are those who, albeit unconsciously, at the same time as helping and protecting their employees, confirm their inferiority and, by extension, that of all people belonging to their social category (migrants, blacks, poor, etc.).

The topic of helpful gestures and feelings of gratitude between employers and employees also connects to previous studies in this field concerning the meaning of the gifts that employers typically give to domestic workers. Scholars have been quite divided on this issue. Jacqueline Cock, for example, is very critical of this practice, saying 'Gifts help to reinforce the social hierarchy by promoting feelings of loyalty, faithfulness and gratitude. (…) This kind of paternalist relationship is intensively demeaning for the dependent servant' (Cock, 1989, p. 82). Equally critical of gift-giving as a strategy that ultimately damages domestic workers are Mary Romero (1992, p. 152) and Elaine Kaplan (1987). Other scholars are more cautious, as is Rhacel Parreñas, who takes the standpoint of Filipina domestic workers to highlight that they 'have gained tremendous material benefits from the inclination of employers to give gifts' (Parreñas, 2001, p. 187).

Turning to more recent scholarship, I find it interesting that a Filipina scholar, Janet Arnado, picks up the concept of maternalism and uses it in her analysis of interviews held in Manila, where domestic workers are mainly young women migrating from rural areas to the city (Arnado, 2003). Arnado identifies four types of maternalism that Filipina employers adopt in relation to their employees. These are (1) maternalism as a 'part of the family' ideology (which is basically Rollins' view of maternalism); (2) maternalism as a form of emotional labour; (3) maternalism to enhance the worker's social network; and finally (4) maternalism based on the value of *utang na loob* (i.e. a 'debt of gratitude').

In the following pages, I will use a combination of the first (maternalism as a 'part of the family' ideology) and the fourth type (maternalism based on a debt of gratitude) for the analysis of the interviews. Thus, my aim is to establish a connection between maternalistic attitudes on the part of employers and the response of workers in terms of moral indebtedness and gratitude to support my analysis of maternalism as involving ambiguities.

Filipina Domestic Workers and the Concept of Citizenship

Filipino men and women have been leaving their country in large numbers to take up cleaning and caring jobs in many parts of the world since the 1970s, such as in the USA and Canada, and also in the Gulf States and the Middle East (Constable, 1997; Lan, 2006; Parreñas, 2001, 2008; Pratt, 2012; Yoeh & Huang, 1999). In the European context, the Filipino diaspora in Italy has been researched by various authors (e.g. Anderson, 2000; Banfi, 2008; Cominelli, 2003; Magat, 2004; Zontini, 2010), whilst, for the Netherlands, few studies exist (Botman, 2011; Marchetti, 2006; Tubadji, Nijkamp, Gheasi, & Rietveld, 2014; Van Walsum, 2011).

In this literature, Filipino migrants come into sight as a transnational workforce mainly employed at the global level in the industry that has increasingly developed around the commodification of care and domestic tasks in the service and health sectors (Yeates, 2009). This transnationalism does not go without repercussions in terms of the individual experiences of Filipino migrants, including, amongst other things, the question of legal constraints on citizenship rights that they face in the destination country. The exclusion of migrant domestic workers from citizenship rights has attracted the attention of several political and social scientists (Bosniak, 2008; Lutz, 2011; Ong, 2006; Sarti, 2005; Triandafyllidou, 2013). Others have focused on this group's social mobilisation to claim access to more citizenship rights in their countries of residence (Constable, 2009; Gutierrez-Rodríguez, 2010).

The question of citizenship is not, however, clear cut. The burgeoning debate that has flourished around the notion of citizenship in recent years has resulted in many and often contrasting definitions (Isin, Neyers & Turner, 2013). Citizenship has been seen as something 'flexible' (Ong, 1993), as a 'lived' experience (Hall & Williamson, 1999) or as the result of 'acts' of citizenship (Isin & Nielsen, 2008). Additionally, it has been seen as a multi-layered 'package' of practices, rights and identities that is composed in different ways depending on the historical and geographical context (Joppke, 2007; Yuval-Davis, 1999). As Sandro Mezzadra (2006) emphasises, migrants' stories address the question of rights and legal entitlements, but they also go beyond the mere institutional dimension of citizenship. It is in this sense that citizenship is an object of negotiation: it is a field in which people with different positions and different trajectories enact their strategies for the acquisition of better status, renegotiate social boundaries or enhance/reduce the distance between them. As I will show, the relationship between migrant domestic workers and their employers is an exemplary context for the deployment of such moves.

Finally, it is also important to mention the feminist debate on citizenship, which has concentrated on the measure to which *all* women are, by definition, excluded by the concepts of citizenship, justice and democracy in modern nation states (see for example Fraser, 2003; Lister et al., 2007; Mouffe, 1992; Young, 1990). Here, however, I am interested less in the way all women are excluded by dominant conceptions of citizenship and more in the way women may have different positions in relation to the entitlements connected to it—in other words, in the differences between women who have access to different degrees and configurations of the practices and the rights related to citizenship, especially in a migratory setting.

In this perspective, the use of the expression 'partial citizenship' (Bauböck, 2011; Parreñas, 2001) is particularly apt to describe the differences between Filipina domestic workers and their employers, both in Italy and in the Netherlands. The idea of a 'partiality' of citizenship indeed emphasises that there are various degrees and forms of access to citizenship entitlements. Against this background, it is not only that Filipina domestic workers in general and their Italian/Dutch employers have different degrees of access (the first as migrants vs. the latter as non-migrants) but there is also a difference *among* Filipina workers on the basis of their different migratory statuses (temporary, permanent, undocumented and so on). This is, in turn, crucially conditioned by different national legislation on migration, labour and citizenship rights across Europe.

In the Netherlands, it is not possible to obtain a residence permit to work in cleaning and care services on a private basis. Hence, the majority of foreigners who are active in this sector are undocumented migrants. They are thus in a position in which they can be detained and forcibly repatriated at any moment; they do not have access to health care (with the exception of life-threatening cases); and they cannot open a bank account, sign a rental contract for their accommodation or buy a season ticket for local transportation. Of course, they cannot leave the Netherlands to visit the Philippines, because this would prevent them from returning. Likewise, they cannot invite their relatives to visit them.

In Italy, domestic work is a valid reason for applying for a residence permit. The employment of foreigners in this sector is heavily regulated through the establishment of yearly quotas for their entry. These limitations are the reason why many foreign domestic workers still lack a regular residence permit. Large numbers, however, do have a permit to stay and work.[1] These people are formally entitled to the same rights and protection as Italian citizens. In reality, however, there are many instances in which their rights are limited: migrants in Italy cannot vote in general elections, and they have difficulty accessing work and financial opportunities (Basa, De Guzman, & Marchetti, 2012). Their residence permits are only temporary and the renewal of these permits is crucially based on the support of their employers, who must declare their intention of hiring them, sometimes hosting them and supporting them financially. Another troublesome issue is that of family reunification, to which, in practice, many migrants do not have access due to income-based requirements in the regulations (see Ambrosini, 2014). In the light of these and other limitations, migrant domestic workers in Italy have been defined as 'partial citizens' (Parreñas, 2001).

These different migration policies determine different citizenship statuses for Filipina domestic workers in Rome and Amsterdam. Given this context, understanding and help from their employers is often the only way for these workers to manage years of distress and their lack of rights. As I will discuss further, this does not go without negative consequences

---

[1] The actual official number of migrant domestic workers in Italy is 807,000; 75,000 of whom are from the Philippines (INPS, 2012).

and it makes one wonder whether this is a situation in which—as Bridget Anderson (2000) writes—states give employers 'the authority to dominate their employees', given the dependency of the latter on the goodwill of the former.

Maternalism from the Employers' Perspective

In this section, I will show the maternalism that is played out on the part of the employers of domestic workers. As mentioned, this is done with reference to two main issues: (1) employers expressing feelings of pity towards the workers and (2) practical involvement by employers in the workers' lives to help them cope with the difficulties caused by their lack of citizenship rights. It is important to underline that the workers I interviewed for this research project did not report overt exploitation or bad treatment (as could have been the case had their employers taken personal advantage of their vulnerability), but instead a willingness of their employers to support them. Nevertheless, as I will show, this still placed employees in an inferior and weaker position, reinforcing their position as 'partial citizens' who were dependent on the goodwill of someone else.

The first step in my argument is to show the extent to which pity and compassionate tones came into the portrayals that employers offered of the Filipina women working for them. The following example comes from an interview gathered in Amsterdam with Hanneke, who was 36 years old and the mother of two children. She had recently returned to paid work with a part-time job and, since then, she had been employing a Filipina woman called Carmen. In reply to my question 'What are your feelings for Carmen?', Hanneke offered the following depiction of Carmen's life and, at the same time, the compassion that this provoked in her:

> I really respect the way she is living; I can't imagine I could live the way she does, and also considering the constant fear of being caught by the police… I think I could not live in that way… I really respect how she does it: she never complains, she is happy. But she tells a lot of sad stories about her family: when her father died she couldn't go, and now about her daughter's pregnancy, it is terrible that she cannot go there! (Hanneke, 36, employer, Amsterdam)

7 Citizenship and Maternalism in Migrant Domestic Labour ...

In this excerpt, Hanneke first of all expresses profound esteem and 'respect' for Carmen. She also emphasises her concern for her employee's situation and how dreadful it is. All of Carmen's problems seem to mainly derive from her lack of citizenship rights due to being undocumented, such as the continuous risk of being deported and the fact that she cannot freely go back to the Philippines for a visit, which seems to provoke much compassion in Hanneke ('she tells a lot of sad stories'). However, I find that boundary-making is also at play in this quotation, when Hanneke says that she cannot imagine being in Carmen's (difficult) position ('I could not live the way she does'). This means, in my view, that fundamentally Hanneke could not imagine ever finding herself in the same personal and socio-economic situation of women like Carmen (i.e. being an impoverished migrant or a transnational mother and lacking citizenship rights). As I will further illustrate when commenting on the next interview excerpts, this coexistence of compassion and boundary-making was typical of the employers' maternalistic attitudes, in which benevolence and affection went hand in hand with hierarchy and inequality.

It is important to note that during the making of the interviews analysed here, I paid special attention to this issue of the possibility/impossibility of the workers and employers to reverse roles, or at least the possibility of them having a peer-to-peer relationship. I addressed these issues in the concluding part of the interviews through questions such as 'Could you imagine being in her place for one day?' and 'Could you imagine being friends, one day?' This was my strategy to tackle the way in which the interviewees conveyed asymmetric representations of themselves and of their counterparts along the axes of gender, ethnicity and citizenship differences.

In relation to the question of pity that I discuss here, I find the answer to my question 'Can you imagine taking her place for one day?' that I received from an Italian employer called Lorenza, particularly telling. She replied:

> No! Not at all! She lives a life of sacrifices, that's why I pity her... I pity her a lot: far away from the children that she adores... a life of sacrifice! (...) To leave your country... I thank God that it did not happen to me! (...) The poor woman, a misfortune in life! (Lorenza, 60, employer, Rome)

Even more than Hanneke, Lorenza did not hesitate to offer a pitiful depiction of the woman working for her. In the above quote, Lorenza describes the employee as a victimised character, suffering to sacrifice for her children and her family. In this narrative, the worker's decision to migrate is emptied of any voluntary character and instead becomes 'a misfortune in life' of which she cannot but be a victim. Lorenza thus (unwillingly) enhances a representation that is in line with the normative gendered model imposed on Filipina women of becoming *bayani*, the 'modern-day heroes' of the Philippines, by embarking on transnational migration for the good of their family and, ultimately, their country (see Parreñas, 2008). It is because of these compassionate feelings towards her employee that Lorenza told me she had done everything possible, in her view, to help the woman at the practical level, especially with bureaucracy and everything connected to her residence status.

Regarding the practical involvement of employers in their workers' lives, it is interesting to consider the following quote from the interview with Ilse, a Dutch employer from Amsterdam. Ilze was a young professional, and after she and her husband had moved into a bigger house, they started to employ a Filipina domestic worker for a few hours every week. During the interview, Ilse appeared particularly concerned about the situation of undocumented migrants in the Netherlands. Her views and attitudes towards her employee emerge in this long quote:

> I admire her for her strength to work hard in a situation that cannot be easy! I remember we talked about her status in the Netherlands, because she doesn't have a permit, so she is illegal here. We talked several times about that and things like the insurance or getting the children here, or how the children are doing, or her housing problems. I looked up this organization that helps undocumented people. I tried to advise her on the rules in the Netherlands, what it is wise to do and what isn't. We signed a letter to get her son to come over here. (…) I try to do anything I can—which is very little—to make it nicer for her. I find the concept of being illegal somewhere… I find it ridiculous! How can you as a person be illegal? (…) So when I met her and I heard her story from a friend of mine, I thought that she could solve my problems cleaning the house, but then the special thing was that I could do something for somebody in a situation I really thought should not exist! So it is my way of resisting against a rule that—I think—is ridiculous! (Ilse, 42, employer, Amsterdam)

In this quote, Ilse simultaneously expresses her concern for her employee's situation and her passionate criticism of the Dutch government concerning migration matters. Moreover, she also relates all the actions that she has undertaken to improve the situation of her worker: she has advised her, directed her to a support group, collected information and discussed her problems. This activity seems to have taken up much of Ilse's energy and to have been the subject of most of the conversations between her and her employee.

In my view, this employer can be seen as an example of a maternalist, particularly in relation to the second type of fundamental maternalistic attitudes previously listed (i.e. intervention by employers helping workers to cope with the restriction of their citizenship rights). The quote illustrates how this intervention is accompanied by the construction of a personal and intimate relationship between employers and employees, based on the employer's benevolence in helping, listening and finding practical solutions. However, as was the case before, in the quote from Hanneke, this attitude not only testifies to the worker's dependence on the benevolent employer, but it is also accompanied by a reaffirmation of the distance between the two women. This boundary-making can be seen to be at play, for instance, when Ilse says 'she could solve my problems cleaning the house [...] I could do something for somebody in a situation I really thought should not exist'. Notwithstanding Ilse's positive intentions, this formulation contains an affirmation of a socio-economic difference between the two women, since the 'problems' that each woman solves for the other are substantially different: for one (Ilse), the problem is having a dirty home; for the other (the Filipina worker), it is being deprived of individual rights because of a lack of a residence permit in the Netherlands as an undocumented migrant.

In conclusion, narratives by employers in which they talk about pitying compassion for their workers and their care in helping and supporting them only apparently describe an equal relationship of solidarity between women. They are actually an opportunity for employers to reinforce their status as women in a position that is constructed as racially and socio-economically superior to that of the women working for them. This difference is articulated, in particular, in narratives by employers that offer a victimised depiction of the other women (especially as sacrificing transnational mothers), and through which they emphasise the dependency of the workers on their goodwill as supportive employers. All of this, together, shapes the maternalistic attitude that I find at play amongst the employers that I interviewed and which is reinforced by the context of a lack of citizenship rights for migrant domestic workers in Italy and the Netherlands.

Negotiations Around Gratitude in the Views of Employees

Recalling Rollins' definition of maternalism, it is important to emphasise that maternalistic attitudes correspond to the expression of gratitude on the part of those who have received favours and protection (Rollins, 1985, p. 186). Along these lines, in this section I will discuss the Filipina interviewees' grateful behaviour towards the employers who helped them circumvent the obstacles set against them by the limitations of their citizenship rights. In the course of this, the other side of the stories previously told by the employers will come into sight. The analysis of these accounts substantially mirrors the previous one in highlighting the recurring elements of (1) dependency on the goodwill of the employer and (2) representation of Filipina migrant women as victimised subjects, particularly because they are 'suffering transnational mothers'.

In general, the Filipina interviewees described intervention by their employers as a unique opportunity to access certain services (precluded to the undocumented) or to navigate complex migration regulations. Therefore, they said that they particularly valued those employers who were willing to help them in these matters. This was poignantly illustrated by Fanny, a worker in Amsterdam, who to my question 'What do you like best about your employer?' simply replied: 'that she always advises me on everything'.

Let us see other examples of how support by employers was perceived by their workers. For instance, Minda, a Filipina worker in Rome, explained how her employer helped her reunite with her husband, who was, at that time, also living in Rome after many years of separation:

> Since I'm regular, I could go through the reunion procedure with my husband. But after the first application failed, I said 'I'll go back to the Philippines'

because being here alone is not nice. (…) So I told my employer 'I'm going back to the Philippines at the end of December'. But she said 'Why don't we make a second application and I'll help you?' I told her all my problems. (…) She solved everything. We went to the police station, both of us, and it seemed that everything was easy! Everything I asked her… she gave me! (Minda, 38, worker, Rome)

Minda described the intervention by the employer as *the* solution to smooth the otherwise complicated procedure for family reunification. Her employer emerged as a personal confidant ('I told her all my problems') and a spontaneously generous person testified by the fact that she was the one to suggest a second application when Minda was thinking of leaving the country.

A similar perspective was offered by Nelly, an undocumented migrant employed in Amsterdam by a woman called Marieke:

When I had problems with the rent and everything, because the husband is an attorney… so he gave me some advice. About the doctor… when my husband was sick, she was the one to call the doctor. They are very helpful to me and every time she tells me 'I'm willing to help you' and then she helps me. (Nelly, 55, worker, Amsterdam)

Here again, the interviewee emphasises the spontaneous generosity of her employer and her helpfulness in critical situations. Interestingly, we see that Nelly refers to the whole network of people (the husband/attorney, the doctor) whom she can access thanks to the intermediation of her employer. This shows that, for people like Nelly, employers are even more valuable when they have high social capital and connections with the 'right' people; this was the case for Marieke, who was married to an attorney and, from what I understood, had very good connections.

The gratitude of workers like Minda or Nelly finds expression in a sentiment of indebtedness towards the employers from whom they have received support. Indeed, the Filipina workers that I interviewed emphasised how their relationship with their employers was based on a bond created by their gratitude and their desire to reciprocate the support they had received. In many cases, this desire to compensate urged them to perform unpaid services, such as working extra hours, assisting with the planning of a party or other tasks not included in the initial contract.

This dynamic recalls what Janet Arnado (2003) defines as a 'debt of gratitude' (*utang na loob*) and which, as I have previously discussed, she finds to be one of the key elements of a maternalistic relationship between domestic workers and their employers in the Philippines. Despite the difference that characterises the Filipino versus the European context, the perspective of the 'debt of gratitude' can still be useful to support the interpretation of the interviews with some of the workers, as I will show.

Fanny's story may serve as a first example. Fanny had been working for Monika for many years. During this time, although her job was originally to babysit Monika's child, it changed to a mixed situation that combined paid and unpaid tasks. She explained:

> Officially they called me as a babysitter, but I do everything and I clean the house, but this is not part of my job. (…) They treat me like family. They are very close. (…) She helped me to find my apartment. I go for 3, 4 hours but I don't want money (…). I told her: 'When I need money I will tell you'. (Fanny, 50, worker, Amsterdam)

The fact that Fanny's employer helped her to find an apartment, which is particularly difficult for undocumented workers in Amsterdam, gave rise to a series of gestures of gratitude on the part of Fanny, who did not hesitate to make use of the 'family analogy' to describe her relationship with Monika's family ('They treat me like family'). So, although initially employed as a babysitter, Fanny ended up doing everything in the house while, as she told me, the employer sat at home watching television. At the time of the interview, Fanny was still babysitting Monika's child without being paid after having found a permanent job elsewhere. The 'debt of gratitude' between Fanny and Monika was the ground for the employers' request for some hours of babysitting when Fanny had free time from her new job.

Again, from the interview with Minda, we see the connection between a willingness to do unpaid jobs and gratitude towards employers. In Minda's case, this was because of her employer's fundamental role in solving her problems, such as her husband's permit and her health issues. To my question 'Do you do some extras without being paid?', she replied:

> Yes, yes. And you will wonder why. Because she has done so many things for me that she does not even want to mention. I mean, that she never

needs to mention. She does not ask me for things in exchange for what she did. And I don't ask for things in exchange for what I do. (...) [Because] everything I needed from her—statements, etc.—she gave me. (...) In exchange for this... look... Even if you don't pay me, why shouldn't I go? I never asked [for money]. (Minda, 38, worker, Rome)

In these lines, I find the absence of a direct mention of the nexus between the favours received and the extra jobs performed particularly interesting ('she never needs to mention', 'she does not ask'). The unspoken nature of the performance of extra jobs signals a tacit consensus between employers and employees surrounding their 'debt of gratitude'. It is also true that, over time, the 'debt' becomes reciprocal: the more unpaid tasks Minda does, the more her employer also feels indebted towards her, which explains Minda's saying 'I don't ask for things in exchange for what I do'.

A similar negotiation emerges from the interview with Nelly, an undocumented worker in Amsterdam, who explained:

I'm also doing the laundry even if she didn't say to do that because sometimes I say to myself ... because I want to help... because they are so nice ... It depends on me also. If I can do something... I do everything nicely. Because she helped me get my son come to visit me. (Nelly, 55, worker, Amsterdam)

Similar to Minda, Nelly emphasised that she had not received an explicit request for unpaid work from her employer. Doing some small extras was presented as her own spontaneous initiative to compensate for the kindness of her employer and the favours she had received in the past. However, this was also something that Minda and Nelly did with the purpose of cultivating a good relationship in the light of possible future benefits. In other words, they did it to strengthen the debt relationship that existed with their employers over time. This is in line with Mary Romero's (1992) observation that domestic workers are keen to perform small gestures as an 'investment' in the hope of being repaid with favours and support from their employers.

These negotiations assume a specific connotation in the context of the 'partial citizenship' of the Filipina migrants that I interviewed. Support from their employers became necessary for them to pursue basic goals such as health assistance, accommodation or family life. This was particularly the case for the undocumented workers in the Netherlands, who, as mentioned, were formally excluded from care and health assistance and were not entitled to sign a rental contract, open a bank account and so forth. This created a number of obstacles in their everyday lives, and intervention by their employers often provided a unique opportunity for alternative solutions. Employers helped them informally to find health care, legal support, accommodation and so forth. In this light, the willingness of workers to do unpaid work as a sign of gratitude testifies to their vulnerability as 'partial citizens' and their dependency on supportive non-migrant people in order to gain some comfort and safety in their everyday lives.

Before concluding, I will illustrate a specific type of support that domestic workers receive from their employers, pertaining to reunification with their families. As emerged from several interviews, reunification is difficult to achieve and yet a highly desired goal for Filipina migrant women, who live separated from their husbands and children for many years. For undocumented workers, permanent reunification is impossible to achieve since they have no legal status in the host country. For the same reason, they cannot apply to have their children come for a short visit. In Italy this is possible in principle for the Filipina domestic workers who have a residence permit. But in practice it is often difficult for them to invite their family members to come for a visit or to reunify because of the requirements set in reunification regulations in terms of the size of their accommodation and income.

I have already quoted excerpts mentioning family reunification, but I believe that the following quote adds one important layer to the analysis and sheds light on the role of gendered values in the bond between employers and domestic workers asking their help. The quote relates to the fact that Nelly asked her employer to help her daughter come to the Netherlands on the occasion of her 50th birthday party. The employer had to pretend that the girl was a friend of hers who wanted to come to the Netherlands for tourism. This is how Nelly told the episode:

> Because she is also a mother, she knows I miss my children. When I told her about my plan for my 50th birthday, I asked if she could invite my

younger daughter. When I asked her, she never refused me: 'Yes! Yes! I am pleased to invite her'. (Nelly, 55, worker, Amsterdam)

For Nelly, the mirroring between herself and her employer as loving mothers made it possible for her to overcome the hierarchy between employer and employee. In other words, the assumed recognition between the women *as* mothers ('because she is also a mother') was seen as a tool to strengthen the woman solidarity between them and overcome the difficulties set by immigration laws.

I argue, however, that focus on the difficulties of migrant domestic workers as mothers, which is articulated here in negotiations around pity and gratitude, ultimately emphasises the boundaries between employers and workers as different types of mothers: on the one side, women who can totally fulfil their mothering role with no obstacles, and on the other side, mothers who care for their children at a distance and therefore are only 'partially' mothers. The women in the second group mother by supporting their children through remittances and distance care, but they miss the dimension of physical presence. In the story of Nelly, this physical dimension can be (temporarily) recuperated thanks to the support of a woman from the former group (non-migrant employers). Here again, dependency on the goodwill of employers is crucial. Moreover, this also confirms the victimising representation of Filipina women as *bayani*—heroic sacrificing migrants—which is a detrimental representation for them in that it promotes the strong expectation of them, as caring mothers and dutiful daughters, to financially support their families through long years of emigration, at the cost of renouncing their own well-being (Basa, De Guzaman, & Marchetti, 2012).

To sum up, in this section I have illustrated the way in which desire to compensate for favours received from employers represents a common attitude among the Filipina domestic workers that I interviewed. Nevertheless, employees willing to work without being paid might sustain the view of migrant women as vulnerable subjects. For this reason, the maternalistic attitude of employers that we saw in the previous section risks undermining the status of domestic workers and reinforcing the boundaries between employers and employees in their asymmetrical social positions. It has the demeaning effect of making employees dependent on the goodwill of employers, implying an impossibility of autonomously achieving better rights in the host society.

Conclusions

In this chapter, I have described the establishment of a maternalistic relationship between employers and the migrant domestic workers they employ, in that these migrants are positioned as 'partial citizens' and are therefore dependent on the goodwill and support of their employers to solve certain everyday problems. I have described this relationship as articulated around the expression of sentiments of pity (on the part of employers) and gratitude (on the part of the workers). I have also explored negotiations between them by saying that they risk promoting the representation of Filipina migrant women as vulnerable victims of their migration, and as suffering mothers who reinforce the compulsory model for Filipina women of the sacrificing *bayani*.

The employers and employees that I interviewed believed their feelings to be proof of the special character of their relationship, in contrast with models of exploitation and abuse that one may find in similar situations. However, as the relationship is embedded in a *maternalistic* setting, the employers' willingness to help ultimately reinforces their own superior socio-economic position as non-migrant women. This is especially so when, albeit unwillingly, they promote a victimising depiction of their employees, particularly as transnational mothers who are dependent on their goodwill to maintain their caring commitments.

On the other side, Filipina employees who benefit from the supportive role of their employers engage in negotiations with the purpose of enhancing this support. Their ability to provoke the personal involvement of their employer is important for them. For this reason, they also provide their helpful employers with a series of compensatory gestures to show their loyalty and faithfulness, most concretely in the performance of extra unpaid tasks. The problem is that doing unpaid work falls back on the employees. With this conduct, they maintain an image of migrant domestic workers as easily exploitable subjects, blurring the boundary between what is licit or illicit for employers to require.

In conclusion, employers and employees' reciprocal exchange of favours represents the creation of a space for negotiating the 'partial citizenship' superimposed on Filipina migrant domestic workers. However, the maternalistic character of the relationships that I have described invites the problematisation of the notion of solidarity among women, particularly in relation to shared assumptions about motherhood as a terrain for mutual recognition among them. Indeed, the differences in citizenship status and socio-economic situation between migrant and non-migrant women lead to a series of negotiations at different levels that do not manage to eliminate, and probably even emphasise, the hierarchies between them.

References

Ambrosini, M. (2014). Parenting from a distance and processes of family reunification: A research on the Italian case. *Ethnicities, 15*, 440–459.

Anderson, B. (2000). *Doing the dirty work? The global politics of domestic labor*. London: Zed Books.

Anderson, B. (2014). Nations, migration and domestic labour: The case of the UK. *Women's Studies International Forum, 46*, 5–12.

Arnado, J. M. (2003). Maternalism in mistress-maid relations: The Philippine experience. *Journal of International Women's Studies, 4*(3), 154–177.

Banfi, L. (2008). Lavoro domestico, politiche migratorie e immigrazione filippina. Un confronto tra Canada e Italia. *Polis, 22*, 5–34.

Basa, C., De Guzman, V., & Marchetti, S. (2012). International migration and over-indebtedness: The case of Filipino workers in Italy. *IIED—Human Settlements Working Paper, 36*.

Bauböck, R. (2011). Temporary migrants, partial citizenship and hypermigration. *Critical Review of International Social and Political Philosophy, 14*(5), 665–693.

Bosniak, L. (2008). *The citizen and the alien: Dilemmas of contemporary membership*. Princeton, NJ: Princeton University Press.

Botman, S. (2011). *Gewoon schoonmaken: de troebele arbeidsrelaties in betaald huishoudelijk werk*. Doctoral thesis, Universiteit van Amsterdam.

Cock, J. (1989). *Maids and madams: Domestic workers under apartheid*. London: Women's Press.

Cominelli, C. (2003). Filippini nel settore domestico: i limiti di una integrazione subalterna. *Sociologia del lavoro, 89*, 52–67.

Constable, N. (1997). *Maid to order in Hong Kong: Stories of Filipina workers*. Ithaca, NY: Cornell University Press.

Constable, N. (2009). Migrant workers and the many states of protest in Hong Kong. *Critical Asian Studies, 41*, 143–164.

Fraser, N. (2003). Social justice in the age of identity politics: Redistribution, recognition and participation. In N. Fraser & A. Honneth (Eds.), *Redistribution or recognition? A political-philosophical exchange*. London and New York: Verso.

Gutierrez-Rodríguez, E. (2010). *Migration, domestic work and affect: A decolonist approach on value and the feminization of labour*. London: Routledge.

Hall, T., & Williamson, H. (1999). *Citizenship and community*. New York: Youth Work Press.

INPS. (2012). Osservatorio lavoratori domestici. Retrieved February 2, 2014, from http://www.inps.it/webidentity/banchedatistatistiche/domestici/index01.jsp

Isin, E. F., & Nielsen, G. M. (2008). *Acts of citizenship*. New York: Zed Books.

Isin, E. F., Nyers, P., & Turner, B. S. (2013). *Citizenship between past and future*. New York: Taylor & Francis.

Joppke, C. (2007). Transformation of citizenship: Status, rights, identity. *Citizenship Studies, 11*(1), 37–48.

Kaplan, E. (1987). "I don't do no windows": Competition between the domestic worker and the housewife. In V. Miner & H. E. Longino (Eds.), *Competition: A feminist taboo*. New York: The Feminist Press.

Kofman, E. (2005). Citizenship, migration and the reassertion of national identity. *Citizenship Studies, 9*(5), 453–467.

Lan, P. C. (2006). *Global cinderellas: Migrant domestic workers and newly rich employers in Taiwan*. Durham, NC and London: Duke University Press.

Lister, R., et al. (2007). *Gendering citizenship in Western Europe: New challenges for citizenship research in a cross-national context*. New York: Policy.

Locher-Scholten, E. (2000). *Women and the colonial state: Essays on gender and modernity in the Netherlands Indies, 1900–1942*. Amsterdam: Amsterdam University Press.

Lutz, H. (2011). *The new maids: Transnational women and the care economy*. London: Zed Books.

Magat, M. (2004). Women breadwinners in the margins: Filipina domestic workers in Rome, Italy. In A. Fauve-Chamoux (Ed.), *Domestic service and the formation of European identity. Understanding the globalization of domestic work, 16th–21st Centuries.* Bern: Peter Lang.

Marchetti, S. (2006). *'We had different fortunes': Relationships between Filipina domestic workers and their employers in Rome and Amsterdam*. Master's thesis, Utrecht University.

Mezzadra, S. (2006). *Diritto di fuga: Migrazioni, cittadinanza, globalizzazione.* Verona: Ombre Corte.

Mouffe, C. (1992). Feminism, citizenship and radical democratic politics. In J. Butler & J. W. Scott (Eds.), *Feminists theorize the political*. New York and London: Routledge.

Näre, L. (2011). The moral economy of domestic and care labour: Migrant workers in Naples, Italy. *Sociology, 45*(3), 396–412.

Ong, A. (1993). On the endge of empires: Flexible citizenship among Chinese in diaspora. *Positions, 1*(3), 745–778.

Ong, A. (2006). *Neoliberalism as exception: Mutations in citizenship and sovereignty.* Durham, NC: Duke University Press.

Parreñas, R. S. (2001). *Servants of globalization: Women, migration and domestic work.* Stanford, CA: Stanford University Press.

Parreñas, R. S. (2008). *The force of domesticity: Filipina migrants and globalization.* New York: New York University Press.

Pratt, G. (2012). *Families apart: Migrant mothers and the conflicts of labor and love.* Minneapolis: University of Minnesota Press.

Ray, R., & Qayum, S. (2009). *Cultures of servitude: Modernity, domesticity, and class in India.* Stanford, CA: Stanford University Press.

Rollins, J. (1985). *Between women: Domestics and their employers.* Philadelphia, PA: Temple University Press.

Romero, M. (1992). *Maid in the U.S.A.* New York: Routledge.

Rothenberg, P. (2000). *Invisible privilege: A memory about race, class and gender.* Lawrence: University Press of Kansas.

Sarti, R. (2005). Freedom and citizenship? The legal status of servants and domestic workers in a comparative perspective (16th–21st centuries). In S. Pasleau & I. Schopp (Eds.), *Proceedings of the servant project*. Liège: Editions de l'université de Liège (Vol. 3, pp. 127–164).

Triandafyllidou, A. (2013). *Irregular migrant domestic workers in Europe: Who cares?* Aldershot: Ashgate.

Tubadji, P. J. M., Nijkamp, D., Gheasi, M., & Rietveld, P. (2014). A study on undocumented migrant workers in the Dutch household sector. *International Journal of Manpower, 35,* 103–117.

Van Walsum, S. (2011). Regulating migrant domestic work in the Netherlands: Opportunities and pitfalls. *Canadian Journal of Women and the Law, 23*(1), 141–165.

Yeates, N. (2009). *Globalizing care economies and migrant workers: Explorations in global care chains.* New York: Palgrave Macmillan.

Yoeh, B., & S. Huang. (1999). Singapore women and foreign domestic workers: Negotiating domestic work and motherhood. In J. H. Momsen (Ed.), *Gender, migration, and domestic service.* London: Routledge.

Young, I. M. (1990). *Justice and the politics of difference.* Princeton, NJ: Princeton University Press.

Yuval-Davis, N. (1999). The "multi-layered citizen". *International Feminist Journal of Politics, 1*(1), 119–136.

Zontini, E. (2010). *Transnational families, migration and gender: Moroccan and Filipino women in Bologna and Barcelona.* Oxford: Berghahn Books.

8

Paid Migrant Domestic Labour in Gender-Equal Norway: A Win–Win Arrangement?

Guro Korsnes Kristensen

> In a global perspective it is absolutely horrible that they have to leave their children behind to come here and give love to my children. On a smaller scale however it is a win-win arrangement. (Norwegian au pair host mum)

Introduction

The aim of this chapter is to explore the increasing occurrence of paid migrant domestic labour in Norwegian families, with a focus on gender arrangements and the intersections of gender, social class, and national background. The chapter's empirical point of departure is Norwegian

---

G.K. Kristensen
Department of Interdisciplinary Studies of Culture, Centre for Gender Studies, Norwegian University of Science and Technology (NTNU), Trondheim, Norway

women and men's perceptions of and experiences with paying migrant women to undertake what has traditionally been perceived of as gendered family tasks, which, in line with today's political and cultural ideals of gender equality, should be shared equally between the sexes. The chapter's analytical point of departure is the neoliberal win–win narrative, which is often identified in discussions of paid migrant domestic labour, including in the empirical material this chapter is based on (see also Näre, this volume). I critically pursue this narrative by asking how the Norwegian employers envisioned the gains of paid domestic labour—both for themselves and for the migrant domestic labourers. In particular, I turn the reader's attention to the complex intersections of gender equality and citizenship, and to the ways in which the implementation of a specific model of gender equality is closely related to specific forms of citizenship, and to specific notions of 'the good citizen'.

Background

Norway is perceived of as a pioneer nation in gender equality, and gender equality is at the core of Norwegian cultural identity (Berg, Flemmen, & Gullikstad, 2010; Danielsen, Larsen, & Owesen, 2014; Gullestad, 2002, 2010; Kristensen, 2010). Norway's main strategies for achieving gender equality have been to strengthen women's economic independence through increasing their labour market participation and to normalise men's involvement in domestic and care work (Brandth & Kvande, 2013; Danielsen et al., 2014). This is particularly evident in policies related to the family, whereby childcare leave-sharing regulations,[1] the paternity leave quota,[2]

---

[1] In Norway the statutory parental leave is either 49 weeks at 100 % salary or 59 weeks at 80 % salary, to be divided between both parents. By law, the mother must take nine weeks of parental leave. The father is entitled to 2 weeks paid leave when the baby is born. In addition, the father must take an additional 10 weeks before the child turns 3 years old. If the father does not take these 10 weeks, they are withdrawn. With respect to the remaining weeks, the parents can decide if the mother takes it all, the father takes it all, or they both work part-time and share it. The National Welfare Office covers an income up to six times the National Insurance basic amount. In addition, most employers top up to the employee's full salary.

[2] The paternity leave quota was introduced in Norway in 1993. In the first years, the quota was 4 weeks. Over the years to come, it was gradually extended to 14 weeks before it was reduced to 10 weeks by the new conservative government in 2013.

and the development of day care facilities[3] enable the implementation of the dual-earner/dual-carer model for gender equality (Ellingsæter, 2014). As a result of these policies, Norwegian women's current employment rate is nearly as high as men's (Statistics Norway, 2015),[4] and Norwegian time-use surveys show a more gender-equal sharing of both paid and unpaid work among fathers and mothers (Kitterød & Rønsen, 2014). In particular, fathers have become more involved with childcare (Vaage, 2012) and, today, more than 90 % of Norwegian men stay at home with their children in the weeks that are provided by the father's quota (Brandth & Kvande, 2013).

However, despite increased promotion of policies supporting the dual-carer/dual-earner model of gender equality, it is still mostly women who adjust their participation in working life to accommodate their male partners' careers and their families' needs (Statistics Norway, 2015).[5] Furthermore, women tend to do more housework than men (Kitterød & Lappegård, 2012; Kitterød & Rønsen, 2014), whereas men tend to do more maintenance work (Kitterød & Lappegård, 2012; Vaage, 2002). Also, women are reported to be considerably more dissatisfied with the distribution of household labour than are men (Vaage, 2012), whereas a web-based survey found that disagreement over the distribution of domestic duties is a common reason for Norwegian heterosexual couples to break up the relationship (Træen, 2010).

One way to understand these numbers is to conclude that the dual-carer/dual-earner model is difficult to achieve in practice (Aarseth, 2011; Smeby & Brandth, 2013), and the normative basis of this model and its position in hegemonic discourses on gender equality are more contentious than they are often expressed in the story of gender-equal Norway (Berg et al., 2010; Kristensen, 2010). A trend that could be cited in support of this suggestion is the increasing tendency of mothers in resourceful dual-career families to leave working life while their children are young (Aarseth, 2014; Halrynjo & Lyng, 2009; Sørensen, forthcoming).

---

[3] In the last few years, substantial efforts have been made to increase day care facilities in Norway and, today, approximately 90 % of children between the ages of 1 and 5 go to kindergarten. *Source*: http://www.ssb.no/utdanning/statistikker/barnehager

[4] In 2013, the employment rate for women (20–66 years) was 77.1 %, and 82.7 % for men.

[5] In 2013, 34.7 % of women aged 20–66 worked part-time, compared to 13.9 % of men.

Another trend that seems to be relevant is the recent increase in paid domestic labour.

After a long period in which having live-in young women help out with cleaning, caring, and cooking was a normal way to organise family life in Norway (Sogner & Telste, 2005), the post-war era—with its social democratic ideology and comprehensive welfare model—introduced a strong focus on equality and sobriety and an explicit negative attitude towards social hierarchies and servitude (Gullestad, 2002; Myhre, 2010).[6] According to the Norwegian historian Sølvi Sogner, paid domestic labour was put particularly high on the list of unacceptable activities, not least in the radical 1970s (Sogner, 2004). However, in recent years, this seems to have changed as paid domestic labour is yet again becoming more widespread—though with a global twist as many new domestic labourers are women from other parts of the world (Isaksen, 2010).

The most prevalent forms of paid migrant domestic labour in contemporary Norway are home cleaning and au pairing. In 2007, 7 % of the adult population reported paying someone to clean their home, and among families with young children (up to the age of 6), the prevalence was 13 % (Kitterød, 2009). The typical consumers of home cleaning services are middle-class dual-earner urban families and, in particular, families in which both adults work long hours, in addition to single elderly men (Kitterød, 2009). As non-registered home cleaning work is widespread (Trygstad et al., 2011), information about those doing the work is inadequate. However, there are indications that a substantial proportion of cleaners are women from Eastern Europe (Alsos & Eldring, 2010; Friberg & Tyldum, 2007; Trygstad et al., 2011). Moreover, since many of them are not registered as employees in Norway, they are not protected by Norwegian labour laws and are not eligible to welfare support if they for some reason cannot work.[7]

When it comes to au pairing, there were 1476 resident permits given to au pairs in Norway in 2013, compared to 370 in 1991; 86 % of these were issued to women from the Philippines (UDI, 2014). In addition,

---

[6] According to Ruth Lister, the comprehensive Norwegian/Nordic welfare model is characterised by a 'passion for equality' (Lister, 2009, p. 246).

[7] In Norway, rights to unemployment benefits and sick leave are dependent on taxation.

8 Paid Migrant Domestic Labour in Gender-Equal Norway ...

an unknown number of people from within the European Union (EU)/ European Economic Area (EEA) (who do not need au pair visas) have taken on work in line with the au pair scheme and official au pair regulations (see also Gullestad and Annfelt, this volume; Stubberud, this volume). Unlike the job of home cleaning, au pairing is not officially defined as work, but as cultural exchange. According to Norwegian au pair regulations, an au pair visa grants residency for a maximum of 2 years, given that the applicant has a host family with which they can stay and for which they should perform light housework in exchange for board, lodging, Norwegian classes, and a minimum of 625 euros a month in 'pocket money' (UDI, 2014).[8] Despite the aim of cultural exchange, it has been documented that au pairs living in Norway perform a considerable amount of housework and care work for the families with which they live (Bikova, 2010, 2015; Kristensen, 2015; Øien, 2009; Sollund, 2010; Stubberud, 2015a, 2015b). It has also been documented that some au pairs working in Norway are breadwinners who send remittances to their families in their home countries (Bikova, 2015).

The described developments mean that more Norwegian families are outsourcing tasks that were traditionally labelled female and that today—in line with the dual-earner/dual-carer model of gender equality—should be shared equally between the sexes. It also means that Norway is facing a situation with an increasing group of migrant women who are working in the grey parts of the labour market, with salaries that are far below normal Norwegian salaries and according to terms and conditions that are not in line with the strictly regulated Norwegian labour market (Øien, 2009; Trygstad et al., 2011).

The overarching aim of this chapter is to reflect upon the concurrence of a strong political and cultural focus on gender equality and the increasing occurrence of paid migrant domestic labour, which is characterised by fundamental social inequalities. Does the implementation of the dual-carer/dual-earner model for gender equality rely on global inequalities and national/racial hierarchies? Does the dual-carer/dual-earner model of gender equality facilitate the (re)production of social and national/racial

---

[8] In comparison, the average Norwegian wage was 5287 euros a month in 2014. *Source*: https://www.ssb.no/arbeid-og-lonn/statistikker/lonnansatt/aar/2015-03-20. Au pairs are granted health insurance that covers medical treatment and return to country of origin, if necessary. The Holidays Act applies to the payment of holiday pay to au pairs.

hierarchies that contradict the political and cultural ideal of social equality? Or does it, by way of paid domestic labour, (also) produce opportunities for empowerment and social equality for migrant women?

Paid Migrant Domestic Work, Gender Equality, and Citizenship

These questions regarding the Norwegian context feed into at least two key discussions with respect to paid domestic labour, gender equality, and citizenship. The first discussion asks whether the commodification of this highly gendered work helps to achieve the political and normative ideal of greater gender equality in paid and household work, or if it is a way to work around this ideal by replacing one woman with another and hence reproducing, rather than challenging, gendered stereotypes related to such work (Bosniak, 2009; Rollins, 1996). For example, Pelechova has shown that, in Great Britain, au pairs are mainly seen as persons assisting or helping the woman—not the man—in the house (2015).

The second discussion asks whether paid domestic labour can be seen as both a way for privileged citizens to pay their way out of some of the challenges related to the 'beings' and 'doings' of gender equality and a way to acquire full and equal citizenship at *the expense of* 'citizenshipless' migrant women, or if it is rather an arrangement in which both the buyers and the sellers come out as winners. Joan Tronto, the author of the *The 'Nanny' Question in Feminism*, states: 'There is no doubt that upper middle-class working men and women benefit greatly from hiring women to work as underpaid, exploited domestic servants' (Tronto, 2002, p. 46). In line with this, Audrey Macklin writes: 'The grim truth is that some women's access to the high-paying, high-status professions is being facilitated through the revival of semi-indentured servitude. Put another way, one woman is exercising class and citizenship privilege to buy her way out of sex oppression' (Macklin, 1994, p. 34).

At the same time, it has also been claimed that domestic workers might experience different kinds of empowerment by taking on this kind of work. For example, Mariya Bikova, who studied Filipino au pairs in

Norway and the Philippines, found that, for some women, au pairing allows them to become an important provider of care for one's family, whereas for others, it allows them to live out an individual project of self-development and self-exploration (Bikova, 2015). In line with this, Stubberud (this volume) shows how au pairing can be a significant migration route and hence also a possibility for achieving formal and informal citizenship for women who have few possibilities for migrating (see also Gullikstad and Annfelt, this volume).

An important backdrop for these discussions on paid migrant domestic labour, gender equality, and citizenship is the strong relation between paid work and formal citizenship rights, which in modern welfare states is strongly related to both the adult worker model and the Western feminist claim that women need to be fully integrated into the labour market to achieve full and equal citizenship (Bosniak, 2009). This is particularly evident in the Nordic welfare states, which are often held up as best practice for gender equality policies due to the successful promotion of a women-friendly, gender-inclusive model of citizenship in which men, as well as women, are able to play a part as citizen-earner/carers and carer/earners (Lister, 2009, p. 249; Näre, this volume).

However, as argued by Linda Bosniak, the aspirational equal citizenship, democratic citizenship, or economic citizenship that women may hope to achieve through paid work 'is not the same social good as the status citizenship that many immigrant domestic workers are lacking' (Bosniak, 2009, p. 138). In other words, even though status citizenship and equal, economic, and democratic citizenship often go together, it is possible to enjoy aspects of equal, democratic, or economic citizenship without being a formal citizen (Bosniak, 2009, p. 144). Furthermore, being a 'non-citizen' in one country does not mean that one is 'citizenshipless', as most migrants are still citizens of their country of origin. This means that even though a great many paid migrant domestic labourers lack citizenship in the countries where they perform domestic work, equal citizenship, democratic citizenship, or economic citizenship are still relevant—in regard to both the country they live in and their country of origin.

Building on this contextual and theoretical background, this chapter studies Norwegian employers' perceptions of and experiences with paid migrant domestic labour. I am particularly interested in the ways in which the employers explain and justify their decision to engage in these at least potentially unequal relationships, and what they envision paid domestic labour to be and do to the women they employ. Is paid migrant domestic labour seen as a way to fulfil the political and cultural ideal of gender equality and thus become a good citizen—for both women and men? What do the employers envision paid domestic labour to be and do to the women they employ with respect to gender and citizenship?

Empirical Data, Methodology, and Analytical Tools

The analyses are based on qualitative research that was conducted in 2012 and 2013 on the employment relations of domestic workers in Norway.[9] The material consists of 22 interviews with 39 adults who were either hiring or about to hire a domestic cleaner or an au pair. Half the interviews were with au pair families and the other half were with employers of domestic cleaners; however, the majority of the au pair families also had experience with home cleaners.

The interviewees lived in different Norwegian cities, and had various kinds of families and work. Thirty-five interviewees were in cohabiting heterosexual relationships and four were single parents (women).[10] All interviewees were parents of relatively young children. With the exception of three babies who were still at home with their mother and/or au pair, the children went to kindergarten, school, and afterschool, though not always full time. The number of children in each household varied from two to five, with a predominance of three. With respect to employment, their working hours ranged from average to very long. Whereas some couples had one partner working long hours and the other working shorter hours, some couples could be classified as what Tronto (2002) describes as 'two-career households'. In relation to social class,

---

[9] The empirical material was produced as part of the research project 'Buying and Selling Gender Equality. Feminised Migration and (Gender) Equality in Contemporary Norway', financed by the Research Council of Norway.

[10] With one exception, I interviewed the couples in pairs.

the interviewees can be classified as middle class and upper class, with considerable variation in income and property.

The interviewees' experiences with employing domestic workers were rather diverse. Some families were employing their first migrant domestic labourer, others had employed several. Altogether, the families had employed between 10 and 15 home cleaners and hosted 26 au pairs. The cleaners' background was not always known by the employers, but of those known, a great majority came from Eastern Europe and none were Norwegian. All but one, who was a man working together with his wife, were women, and their age, to the extent that this was known, was rather varied. The au pairs came from different countries: fifteen from the Philippines, five from other non-European countries, and six from Europe (within the Schengen Area). All au pairs were women, and their ages ranged from 19 to 30 years, with the majority between 25 and 30.

In my analysis of the interviews, I focus explicitly on the way in which interviewees framed their decision to employ migrant domestic labourers and the arguments they put forward to make this decision culturally intelligible and morally acceptable in the Norwegian context. I also identify interviewees' way of presenting themselves compared to the way in which they presented the domestic labourers they employed.

'A Great Help'

Despite rather heterogeneous research material consisting of families living varied lives, the interviewees' ways of framing their decision to employ a home cleaner and to host an au pair had some striking similarities. Most important in this respect was the tendency of presenting the arrangement as a solution to the challenging task of balancing a stressful family life with paid work without compromising rather high expectations of parenthood and housework, and hence as a great help.[11]

---

[11] In the book chapter 'A Fair Deal? Paid Domestic Labour in Social Democratic Norway' (Kristensen, 2015), I also present examples of other, though more marginal, ways of framing the decision to employ domestic labourers than the need for help; these include the wish to get to know new people, to help the children learn more English, and to give another person the opportunity to come to Norway and experience Norwegian culture.

To exemplify this notion of paid migrant domestic labour as a great help, we must look at the interview with the couple Peter and Ann.[12] This couple had three children between the ages of two and nine who were attending school, afterschool, and kindergarten. Whereas Peter had a full-time job in a private company, Ann, who worked in the public sector, was currently working 90 %.[13] This was explained partly by her daily commute of 1 hour, which she felt would make a full-time job stressful and strenuous, and partly by child-related obligations, such as family breakfasts in the kindergarten and dentist visits, which in Ann's words, 'stole' time from her working hours. As we will see, the same reasoning was used to explain the couple's decision to employ paid migrant domestic labour. Two years prior, Peter and Ann had decided to employ an Eastern European woman to clean their house and change the bed clothes every second week. The woman had been recommended by several of their neighbours who were already employing her, and the agreement they had decided on implied payment in cash at an amount between two and three times lower than the price of a similar service offered by a registered company:

> Ann: We could have done it ourselves, but there is so much to do. And it gets so dirty everywhere and it takes such a long time to do it when you have three children. And then you end up doing it very late at night or on Saturdays… Because we do want to keep it rather tidy and clean right? We like to have a certain standard… So actually we are buying ourselves time with the children. And I am buying myself happiness. (…) And it is such a nice feeling to come home and see that the whole house is clean, that the bed clothes are changed…

Here, paid migrant domestic labour is presented as a solution to a stressful everyday life, combined with a wish for quality time with the children *and* a tidy and clean house. In addition, Ann reflects on her own feelings regarding cleanliness and housework, which can be interpreted

---

[12] Due to anonymity requirements, I use aliases for all interviewees.
[13] As a Norwegian working week is 37.5 hours, working 90 % means working 33.75 hours per week.

as an adherence to the stereotypical idea that women care more about housework than do men. In other parts of the interview, however, this claim was partly countered, as the couple generally described themselves as having a shared opinion—both in their wish for a clean house and in their investments in maintaining it as such. This means that the female home cleaner replaced both Peter's and Ann's hands, and helped both of them fulfil their ideals for a happy everyday life that included full (or next to full) employment, quality time with the children, and a clean and tidy home.

The notion of paid migrant domestic labour as a great help was also highly present in the interviews with the au pair host parents. In line with this, the *work*, which included both housework and care work, was presented as the greatest advantage provided by the au pairs—not cultural exchange.[14] Having said that, most of the au pairs seemed to do a substantial amount of work for the families with which they were living, not least when it came to housework. In several families, the au pairs did more or less everything in the house, in addition to more marginal tasks in relation to the children. This is in line with a recurrent claim in the interviews that the parents wanted to outsource housework in order to have more time with their children, rather than the alternative of outsourcing time with the children (see also Sollund, 2010).

This can be exemplified by the interview with Sarah and William. The couple had two children of school-age, and at the time of the interview they were hosting their third au pair. Before taking on an au pair, the couple had tried various home cleaning arrangements:

> Sarah: We decided to employ a home cleaner because cleaning was one such thing that we were arguing about. Like 'You are not hoovering the way I want you to' and I didn't do it like you preferred it.... Such silly arguments.... So we hired a domestic cleaner, and then it was 'Now we have to tidy up' [before the cleaner arrives], and 'So come on then, tidy up'... Troubles....
>
> William: But now it is tidy all the time. (…)

---

[14] This does not mean that cultural exchange did not occur in these families, or that it was not considered important by the host families.

Even though arguments about equal distribution of household tasks were described as the reason for them to employ a home cleaner some years prior, this was not presented as the main reason that the couple decided to take on an au pair. Rather, this decision was framed as a prerequisite for Sarah to accept a job offer that would imply more working hours and more hours away from home, in addition to more money and higher social status:

> Guro: Was your previous job also a full-time job?
>
> Sarah: Yes, but then I was working shifts and my working hours were more predictable. (…) And remember that on Saturdays we often had an arrangement where he [the husband] went outside with the children, whereas I was tidying up and cleaning the house. And if I wasn't cleaning, I was organising the children's clothing and things like that. Managing the household. You see, we used to employ a home cleaner prior to hosting an au pair. So, a lot of things changed when I got that new job. And it was then we realised that this is not going to work without an au pair. So actually, taking on an au pair was a prerequisite for me accepting that job offer.

In line with the notion that it was the change in Sarah's work situation that caused the need for an au pair, it was also Sarah who reported the strongest feeling of being helped (see Pelechova, 2015). Further, even though William did not take on much more household work when Sarah started her new job, the arrival of the au pair led to a more equal sharing of housework and care work in the couple, because the number of tasks was considerably reduced. In other words, the extra pair of hands helped, or made it feasible for the couple to become not only a dual-earner couple but also a gender-equal dual-carer couple—without compromising their high expectations for parenthood and cleanliness.

A somewhat different way of talking about au pairing as 'a great help' is found in the interview with Trude and Thomas. The spouses had three young children and both had rather demanding, though flexible and well-paid jobs, which they also claimed to find interesting and meaningful. In addition, both Trude and Thomas were engaged in time-consuming work-related leisure activities. The children attended either school and afterschool or kindergarten, though not full time. At the time of the interview, the family was hosting their third au pair.

In the interview, the couple's decision to take on an au pair for the first time was explained as a solution to a demanding situation with three small children causing very little sleep and a growing dissatisfaction related to housework not being done and/or not being fairly shared; this was combined with their feeling of not being able to invest as much time and energy in paid work as they wanted to. As we will see in the quotation below, the wish for more help had practical, relational, and emotional aspects:

> Guro: Why did you want an au pair in the first place? What did you try to achieve by taking on an au pair?
> Trude: Happiness. Calmness. Harmony. Love.
> Thomas: Ok, ok…
> Trude: Avoiding a divorce…
> Thomas: Yes…. By taking on an au pair you do not have to do as much housework. And you get one more adult to help out with the children. That way it makes life… It gives us a kind of flexibility that I think we need. We could not have been living this way had it been only the two of us. It would not have worked.

According to Trude and Thomas, having an au pair made it possible for them to 'have it all'. By talking about 'us' rather than 'I', Thomas indicated that, for them, the au pair had not come to replace the woman, but rather to make it possible for both parties to combine family life with paid work and leisure activities rather than having to do the housework that none of them really appreciated. Later in the interview, the idea that domestic work is women's work was challenged more explicitly:

> Guro: But were the two of you equally positive to take on an au pair or were one of you more positive?
> Thomas: I think we had the same opinion about it. You see, my wife has been, and still is, so bad at everything that has to do with house work. And because of that I have to do more or less everything. And then I get more and more grumpy, and then….

When framing the decision to take on an au pair in this way, Thomas was on the one hand claiming that equal distribution of domestic labour within the couple was ideal, and on the other hand challenging traditional gendered divisions of labour where women do (or should do) more housework than men. Later in the interview, Trude also claimed that her priorities with respect to paid and unpaid work and the decision to employ a domestic labourer were part of her 'personal feminist project':

> Trude: (…) My personal feminist project is based on the idea that women should be allowed to have it all. But at the same time I do realise, that for women to have both a career and have children, you need to have some help in the house. Or, alternatively we would have needed to work part-time both of us, but you [the husband] would never agree to that. And neither would I. It is absolutely unthinkable. To wash your own house! [laughing] As I see it I have such a long education and such an expertise that it is a waste of time if I am cleaning and tidying up. Besides, I am so bad at it. My husband can confirm that.

Here, Trude explicitly links feminism to participation in paid work and counters the widespread practice of *women* reducing their working hours to solve the time bind whereas men work full time. In addition, she, in the same manner as Thomas in the explanation cited above, challenged a gender stereotype when claiming to be bad at domestic work. Furthermore, while normalising equality between the genders, Trude takes a different stance when it comes to social class by supporting social hierarchies and *in*equality. By claiming that people with education should not need to do housework and solving this by hosting au pairs, Trude makes nationality a part of the same cluster. One could claim that this couple, by taking on female au pairs who were carrying out what they used to organise in this untraditional way in regard to gender, actually ended up enforcing a traditional gendered division of labour.

To summarise, the Norwegian employers tended to frame their decision to employ a home cleaner or become an au pair host family as a way to live up to the ideals of the dual-carer/dual-earner model of gender equality. Paid migrant domestic labour was presented as a help or prerequisite for both genders to engage more equally in paid work and unpaid housework and care work—which, in practice, meant doing equal paid work and, to a certain extent, care work, and equally little housework—while at the same time ensuring that at least the housework remained women's work (or, to be more precise, *some* women's work). This supports the contention that paid migrant domestic labour is a way to acquire full and equal citizenship for Norwegian middle- and upper-class women—by way of paid work—and that it is also a way for Norwegian women and men to fulfil the citizenship ideals of not only equal participation in paid work, but also equal participation in unpaid housework and care work.

In the next section, I turn to the domestic labourers and examine how the employers talked about the workers' situation and the potential gains they experienced from their arrangement with the Norwegian families.

'Better than Nothing'

Although the interviews with the employers were primarily focused on the positive effects paid migrant domestic labour had on their everyday life, the interviews also conveyed information about what they envisioned the home cleaning—and au pair arrangements—to mean and do to the labourers they employed.

An important finding in this respect is a widespread ambivalence wherein the employment conditions and the labourer's situation in Norway and in the family were simultaneously described as both good and not so good. And as we will see, the cited gains and pains of the migrant domestic labourers were closely related to their assumed reasons for being in Norway and for taking on this work.

As in the previous section, I will start with the interviewees' perceptions of the home cleaners. We have already seen that most of the home cleaners employed by the interviewees came from Eastern Europe, and most were paid in cash at a low price. Furthermore, there were no written contracts regulating the arrangement, which meant that both parties were free to cancel an appointment and terminate the agreement at any time. This had been done by some of the interviewees who had not been satisfied with the work.

When the employers spoke about the home cleaners, however, the overall message was that the arrangement was a good deal for the workers, as well as the employers. This was because the payment was as good as or better than the workers would get in other houses, because the houses and flats were not big and because they were not very untidy and dirty. In addition, there seemed to be an underlying understanding that the women doing the work did not have better alternatives for earning money—in either Norway or their home country. It was assumed that, if they did, they would not have accepted the job offer. As we will see, this does not mean that the employers did not see that the undeclared home cleaning arrangement also had some problematic side effects on behalf of the cleaner. As Ann put it:

> I have decided to think that this woman is really helping us… At the same time I realise that she might not have any alternatives, and that we somehow contribute to the maintenance of this kind of bad work arrangements by engaging in undeclared work. However, I can rather easily persuade myself into thinking that this is a good deal after all, and that this is a choice the cleaners themselves have taken.

Here we see that Ann was aware that the deal they had with the home cleaner could be seen as exploitative, and that she and Peter could be understood to be supporting a system that she did not approve of. However, what is also clear is that these critical reflections were overridden by her wish for a clean house at a cheap price and, as I read it, the understanding that the deal was as good as or better than the alternatives the cleaner could hope for. In other words, payment in cash for a rather easy job was better than nothing—even though it was not ideal. It is also interesting to note that neither Ann nor Peter reflected upon the fact that they were actually committing a crime by using undeclared labour.

Au pairing is a legal arrangement, but it has been criticised by Norwegian politicians and the media for being unfair and potentially exploitative (Gullikstad and Annfelt, this volume; Stubberud, 2015b). The overall story was the same as for the home cleaners: the deal was good not only for the host families, but also for the au pairs. As we will see, the gains the employers envisioned the au pair to have were closely related to their assumed reasons for becoming an au pair and to the employers' ideas about their situation back home.

When working with the interviews, I found that the au pairs were divided into two categories: those working as au pairs 'because they wanted to' and those doing it 'because they had to'. In the first category were mainly European young women, but in some cases also women from other parts of the world in which they were members of the privileged classes; they had all come to Norway to experience another culture and maybe also to learn another language—not to earn money. For these women, the gains of au pairing were presented as self-evident, in the sense that just being in Norway and living with a particular family was expected to be good—otherwise, they would have left. Furthermore, these au pairs did not seem to be persons who would easily be taken advantage of or exploited. In addition, they were often described as capable of ignoring some of their host parents' instructions, and hence resisting the relative subordination that tended to stick to this kind of work.

But I also identified some ambivalence; to the extent that these feelings were related to the au pairs, they revolved around possible unhappiness and loneliness. Again, this was partly related to their lack of family and friends, as well as the situation in Norway with a foreign language, an unknown culture, and cold weather.

However, for the other kind of au pairs, those who, according to the host parents, were in Norway 'because they had to', the ambivalence was more striking. On the one hand, these au pairs were generally thought of as more helpful than those in the other category, in the sense that they would do all the housework with hardly any instructions, and even ask for new tasks when they considered their work done. In general this diligence was considered to be very positive, but there were also some employers who claimed that they found it somewhat problematic. For example, Maria, told me that her Filipino au pair would always say 'Yes' when asked to do something, which Maria claimed that she 'as a Norwegian woman found a bit difficult to cope with'.

On the other hand, these au pairs were, compared to other au pairs, assumed to be in a much more difficult situation. This was partly related to the fact that they lacked language qualifications and cultural knowledge and were assumed to experience the greatest isolation and culture shock, and partly related to their situation back home. For example, some employers told me that they had learned that their au pair was not free to return to her home country until she had repaid the debt accrued when she had bought her ticket to Norway. Others had au pairs who had come to Norway to raise money so that their younger siblings could go to school, or to support their own children financially.[15] Several host parents also admitted that they—at least in periods—had been worried about their au pair's situation and wellbeing. These worries typically revolved around the au pair's social life, health, resident permit, and economic situation—including her obligations to pay off debt and support a family with her 'pocket money'. In several interviews, the employers gave detailed descriptions of the difficulties their au pair had experienced before coming to Norway and what she would expect to return home to after 2 years of au pairing. An example of this is found in the interview with Maria, who gave this answer when asked about what she knew about her au pair's life in the Philippines:

> She has told us a few things. She is rather shy, but I have been around so much so that I know that she has got a brother and parents, and that she will turn 30 this year. And that is the maximum age at which one can be an au pair. That means that she in her culture is too old to have children, and it means that she is positioned at the very, very bottom of the hierarchy. And then her mission in life is to take care of the family, and that includes not only her parents and brother, but also cousins and those having children. So she sends her money to her family back home, and sets aside a bit for herself.

Here, the au pair is considered to be in a difficult situation, both because of her age and because of her family situation. However, as Maria saw it, and this was also the case for the other interviewees who had been or were employing au pairs who were working as such 'because they had to', this did not imply that the au pair was exploited or that au pairing was disadvantageous to the worker. Quite the contrary, the more

---

[15] As several of the au pairs had come to Norway before the Norwegian government in 2012 decided that au pairs could not have children, several of my employers had experience with hosting au pairs who had children in their home country.

unfortunate and vulnerable the au pair was considered, the more positive the arrangement was assumed to be.

An important part of these gains, as seen through the eyes of the employers, was economic empowerment and the social status that followed in the wake of increased wealth. Even though the pocket money the au pairs were given in a Norwegian context was very low compared to normal salaries, it was seen as significant for the au pair and her family. Several host families told me that their au pairs did not spend any money in Norway, and that they—by saving their pocket money and taking on extra work—were able to send a lot back home; hence, they were able to significantly improve their situation. Thomas put it like this when I asked him whether he had any objections to the au pair arrangement:

> No, I don't really have any objections. We get.... Or we buy a kind of service.... And at Christmas she was back in the Philippines, buying a fridge and throwing a big party. That is.... As I see it this is she being empowered through this arrangement. Back home she is the breadwinner in her family and.... And we buy her services. She saves more or less all her money. In reality it is probably nearly 500 euros a month, which we are providing that way and hence creating something more.[16]

Here, Thomas speaks very positively about what a woman coming from poor conditions can achieve through au pairing in Norway. The achievements are not only described as something the au pair acquires, but also something the host family gives her. In other words, as I read this answer, Thomas indicates that, by hosting an au pair, he and his wife actually help someone. This means that the au pair helps them by facilitating the implementation of the dual-earner/dual-carer model of gender equality—which they really want to implement—whereas they give her the opportunity to provide for her family and improve her position in the family and probably also in society. This can also be described as a way for the au pairs to achieve full and equal citizenship in their country of

---

[16] When this interview was done, the minimum wage was approximately 500 euros (4000 NOK).

origin while living in a country where they are categorised as 'non-citizen' (Bosniak, 2009).

This brings us to the other positive outcome the host parents talked about in regard to the au pairs, which pertains to cultural knowledge and experience of democracy and gender equality, and resembles to what Bosniak labels 'the aspirational equal citizenship, democratic citizenship and economic citizenship' (Bosniak, 2009, p. 138). An example of this is found in the interview with Thomas, who spoke about the interest their au pairs had in the Norwegian parliamentary election and the fascination they expressed towards the transparent and strictly controlled democratic system. Another example, which revolves around gender and gender equality, is found in the interview with Maria, who talked about the importance of introducing the au pairs to the Norwegian gender regime, in which women are not regarded as second citizens and are free to say and do whatever they like, and the nice feeling she got when observing the au pair becoming increasingly confident as time went by. Yet another example is Trude's narrative about their first au pair, who, in her home country, had been in a non-functioning marriage and had been controlled by her parents-in-law, but had managed to prolong her stay in Norway after the au pair period and was building up a new life that included both paid work and aspirations for a gender-equal organisation of family life.

Whereas democracy was used in regard to both the political system and a more vague manner of behaviour, wherein all individuals were given the same right to express their meanings and feeling, the notion of gender equality was spoken of both as a system that Norway had accomplished and as a cultural mentality in which women were perceived of as equal to men and free to behave more or less in the same manner as men. An example of this is Maria's already cited comment on how she 'as a Norwegian woman' reacted to the au pair's submissiveness. And whereas the positive effect of learning about democracy—according to the employers—was to counter the au pairs' previous experiences with corrupt and non-functioning political systems in their home countries, the benefits of gender equality was justified mostly by implicit allusions to the traditional, unenlightened, and gender-oppressive cultures the au pairs were raised in and normally living under.

The Good Norwegian Citizens and the Empowered Migrant Women

In this chapter we have seen that the Norwegian employers described paid migrant domestic work as an available and efficient way to solve some of the challenges related to the dual-carer/dual-earner model of gender equality. In particular, home cleaning services and au pairing seem to have made possible the implementation of the dual-*earner* organisation of family life, without compromising high expectations for parenting and the household. But as we have seen, paid migrant domestic labour also smoothed the implementation of the dual-*carer* aspect of the gender equality ideal by reducing the number of tasks and hence preventing (too much) inequality within couples.

Considering the central position of paid work in Norwegian society, one could say that paid migrant domestic labour facilitates full and equal citizenship for the Norwegian women who buy their services. Traditionally, Norwegian women have performed the majority of the domestic tasks which some families (predominantly from the middle- and upper social classes) now outsource to migrant women. This outsourcing enables Norwegian women to perform more rewarding work outside the home. Since both the dual-earner and the dual-carer aspects of family life are important to the Norwegian model of citizenship, one could also say that paid migrant domestic labour simultaneously facilitates full and equal citizenship for Norwegian men—who, due to the substantial reduction in the household tasks, are able to do a more equal share of the caring, cleaning, and cooking in the domestic setting, compared to their female partners. In other words, Norwegian employers of domestic services are essentially buying themselves the opportunity to live up to the dual-earner dual-carer model of gender equality and hence also live up to the ideal of the 'good Norwegian citizen', while their cleaners and au pairs are the means who make this possible.

Furthermore, because the migrant domestic labourers are employed with conditions that clearly violate Norwegian labour law and established standards for decent employer–employee relations, it is easy to read the practice as a (re)introduction of social and national/racial hierarchies that contradicts the political and cultural ideal of social equality. In other words, gender equality is given priority over social equality, and the implementation of the dual-earner/dual-carer model for gender equality relies on global inequalities and national/racial hierarchies.

However, as seen through the eyes of the Norwegian employers, paid migrant domestic labour is also positive for the women doing the work, who, through this work, experience monetary and cultural empowerment. This empowerment, though, which I have argued is related to economic, democratic, and equal citizenship, is mainly applicable in the country in which the migrants are already formal citizens—not in Norway, where they can be described as 'citizenshipless' (Bosniak, 2009). Nevertheless, by focusing on the potential for empowerment (in the country of origin) rather than the risk of exploitation and subordination (in Norway), the Norwegian employers create a version of the win–win narrative in which paid migrant domestic labour is made compatible with the Norwegian citizenship ideals of gender equality and social equality. This means that, even though paid migrant domestic labour challenges important Norwegian political and cultural ideals, the win–win narrative provides an opportunity to veil these problematic aspects and turn the focus towards the arrangement's possible positive side effects.

References

Aarseth, H. (2011). *Moderne familieliv. Den likestilte familiens motivasjonsformer*. Oslo: Cappelen Damm.
Aarseth, H. (2014). Finanskapitalismens kjønnsromantikk: Næringslivselitens kjønnskomplementære familiekultur. *Tidsskrift for kjønnsforskning, 38*(3–4), 208–219.
Alsos, K., & Eldring, L. (2010). Husarbeid uten grenser. *Tidsskrift for kjønnsforskning, 34*(4), 377–393.
Berg, A.-J., Flemmen, A. B., & Gullikstad, B. (2010). *Likestilte norskheter: Om kjønn og etnisitet*. Trondheim: Tapir Akademisk Forlag.

Bikova, M. (2010). The snake in the grass of gender equality. In L. W. Isaksen (Ed.), *Global care work: Gender and migration in Nordic societies*. Lund: Nordic Academic Press.

Bikova, M. (2015). In a minefield of transnational social relations: Filipino Au pairs between moral obligations and personal ambitions. In R. Cox (Ed.), *Au pairs' lives in a global context. Sisters or servants?* Basingstoke: Palgrave Macmillan.

Bosniak, L. (2009). Citizenship, non-citizenship, and the transnationalization of domestic work. In S. Benhabib & J. Resnik (Eds.), *Migrations and mobilities: Citizenship, borders and gender*. New York: New York University Press.

Brandth, B., & Kvande, E. (2013). Innledning—velferdsstatens fedrepolitikk. In B. Brandth & E. Kvande (Eds.), *Fedrekvoten og den farsvennlige velferdsstaten*. Oslo: Universitetsforlaget.

Danielsen, H., Larsen, E., & Owesen, I. W. (Eds.) (2014). *Norsk likestillingshistorie 1814–2013*. Oslo: Fagbokforlaget.

Ellingsæter, A. L. (2014). Nordic earner-carer models—Why stability and instability? *Journal of Social Policy, 43*(3), 555–574.

Friberg, J. H., & Tyldum, G. (Eds.). (2007). *Polania i Oslo. En studie av arbeids- og levekår blant polakker i hovedstadsområdet*. Fafo-rapport nr. 27, Oslo.

Gullestad, M. (2002). *Det norske sett med nye øyne. Kritisk analyse av norsk innvandringsdebatt*. Oslo: Universitetsforlaget.

Gullikstad, B. (2010). Når likestilling blir ulikhet. Interseksjonalitet i arbeidslivet. In A.-J. Berg, A.-B. Flemmen, & B. Gullikstad (Eds.), *Likestilte norskheter. Om kjønn og etnisitet*. Trondheim: Tapir Akademisk Forlag.

Halrynjo, S., & Lyng, S. T. (2009). Preferences, constraints or schemas of devotion? Exploring Norwegian mothers' withdrawals from high-commitment careers. *British Journal of Sociology, 60*(2), 321–343.

Isaksen, L. W. (Ed.) (2010). *Global care work: Gender and migration in Nordic societies*. Lund: Nordic Academic Press.

Kitterød, R. (2009). Rengjøringshjelp i norske husholdninger. Vaskehjelp vanligst i høystatusgrupper. *Samfunnsspeilet, 23*(1), 58–62.

Kitterød, R. H., & Lappegård, T. (2012). A typology of work-family arrangements among dual-earner couples in Norway. *Family Relations, 61*(4), 671–685.

Kitterød, R. H., & Rønsen, M. (2014). Jobb og hjem i barnefasen. Nå jobber også far mindre når barna er små. *Søkelys på arbeidslivet, 31*(1–2), 23–41.

Kristensen, G. K. (2010). Trad eller trendy med tre. Om barnetall, likestilling og "norskhet". In A.-J. Berg, A.-B. Flemmen, & B. Gullikstad (Eds.), *Likestilte norskheter: Om kjønn og etnisitet*. Trondheim: Tapir Akademisk Forlag.

Kristensen, G. K. (2015). A fair deal? Paid domestic labour in social democratic Norway. In A. Triandafyllidou & S. Marchetti (Eds.), *Employers, agencies and immigration: Paying for care*. Farnham/Burlington: Ashgate.

Lister, R. (2009). A Nordic Nirvana? Gender, citizenship, and social justice in the Nordic welfare states. *Social Politics, 16*(2), 242–278.

Macklin, A. (1994). On the outside looking in: Foreign domestic workers in Canada. In W. Giles & S. Arat-Koc (Eds.), *Maid in the market: Women's paid domestic labour*. Halifax: Fernwood Publishing.

Myhre, A. S. (2010). *Herskap og tjenere*. Oslo: Forlaget Oktober.

Øien, C. (2009) *On equal terms?: An evaluation of the Norwegian Au pair scheme*. Fafo-rapport 2009:2, Oslo.

Pelechova, L. (2015). Au pairs and changing family needs in the United Kingdom. In A. Triandafyllidou & S. Marchetti (Eds.), *Employers, agencies and immigration. Paying for care*. Farnham/Burlington: Ashgate.

Rollins, J. (1996). Between women: Domestics and their employers. In C. L. Macdonald & C. Mariaanni (Eds.), *Working in the service society*. Philadelphia: Temple University Press.

Smeby, K. W., & Brandth, B. (2013). Mellom hjem og barnehage: Likestilling i det tredje skiftet. *Tidsskrift for kjønnsforskning, 37*(3–4), 329–347.

Sogner, S. (2004). The legal status of servants in Norway from the seventeenth to the twentieth century. In A. Fauve-Chamoux (Ed.), *Domestic service and the formation of European society*. Bern: Peter Lang AG.

Sogner, S., & Telste, K. (2005). *Ut og søkje teneste. Historia om tenestejentene*. Oslo: Det norske samlaget.

Sollund, R. (2010). Regarding Au pairs in the Norwegian welfare state. *European Journal of Women's Studies, 17*(2), 143–160.

Sørensen, S. Ø. (forthcoming). The performativity of choice. Postfeminist perspectives on work-life balance. *Gender Work & Organization*.

Statistic Norway. (2015). Nøkkeltall for likestilling. Retrieved from http://www.ssb.no/befolkning/nokkeltall/likestilling

Stubberud, E. (2015a). "It's not much". Affective (boundary) work in the Au pair scheme. In R. Cox (Ed.), *Au pair's lives in global contexts. Sisters or servants?* Basingstoke: Palgrave Macmillan.

Stubberud, E. (2015b). Framing the Au pair: Problems of sex, work and motherhood in Norwegian Au pair documentaries. *Nordic Journal of Feminist and Gender Research, 23*(2), 125–139.

Træen, B. (2010). Sexual dissatisfaction among heterosexual norwegians in couple relationships. *Sexual and Relationship Therapy, 25*(2), 132–147.

Tronto, J. C. (2002). The "nanny" question in feminism. *Hypatia, 17*(2), 34–49.
Trygstad, S., et al. (2011). *Til renholdets pris.* Fafo-rapport 2011:18, Oslo.
UDI. (2014). Oppholdstillatelse til au pair. Retrieved from https://www.udiregelverk.no/no/rettskilder/udi-rundskriv/rs-2012-015/
Vaage, O. F. (2002). Til alle døgnets tider. Tidsbruk 1971–2000. *Statistical Analyses 52.* Oslo-Kongsvinger: Statistics Norway.
Vaage, O. F. (2012). Tidene skifter. Tidsbruk 1971–2010. *Statistical Analyses 125.* Oslo-Kongsvinger: Statistics Norway.

9

The Intouchables: Care Work, Homosociality and National Fantasy

Priscilla Ringrose

Introduction

In Olivier Nakache and Éric Toledano's 2011 movie *The Intouchables*[1] [*Intouchables*] a wealthy disabled aristocrat employs a roguishly charming black street stud as his care worker. The movie charts the blossoming friendship between the 'superficially mismatched' pair Philippe (François Cluzet) and Driss (Omar Sy) as barriers of class, race, age and dis/ability are (apparently) broken down, implying that life is actually beautiful (Alberge, 2012). *The Intouchables*, distributed in 66 countries, the highest ever grossing movie in a language other than English, won a slew of prizes, not least the African-American Film Critics Association Best Foreign Film award and the National Association for the Advancement

---

[1] The film is inspired by *Le Second Souffle* (Bayard, 2001), an autobiography by Philippe Pozzo di Borgo, which gives an account of relation with his care giver, Abdel Yasmin Sellou.

P. Ringrose
Department of Interdisciplinary Studies of Culture and Department of Language and Literature, Centre for Gender Studies, Norwegian University of Science and Technology (NTNU), Trondheim, Norway

© The Editor(s) (if applicable) and The Author(s) 2016
B. Gullikstad et al. (eds.), *Paid Migrant Domestic Labour in a Changing Europe*, DOI 10.1057/978-1-137-51742-5_9

of Colored People prize for Outstanding International Motion Picture (AAFCA, 2012; NAACP, 2013). The film's universal appeal rests on its standard exploitation of an unlikely friendship between a mismatched pair. Yet the context of the film, contemporary France, with its republican model of citizenship and vexed relation to immigration, raises particular questions about the racial and gendered framing of the central employee–employer relation.

Film here is understood as a social practice which 'constructs narratives and meanings, which enable us to locate evidence of the ways in which [a] culture makes sense of itself' (Turner, 2012, p. 3). Nakache and Toledano's *The Intouchables* constructs a narrative centred around the black migrant labour which enables us to locate evidence of the way in which France makes sense of itself and its migrants. This chapter first focuses on the representation of Driss,[2] the black migrant care worker, within the assimilative framework of the French model of citizenship. Secondly it investigates the employee–employer relation with reference to the workings of homosocial relations. While homosociality, 'a concept used to refer to nonsexual interpersonal attractions,' is predominantly used in the context of group dynamics, it is useful for identifying the mechanics of the relation between the film's two main protagonists (Bird, 1996, p. 120).

The film's central story moves the main character Driss from partial precarious citizenship, as a young, uneducated, unemployed ex-con with an insecure housing situation, to apparent full citizenship, as carer but also a friend and confidant to his ultra-wealthy paraplegic middle-aged employer, living in sumptuous quarters and pocketing a good salary. To what extent does this change of citizenship status depend on the French universalist model of citizenship, based on the premise of cultural assimilation? Is the black care worker produced, in Étienne Balibar's genealogical terms, as the social and symbolic heir of the colonial servant, assimilated into the civilised French home (2001)? Or does the evolving homosociality between Driss and his employer not only defy the colonial paradigm,

---

[2] Driss confides to Philippe that his aunt and uncle, who were childless at the time, adopted him at the age of eight, when he moved from Senegal to France to live with them.

but also the parameters of care work itself, including its gendered and sexualised aspects? This question, as we will see, interpellates the debate around the feminisation of care work and around care workers' relation to the sexual citizenship of disabled employers.

I first suggest that the film can be read as in an orientalist vein, in Balibar's genealogical terms, but then argue that the bond between employer and employee problematises such an approach. The plot can rather be read as a carefully synchronised attempt to undermine the assimilative logic of the French republican model, skilfully orchestrating a fantasy of nation in which Old and New France meet half way. Finally, following Anne-Marie Fortier (2008, p. 11), I discuss the film's cultural imaginary in the context of Lauren Berlant's (1991) notion of 'national fantasy' and Jacqueline Rose's idea of 'protective fiction' (Rose, 1998, p. 3). What fantasy of nation does this film produce? Can it be conceived of as protective fiction? And if so, who is being protected and why?

Background

Care work and domestic labour, like other feminised employments, are closely associated with the mobilisation of so-called 'feminine qualities of patience, caring, dexterity, acquired via socialisation in the private sphere. These capacities and qualities are not socially recognised: they are naturalised' (Scrinzi, 2013, p. 23).[3] The notion of 'feminised employment' can be understood in terms of both the symbolic social devaluation of employments which are predominantly occupied by women and, in a quantitative sense, the over-representation of women in certain sectors (Zaidman, 1986 in Scrinzi, 2013). In France, for instance, women constitute 98 % of care workers (Dussuet, 2005, p. 198).

Studies relating to the male domestic workers in the French context suggest that they perceive their work as a form of labour that is 'unnatural for a man', or, in other words, as work which cannot be assimilated to 'traditional and hegemonic forms of masculinity' (Näre, 2010; Scrinzi,

---

[3] All translations from French in this article are the author's.

2010). One such study suggests that as a result these workers tend to feel the need to 'prove their masculinity, as well as their competence' (Scrinzi, 2010, p. 55). They used various strategies to achieve this, such as 'emphasizing the "masculine" aspects of the job', constructing masculinity as a 'professional specialization' (focusing on aspects of the work that require physical strength) or distancing themselves from domestic service by stressing that they had entered the sector only because they 'could not find any other job or because they were migrants' (Scrinzi, 2010, pp. 56–57).

Since domestic and care work in the feminised private sphere is predominantly undertaken by women, it is often perceived of by employers as a 'labour of love', an extension of women's unpaid domestic labour (Lutz, 2007; Scrinzi, 2013). This not only serves to open their labour for exploitation, but also, from the employer's perspective, helps to counter the awkwardness arising from a commercial exchange in the intimacy of the home. In the context of the care of 'dependent' clients, Scrinzi points to the fact that this labour of love often translates into employers' expectation that carers undertake emotional labour. As Hochschild (1983) has shown, these workers 'do not only sell their labour, but rather directly sell their "selves", or even their emotions and personal and "private" experiences' (Scrinzi, 2013, p. 62). This implies a personalisation of the relationship which blurs the distinction between the person that accomplishes the work and the work itself (Scrinzi, 2013, p. 62).

The personalisation of the employee–employer relation can be positive, in the sense that it can attribute feelings of usefulness and meaning to work that is socially devalued (Scrinzi, 2013, p. 64). On the other hand, in order to fulfil its function, emotional labour has to be denied as work and take on the appearance of spontaneous emotion (Hochschild, 1983, p. 18). In the context of care jobs involving intimate interventions, Rivas shows that the most appreciated quality is invisibility, and that 'immigrant women are the caregivers par excellence because both they and their work are often rendered invisible' (2004, pp. 76–77). The capacity of making oneself socially invisible is aimed at making the individuals who are being cared for think that they are (more) independent, but also to make tasks involving bodily functions less awkward (Rivas, 2004, p. 77). While the requirement for emotional labour is understood as part and parcel of the care work, the worker's own emotions often go unrecognised—for example, care workers might be expected to hide their close relation to their client when certain family members are present (Scrinzi, 2004 in Scrinzi, 2013, p. 67).

The construction of the employer–employee relation within a familial or friendship rubric is another strategy employers use to manage the tension and awkwardness produced by the introduction of a commercial transaction into a private space. Racist stereotypes are also mobilised to help to manage this tension, with the migrants regarded as needy, in need of education, or of help with integration. Some employers use the word 'help' rather than 'employ' when referring to employees (Scrinzi, 2004 in Scrinzi, 2013, p. 67). Balibar (1991) points to the way cultural racism becomes a way of naturalising such unequal social relations. When culture is understood as a fixed entity, and individuals as 'the exclusive heirs and bearers of a single culture', then to avoid racism, 'you have to respect "the tolerance thresholds", maintain "cultural distances"' (Balibar, 1991, pp. 22–23). The shift from the biological to immutable cultural difference means that cultural racism 'naturalises not racial belonging but racist conduct' (Balibar, 1991, p. 22). In this vein, migrants are defined in terms of their belonging to a 'cultural group' or 'tradition', feeding the idea that it is 'natural for humans not only to have a specific culture, but to feel hostility towards those whose integration to another culture is bound to fail' (Scrinzi, 2013, pp. 50–51). Scrinzi, following Lewis (2006), suggests that such rhetoric is founded on the assimilation of the national public sphere to the private sphere of the family, with the metaphors of house and family employed to represent the nation, legitimising 'internal' solidarity on the one hand, and xenophobia on the other (2013, p. 51).

While the idea of nation can be invoked in a legitimising function to exclude the nation's others, it can also, according to Berlant (1991), have another (but complementary) protective function to produce an idea of the nation/al that denies the 'horrors of the real'. This construct of nation is described as a fantasy, brought into being 'in the public domain by repeatedly imagining that it exists and iterating it as something real, out there, that binds the "national people" together' (Fortier, 2008, p. 11). As Fortier elaborates, following Berlant (1991): 'Fantasy, here, is more than its popular conception suggests—as escape, make believe, whimsical fabrication' and is rather a form of protection, 'a narrative support, a story that gives consistency to the nation and its subjects' (2008, p. 11). In this sense, fantasy is not a means of escape, not 'antagonistic to social reality' but rather the necessary 'psychic glue' (Rose, 1998, p. 3) which 'protects the nation/al from the horrors of the "real" that threaten the disintegration of the self; it keeps it whole' (Fortier, 2008, p. 12).

This article looks at the cultural imaginary of the film as a narrative which projects a certain fantasy of nation, in which Old France, represented by the film's aristocratic employer, meets New France, the renegade migrant care worker. The relation between France and its migrants on the everyday level is closely imbricated in wider discourses and policies on migration, framed within the French republican model of citizenship. This model of citizenship, founded on individualism, is opposed to 'communalism', the idea that group identities take precedence over national identity in the lives of individuals. In France 'there is no possibility of a hyphenated ethnic/national identity—one belongs either to a group or to the nation' (Scott, 2007, p. 11). In French political theory, equality is equivalent to the erasure of one's social religious ethnic and other origins from the public sphere—'it is as an abstract individual that one becomes a French citizen. Universalism—the oneness, the sameness of all individuals—is taken to be the antithesis of communalism' (Scott, 2007, p. 11). Scott points to the paradox of a particularly French form of universalism:

> France insists on assimilation to a singular culture, the embrace of shared language, history and political ideology. The ideology is French republicanism. Its hallmarks are secularism and individualism, the linked concepts that guarantee all individuals equal protection by the state against the claims of religion and any other group demands. (Scott, 2007, p. 12)

While the sameness at the heart of French equality is an abstraction, a 'philosophical notion meant to achieve the formal equality of individuals before the law', when applied in practice, assimilation equates to the eradication of difference:

The norms of the culture, of course, are anything but abstract, and this has been the sticking point of French republican theory. Abstraction allows individuals to be conceived as the same (as universal), but sameness is measured in terms of concrete ways of being (as Frenchness). And ascriptions of difference, conceived as irreducible differences, whether based on culture, or sex or sexuality, are taken to preclude any aspiration to sameness. If one has already been labelled different on the basis of any of these grounds, it is difficult to find a way of arguing that one is or can become the same. (Scott, 2007, p. 13)

Scott points to the continuing legacy of colonialism in contemporary France, 'its traces [...] visible in debates about the status of "immigrant" Arab/Muslim populations' (Scott, 2007, p. 88). The fact that the term 'immigrant' is never used to refer to those with European origins, no matter how long they have been resident in France, and is reserved for Maghrebis or others from former colonies, signals the very impossibility of integration (Scott, 2007, p. 88). As such, the paradox of a (colonialist-like) civilising mission aimed at the uncivilisable lives on: 'Even if the characteristics attributed to non-ethnic French nationals with North African backgrounds have changed over the years, the stigma of their origin still attaches to them' (Scott, 2007, p. 88). As Balibar observes,

> a quality like 'migrant' (which is in fact a stigma and a pejorative collective name) becomes absurdly attributed to youngsters, who because, precisely they are discriminated, are seen as a threat but who are only the children or the grand-children of actual migrants, therefore enjoy the national citizenship for most of them, so that the quality 'migrant' becomes socially and symbolically a hereditary quality. (Balibar, 2001, pp. 7–8)

Following Scott, we identify three perspectives on the universalist model of citizenship. The first perspective takes its workings for granted on the basis that cultural assimilation is both favourable and doable. The second considers it paradoxical and unworkable, assuming that immigrant cultures are based on irreducible differences. The third is Scott's own position which points to the unreasonable premise upon which cultural assimilation is founded (giving up differences which are ascribed to you) and to the assumption of French superiority it carries with it. I will now look at the extent to which the film relates to these perspectives, with reference to the representation of the black care worker Driss and of his relation to his employer, Philippe.

From Colonial Chains to Homosocial Bonds

According to Jean Daniel, founding editor of *Le Nouvel Observateur*, 'France is the site of an exciting venture, (...) that of transforming Islam through its contact with French civilization' (Scott, 2007, p. 81). *The Intouchables* can be read, in this vein, as a Cinderella story, the site of an exciting (ad)venture, that of transforming the immigrant through his contact with the civilised French mentor—a bildungsfilm, or coming of age narrative based on a colonial paradigm of assimilation via the eradication of difference. From this perspective, Philippe functions as the master/mentor whose task is to civilise the unruly philistine servant-employee, handicapped by ignorance and immaturity. To the colonial cliché is added the migrant family stereotypes activated as soon as Driss appears on home territory, in a cramped high-rise apartment, crawling with kids of all ages, complete with oppressed mother and missing paternal figure.

The economic and cultural chasm between Philippe and Driss is established at the interview—cut from high-rise HLM to Philippe's Parisian mansion with all the classic exquisiteness of a urban French chateau, weighty antiques, luxurious drapes, priceless artefacts, rows of Fabergé eggs and heavy gilded portraits, alongside a retinue of 'servants'—housekeeper, assistant, physiotherapist and cooks, and a courtyard filled with a fleet of top-end cars. When Driss is led into the interview, he offhandedly asks for the signature on his unemployment papers, since, as he says he 'will obviously not get the job'. He seems oblivious to the cold patronising gaze of Philippe's haughty flame-haired assistant, or to Philippe's intense stare, or indeed to his wheelchair. Philippe's request for references is met with a nonchalant rejoinder:

Magalie: Have you got references?
Driss: Yep. References Got some.

Magalie: We're listening.
Driss: Kool and the Gang, Earth, Wind and Fire, they are references, aren't they?
Philippe: I don't understand.
Driss: If you haven't heard of them, you don't know anything about music.
Philippe: I don't consider myself a philistine when it comes to music.[4]

The dialogue continues to underscore Driss's cultural deficit by playing on the ambiguity of Philippe's favourite composer Berlioz (also a Parisian district). Driss laughs out loud at Philippe's contention that he is a Berlioz specialist: 'Berlioz! Who do you know there? I bet you don't know anyone there!' Philippe proceeds to enlighten Driss into the mysteries of nineteenth century music. The interview over, Driss lopes off in true delinquent style, with a stolen Fabergé eggs in his pocket. The cultural bankruptcy of the migrant is then hammered in yet again—Driss's aunt dismisses the Fabergé masterpiece as a worthless 'Kinder egg', and Driss, equally, seems to have little idea of its value.

As Driss's aunt gives short shrift to the gift of the Fabergé egg, she also establishes his status as renegade 'son'. She is seen returning from work late in the evening, surveying the dirty dishes still strewn all over the kitchen and wearily putting them away, as Driss sits nonchalantly at the kitchen table, having smoothly whipped away his packet of cigarettes out of sight, and chucked a stub out the window.

Driss: [handing his aunt the egg] Here, it's for you.
Aunt: Where have you been?
Driss: On holiday.
Aunt: On holiday. Do you think people around here don't talk? You think I am a stupid bitch? We haven't seen you for six months. Not one phone call. Nothing. And now you turn up with a Kinder egg? You think your scams will pay the rent, for food? […] You think this is a hotel? Look at me when I talk to you! […]

---

[4] Translations of the film script are the author's, with some reference to subtitles.

Aunt: You know Driss. I have prayed for you a lot. But may God forgive me. I have other children. I still have hope for them. I don't want to have you hanging around here. Just pack your bags and get the hell out.

Driss exits the hellhole of the banlieues and crosses the threshold into a brave new world. As he is drawn into Philippe's refined universe, he receives progressive injections of high culture, from a night at the opera, a private classical concert and exclusive art exhibitions to Philippe's own poetry reading. Interpellating the grammar of class divisions (Bourdieu, 1984), Philippe's high economic and cultural capital makes an exhibition of Driss's low volume variation, and, to paraphrase Bourdieu, nothing classifies Driss more than the way he classifies modern art—the 'masterpiece' Philippe admires at a high-end gallery looks to him 'like a nosebleed on canvas' (Bourdieu, 1984, p. 19). Nevertheless, Driss decides to play Philippe at his own game, and has a go at painting himself (albeit initially in secret), although it is unclear as to whether this is out of an aesthetic or financial motive, or from a 'perverse' desire to uncover contemporary art as a charade. But the implication is still there that 'a black man from the wrong side of town' (Weissberg, 2011) could never really have appreciated real art, not without a proper education. Driss 'obviously' does not appreciate 'real' music either but he is nevertheless paraded in front of Philippe's upper class friends at a classical concert held in Philippe's home in honour of his birthday. As *Variety Magazine* reviewer Jay Weissberg observes:

> In fact, he [Driss] is treated as nothing but a performing monkey (with all the racist associations of such a term), teaching the stuck-up white folk how to get 'down' by replacing Vivaldi with 'Boogie Wonderland' and showing off his moves on the dance floor. It's painful to see Sy, a joyfully charismatic performer, in a role barely removed from the jolly house slave of yore, entertaining the master while embodying all the usual stereotypes about class and race. (Weissberg, 2011)

Driss not only learns culture; he learns morality, teaching us a lesson along the way in what Fortier calls the new 'moral racism' (2008). According to Fortier, writing in the British context, 'the new moral politics that produce a new inflection of cultural racism in which beliefs, values and morals are in the primary site for the marking of absolute difference, rather than "cultural practices" such as customs, traditions and "lifestyles"' (2008, p. 6). In this vein, Philippe has a lesson or two in store for Driss: he shall not steal (the missing Fabergé egg does not go unnoticed), he shall not sponge off the state (Philippe reprimands Driss for being focused on qualifying for his welfare benefits rather than for employment) and he shall not neglect his family (Philippe instructs him to look after his younger brother who is in trouble with the police). Driss combines the moral failings of the colonial servant with his suspect hyper-sexuality, as he invites the haughty Magalie into his bath and suggests to Philippe that he should set up a hooker file alongside his other correspondence. The result echoes '[t]he ambiguity of the Africans' childlike primitivism [...] firmly located [...] in a supposed lack of sexual restraint, which was as much a sign of a dangerous and unbridled savagery as it was that of an undisciplined, "pre-civilised immaturity"' (Ashcroft, 2001, p. 43).

For one of Philippe's relatives, Driss is uncivilised and uncivilisable. Early in the film, this poster boy for cultural racism warns Philippe that Driss is an ex-con, who has done time for theft and is certain to fleece him mercilessly. Such views, which suggest that differences are irreducible and that the civilising mission is unworkable, are undermined by Philippe's refusal to listen to them and by the eventual rewards of his persistent mentoring. In this case, the immature, irresponsible 'child' is bridled: he is repackaged at journey's end as a fully fledged adult who thanks to Philippe realises that his real civic duty is to his family, who need him most. The feckless youth-turned-disciplined-penitent/returning prodigal now meets his aunt coming off a late shift and is seen humbly taking her bags, before walking her home.

On the other hand, one of the final incidents in the film, also featured in the prologue, appears to interpellate an alternative model of citizenship, which departs from the French assimilationist model, and favours acculturation. David L. Sam and John W. Berry, following Redfield, define the 'building blocks' of this form of acculturation, as 'contact, reciprocal influence and change' (Redfield et al., 1936 in Sam & Berry, 2006, p. 14). Contact or interaction should be 'first hand', and reciprocal change 'may include personal characteristics such as values, attitudes and identity' (Sam & Berry, 2006, pp. 14–15). The incident in question and the reciprocity it suggests bring to play an alternative interpretation of the film as a fantasy narrative in which the nation/al and its Other, or Old France and its Banlieues (deprived suburbs) or employer and employee 'meet half way' in carefully synchronised moves. Here the necessary 'psychic glue' (Rose, 1998, p. 3) which keeps the fantasy 'together', protecting the nation/al from the twin horrors of migration and disability—and their 'untouchables'—is, as we will see, constituted by the homosocial bond between Driss and Philippe.

It all starts (and ends) with the two men setting out on the final road trip South, where Driss, unknown to Philippe, has set him up on a date with Éléonore, the latter's mysterious epistolary love interest. Driss is soon caught speeding recklessly through the Parisian quartiers in a Maserati, with Philippe in the passenger seat. While Driss spins a story to the police, angrily protesting that they are on their way to hospital because of a critical medical emergency, Philippe plays along, enacting an epileptic-like fit. Having pulled off the scam, they speed off again having even obtained police escort to the hospital. Philippe is on a high, laughing uproariously, swearing raucously and nodding his head enthusiastically the sounds of *Earth Wind and Fire* blasting out of the car. The upstanding pillar of the establishment is now displaying the kind of social behaviours more often associated with young delinquents—traffic offences, police deception, sound pollution, crude language, and what's more, relishing every moment.

So is *The Intouchables* less colonial throwback and more modern bromance? And if so, how is the emergent homosocial bond between Driss and Philippe achieved? According to Kiesling, homosociality, ultimately guaranteed by the performance of heterosexuality, is dependent on carefully careless social manoeuvring:

> Homosociality puts men in a double bind of their own: To be a man is to be powerful, and to be powerful in the current gender order is, in part, to be heterosexual. But affiliation is often equated with dependence, so homosociality is almost by definition not masculine. To create a masculine identity along the lines of dominant cultural discourses of masculinity, a man must not create love, dependency, nor sexual desire with his 'fellow' men,

but at the same time he must create solidarity with them. (Kiesling, 2005, p. 720)

Homosociality requires finding 'ratified indirect ways of taking up homosocial stances that are not homosexual stances', for example, via 'socially indirect speech genres, acts, and stances' (Kiesling, 2005, pp. 720–721).

At the outset, both Driss and Philippe's relation would appear to militate against the potential for homosociality, given the latter's foundation in parity—whether of profession, class, age or a combination of these. Can Old France, immobilised in her wheelchair, find common ground with the 'disruptive excess' of its other? Not only is the equivalency upon which homosociality is contingent absent, but so is, more significantly, its very foundation, namely 'a masculine identity along the lines of dominant cultural discourses of masculinity' (Kiesling, 2005). Both Driss's and Philippe's masculine identities are in part compromised by their personal circumstances. In Philippe's case, emasculation is a by-product of the disabling of the body. As Engel and Munger note (2003, p. 217), the masculinity of men with severe physical disabilities is significantly compromised in the eyes of society: 'Paralytic disability constitutes emasculation of a more direct and total nature. For the male, the weakening and atrophy of the body threaten all the cultural values of masculinity: strength, activeness, speed, virility, stamina, and fortitude' (Murphy, 2001, pp. 94–95). Driss's masculine identity on the other hand is threatened by his professional status, namely his employment within a feminised sector, where he does an 'unnatural' job for a man, one which does not correspond to hegemonic and traditional notions of masculinity (Näre, 2010, p. 80; Scrinzi, 2010, p. 55). But at the same time he embodies the stereotypical association of black men as both lacking masculinity and having excess masculinity (Alsop, Fitzsimons, & Lennon, 2002, p. 150).

Since the achievement of homosociality is built around a masculine identity, this means that for Driss and Philippe, it is conditional on the re-masculinisation of the disabled body and the de-feminisation of the care worker's labour. This de- or re-gendering is in the first instance initiated via the interaction between man and machine. According to Mellström, masculine bonds are mediated and communicated through interactions with machines, in particular, motorbikes and cars. In these different social settings, technologies can be understood as means of an embodied communication for forming homosocial bonds. These masculine practices continuously exclude women and perpetuate highly genderized societal spheres where men form communities based on passion for machines. (Mellström, 2004, p. 368)

For Philippe, rehabilitation into the cultural values of masculinity is co-incident with Driss's rehabilitation of his long-abandoned Maserati. Turning up his nose at Philippe's disabled access white van, Driss bundles Philippe into the mean machine, facilitating the latter's instant and more or less direct re-acquisition of (some) of 'the cultural values of masculinity'—speed, virility and activeness (Murphy, 2001, pp. 94–95). The man–machine relation culminates in a subsequent adventure in the Alps involving private jets and paragliders.

The road to homosociality also requires the revision of the forms and contents of Driss's care work, since a 'buddy relation' cannot be based around the kinds of 'feminised' activities related to care which are foregrounded at the start of the film. Scrinzi notes that male domestic workers perceive an expectation to justify their employment in what is seen as a feminised sector, and to prove their masculinity, as well as their competence (2010, p. 55). As a result, they tend to emphasise the 'masculine' aspects of the job in order to legitimise their occupation (Scrinzi, 2010, p. 56). Driss fulfils this stereotype from the start making it clear that he does not want to do 'women's work'.

> Marcelle: [dressed in nurse's white coat, lays Philippe's stretch tights on the bed, then addresses Driss] Are you ok? Will you manage?
> Philippe: Of course he will [...] There—go and eat, Marcelle. Everything's fine.
> Driss: [pointing to the tights with distaste]. So where's the skirt then?
> Philippe: They're support stockings. They help the blood to flow properly. So I don't faint.
> Driss: I'm not going to put stockings on you. There's a problem here. A little problem because if I am not going to do it… we need to see if … to see if … Maybe Marcelle could come back to put them on for you. She

knows how to do it being a girl and all that. I don't even know why we are talking about it. Frankly I'm just not doing it, ok, even for you. You'd be better off fainting. I mean, sometimes, we say no. We refuse to put them on. We're men. [Shouts] Marcelle, we're not putting them on!

[Cut to Driss putting on the stockings and looking at Philippe accusingly]

Philippe: You're good with stockings. Very natural with that cute earring.

Driss: Can we cut the jokes?

Philippe: You're a natural at this. Have you ever thought of working as a beautician? [laughs as Driss glares at him]

As Wolkowitz (2002) following Lawler (2006) points out with reference to the nursing sector, body work occupations are not only highly gendered, they also themselves reproduce divisions of status 'which reflect different relations to the body, sometimes conceptualised as the difference between "basic" and "technical" nursing, the first originating in what are seen as the gross physical needs of the patient, including the "dirtier jobs", and the latter involving "cleaner" tasks and less touching of other people's bodies' (2002, p. 501). Driss intuitively refuses to do the gendered 'dirty work' (Anderson, 2000, p. 142) associated with servicing the physical needs of the body but he also expresses this refusal as a point of principle, as he shuns the plastic gloves he is handed: 'Ready or not: I'm not emptying the ass of a guy I don't know. Or even of a guy I do know. I don't empty anyone's ass in general.'

The feminised care tasks undertaken by Driss are gradually elided as the film progresses. And while the invisibility of care work/ers may be associated with shoring up the client and hiding the emotional bonds between employer and employee (Rivas, 2004), here it serves to make the worker appear more masculine and subsequently enable the evolution of emotional (homosocial) bonds. At the start Driss is pictured showering, massaging or feeding an incapacitated bed-ridden paraplegic in a luxurious but highly medicalised bedroom crammed full of therapeutic paraphernalia, surrounded by a team of health personnel. But this form of care work disappears from view, as the functional interactions in the sphere of the bedroom are supplanted by fun forays into public spaces. The everyday tasks of caring are either gradually backgrounded or made the subject of jokey banter. There is a stark contrast between the early scenes, where a sullen Driss feeds the recalcitrant Philippe in a slow, ungainly manner and the matey exchanges in swish eateries we witness in later sequences. Here Driss smilingly flourishes a cloth in the direction of the Philippe's mouth, before reprimanding him with a buddy-like jibe, reminiscent of the banter of jostling adolescents—'Oh stop that disgusting dribble!' Driss, far from being admonished in return, is met by an equally jocular expression on the face of his dinner companion. Such banter interpellates the indirect declarations of affiliation common to homosocial interactions 'often characterised as humorous interactions involving idioms, nicknames, curses, nonsense talk, aggressive gestures, and embraces' (Kaplan, 2005, p. 571).

Homosociality depends not only on reciprocal expressions of affiliation but also on individual performances of heterosexuality. This means that in the case of Philippe, homosociality is conditional on his disabled body being repositioned as sexual. The transformation of the immobilised, sex-less Philippe, embodiment of Old France's sterility, into a sexual being is achieved thanks to Driss' direct intervention. Driss breathes new life into Old France, but does so in such a way as to challenge the conventional boundaries of the relation between care workers and their (disabled) employers' sexual citizenship.

The relation between sexuality and disability, and its implication for care workers is explored by Margrit Shildrick in the context of a cultural imaginary that fears non-normative sexuality, deferring to the 'unspoken anxiety that takes the form alternatively of denying that sexual pleasure has any place in the lives of people with disabilities or of fetishizing it' (2007, p. 53). Shildrick notes that while homosexuals challenge sociocultural norms and have traditionally been perceived as a threat to the fabric of society, disabled people, who are similarly positioned as sexual outsiders literally, 'cannot fulfil normative expectations by reason of their embodied difference' (2007, p. 57). Although the experience of disability can differ widely, generalised reductive perceptions persist; one, that 'sexual normativities—at least in authorised sexual practice—are set up in such a way that the particularity of each person is largely overridden, with the result that the majority of disabled people are positioned as sexless' and two, that 'to have a severe disability precludes both functional sex, and sexual pleasure and desire' (Shildrick, 2007, p. 57). Shildrick points to the crux of the issue as not relating to differential sexual outcomes but rather to 'the differential form that sexual expression itself must often take for people with disabilities' (2007, p. 57).

Returning to the film, it seems that Driss also appears to grasp the crux of the issue. Just as Philippe challenges the sociopolitical normativities of universalism as he starts to appreciate Driss's 'difference', Driss defies the sexual normativities which eradicate Philippe's corporeal particularity. He neither assumes that Philippe is sexless nor does he appear to share the prevalent 'unspoken anxiety about non-normative sexuality', as he enquires into the potential 'differential form' which Philippe's sexual expression may take:

> Driss: Yes, about that, I wanted to ask you, about women, can you..., I mean how does it work?
> Philippe: You got to adapt.
> Driss: Just tell me, in practice—can you or can't you?
> Philippe: In practice, you may not have noticed, but I feel nothing from the base of my neck to the tips of my toes.
> Driss: So you can't?
> Philippe: It's not that simple. Let's say that I can but it's not always me that decides. And you can also find pleasure elsewhere.
> Driss: Yeah?
> Philippe: You've no idea.
> Driss: You're right. I can't imagine. How, for example?
> Philippe: For example, the ears...
> Driss: What do you mean the ears?
> Philippe: You know it's a very sensitive erogenous zone.
> Driss: So your thing is to get your ears licked. Ha, Ha.... I would never have guessed!

But what Driss then does with that knowledge interpellates discourses around the relation care workers have to the sexual citizenship of their employers. Shildrick points to the fact that the care of disabled persons is directed primarily towards the meeting of needs, with 'mere wishes or desires confined largely to the realm of private provision' (2007, p. 59).[5] She notes that certain disability activists challenge that distinction, and advocate that sexual citizenship should be positioned at the same level as other forms of citizenship, arguing that assistance should include things such as accompanying the disabled employees to sex clubs, negotiating with sex workers and supporting them in achieving sexual satisfaction (2007, p. 60).

In the case of *The Intouchables*, it becomes clear that the care worker is more than willing to provide both sexual and romantic assistance, but in this case, the issue is not the compliance of the care worker, but that of the employer, since Driss's assistance is offered then provided (initially at least) against Philippe's wishes. Philippe, far from soliciting sexual assistance, is safely cocooned in a long-term platonic and purely epistolary relationship sustained only by the most ethereal of poetic compositions, while internalising the unspoken anxieties of the cultural imaginary as regards the (his own) disabled body. Driss soon takes matters into his own hands. Unabashed by Philippe's auricular interests, he calls on the services of two Asian 'massage therapists', who provide for a classic moment of laddish homosocial bonding. Philippe and Driss are pictured sitting side by side in Philippe's' living room, Philippe enjoying auricular stimulation while Driss receiving a chest massage, keeps a paternal eye on Philippe's masseuse's wandering hands 'Hey, stick to the ears!' Driss's mediations in Philippe's romance with Éléonore are initially similarly interventionist but the romance eventually becomes a joint project, with both Philippe and Driss investing themselves in its eventual happy conclusion.

Driss's investment in Philippe's destiny is paralleled by Philippe's investment in Driss's family life. While Driss helps Philippe find a partner and discipline his unruly teenage daughter, Philippe helps Driss to find his place in his family again, concluding that Driss must leave him for good because they need him more than he does. The reciprocities which precede this decision have climaxed to perfect Torvill-and-Dean-style syncopation: Together they laugh at the pretentiousness of high culture and to move to the rhythms of low culture. Together they collude in the passing and selling off of Driss's experimental artwork in the high-price

---

[5] This discussion is made in relation to public policy funding.

art market. Together they laugh, joke and tease each other—on Philippe's private jet, heading to their mountain adventure, Driss, a novice to flying is the terrified wimp ('What's that?' Philippe: 'Oh nothing, just a hole in the fuselage, we won't make it'), while Philippe, who has seen his share of hard times ('Hey, you're used to tragedy, I'm not'), has the 'luck of the Kennedys'. They have fulfilled the linguistic requirements of homosociality, they have found ratified indirect ways of expressing their affiliation, and as they do, Old France is flying high, and New France is along for the ride… and so perhaps are we.

Conclusion

Does the reciprocal basis of Driss's and Philippe's heart-warming camaraderie defy the power dynamics of the assimilationist model of citizenship? I suggest, following Fortier (2008) and Rose (1998), that that the elements of reciprocity simply function as a form of 'protective fiction', a narrative support that gives consistency to the notion of a united French nation, free from the dissentions of class and race. As Fortier asserts, 'the nation is a fantasy that is brought into being in the public domain by repeatedly imagining that it exists and iterating it as something real, out there, that binds the "national people" together' (2008, p. 11). For Fortier, this fantasy is imagined at the interface between reality and horror: as the necessary 'psychic glue' (Rose, 1998, p. 3) 'which protects the nation/al from the horrors of the "real" that threaten the disintegration of the self' (2008, p. 12).

In *The Intouchables*, the elements of reciprocity allied to the evolution of homosociality—Philippe's flippant flirtation with immigrant culture, Driss's successful intervention into his employer's private life, and Philippe and Driss's joint investment in masculine adventures—all protect the viewer from the real, whether that is the real lives of (most) disabled people, immigrants or care workers, or the structural conditions that circumscribe them. As such, *The Intouchables* does after all comply with colonialism by succeeding in sanitising both care work and immigration, while Old France remains in her wheelchair—ultimately untouched.

References

AAFCA. (2012). African-American Film Critics Association. Retrieved from http://aafca.com/wp/wp-content/uploads/2012/11/2012-AAFCA-Award-Winners.pdf

Alberge, D. (2012). Untouchable—Review, *The Guardian*, September 20. Retrieved from http://www.theguardian.com/film/2012/sep/20/untouchable-review

Alsop, R., Fitzsimons, A., & Lennon, K. (2002). *Theorizing gender: An introduction*. Cambridge: Polity.

Anderson, B. (2000). *Doing the dirty work?: The global politics of domestic labour*. London: Zed Books.

Ashcroft, B. (2001). *On post-colonial futures: Transformations of a colonial culture*. London: Continuum.

Balibar, E. (1991). Is there a "neo-racism"? In E. Balibar & I. M. Wallerstein (Eds.), *Race, nation, class: Ambiguous identities*. London: Verso.

Balibar, E. (2001). The genealogical scheme: Race or culture. *Trans-Scripts* 1. Retrieved from http://sites.uci.edu/transscripts/files/2014/10/2011_01_launch.pdf

Berlant, L. (1991). *The anatomy of national fantasy: Hawthorne, utopia, and everyday life*. Chicago: The University of Chicago Press.

Bird, S. R. (1996). Welcome to the men's club: Homosociality and the maintenance of hegemonic masculinity. *Gender & Society, 10,* 120–132.

Bourdieu, P. (1984). *Distinction: A social critique of the judgement of taste*. Cambridge, MA: Harvard University Press.

Dussuet, A. (2005). *Travaux de femmes: Enquêtes sur les services à domicile*. Paris: L'Harmattan.

Engel, D. M., & Munger, F. W. (2003). *Rights of inclusion: Law and identity in the life stories of Americans with disabilities*. Chicago: University of Chicago Press.

Fortier, A.-M. (2008). *Multicultural horizons: Diversity and the limits of the civil nation*. London: Routledge.

Hochschild, A. R. (1983). *The managed heart: Commercialization of human feeling*. Berkeley: University of California Press.

Kaplan, D. (2005). Public intimacy: Dynamics of seduction in male homosocial interactions. *Symbolic Interaction, 28,* 571–595.

Kiesling, S. F. (2005). Homosocial desire in men's talk: Balancing and re-creating cultural discourses of masculinity. *Language in Society, 34,* 695–726.

Lawler, J. (2006). *Behind the screens: Nursing, somology, and the problem of the body*. Sydney: Sydney University Press.
Lewis, G. (2006). Imaginaries of Europe: Technologies of gender, economies of power. *European Journal of Women's Studies, 13*, 87–102.
Lutz, H. (2007). Domestic work. *European Journal of Women's Studies, 14*, 187–192.
Mellström, U. (2004). Machines and masculine subjectivity: Technology as an integral part of men's life experiences. *Men and Masculinities, 6*, 368–382.
Murphy, R. F. (2001). *The body silent*. New York: Norton.
NAACP. (2013). 2013 image awards nominations. Retrieved from http://www.naacp.org/news/entry/2013-image-awards-nominations
Näre, L. (2010). Sri Lankan men working as cleaners and carers: Negotiating masculinity in Naples. *Men and Masculinities, 13*, 65–86.
Redfield, R., Linton, R., & Herskovits, M. (1936). Memorandum on the study of acculturation. *American Anthropologist, 38*, 149–152.
Rivas, L. M. (2004). Caring for the independent person. In B. Ehrenreich & A. R. Hochschild (Eds.), *Global woman: Nannies, maids, and sex workers in the new economy*. New York: Henry Holt.
Rose, J. (1998). *States of fantasy*. Oxford: Clarendon Press.
Sam, D. L., & Berry, J. W. (2006). *The Cambridge handbook of acculturation psychology*. Cambridge: Cambridge University Press.
Scott, J. W. (2007). *The politics of the veil*. Princeton, NJ: Princeton University Press.
Scrinzi, F. (2004). Ma culture dans laquelle elle travaille: Les migrantes dans les services domestiques en Italie et en France. *Genre, travail et migrations en Europe, 12*, 137–162.
Scrinzi, F. (2010). Masculinities and the international division of care: Migrant male domestic workers in Italy and France. *Men and Masculinities, 13*, 44–64.
Scrinzi, F. (2013). *Genre, migrations et emplois domestiques en France et en Italie*. Paris: Petra.
Shildrick, M. (2007). Contested pleasures: The sociopolitical economy of disability and sexuality. *Sexuality Research & Social Policy, 4*, 53–66.
Turner, G. (2012). *Film as social practice*. London: Routledge.
Weissberg, J. (2011). Untouchable: Film review. *Variety*, September 29. Retrieved from http://variety.com/2011/film/reviews/untouchable-1117946269/
Wolkowitz, C. (2002). The social relations of body work. *Work, Employment & Society, 16*, 497–510.
Zaidman, C. (1986). La notion de féninisation. In N. Aubert, E. Enriquez, & V. de Gaulejac (Eds.), *Le Sexe du pouvoir: Femmes, hommes et pouvoirs dans les organisations*. Paris: Épi.

10

Unequal Fatherhoods: Citizenship, Gender, and Masculinities in Outsourced 'Male' Domestic Work

Ewa Palenga-Möllenbeck

Introduction

This chapter discusses the increased outsourcing of stereotypically male domestic work such as repairing, renovating, and gardening, also referred to as the 'phenomenon of (migrant) handymen' (Kilkey & Perrons, 2010). In Germany over the past 25 years, these services have predominantly been provided by Polish men. Unlike the case of migrant female domestic workers in Germany (Polish cleaners, elderly carers, and child minders), the phenomenon of male migrant handymen has, so far, gone largely unnoticed by researchers. Domestic work has tended to be discussed mainly in terms of women's work, and only recently have researchers started to analyse (migrant) men in 'feminised' domestic sectors (see for example Näre, 2010; Sarti & Scrinzi, 2010) and in stereotypically male domestic work sectors (Kilkey, Perrons, & Plomien, 2013; Palenga-Möllenbeck, 2013a, 2013b; Cox, 2010 on non-migrant male domestic work).

E. Palenga-Möllenbeck
Department of Gender Studies, Goethe University, Frankfurt, Germany

© The Editor(s) (if applicable) and The Author(s) 2016
B. Gullikstad et al. (Eds.), *Paid Migrant Domestic Labour in a Changing Europe*, DOI 10.1057/978-1-137-51742-5_10

Drawing on the example of Polish handymen working in German households, the chapter explores the fatherhood practices of Polish handymen and their employers in light of new forms of intra-European inequality based on intersecting dimensions of citizenship, class, and gender. As I will show, the migrant handymen phenomenon in Germany is based on ambiguous patterns of inclusion and exclusion corresponding with processes that *expand, erode,* and *engender* citizenship (Kivisto & Faist, 2007; Lister, 2003). Within the framework of this citizenship model, based on work as the central mode of social inclusion, the outsourcing of domestic work functions as a practical solution for the work–life balance of certain individuals—and is also politically expedient.

The chapter looks at the ways in which the phenomenon of outsourcing stereotypical male labour impacts on questions of masculinity and fatherhood within the context of recent European policy changes in the area of citizenship. How do Polish and German men engaged in the buying and selling of such services negotiate both practices and ideals of masculinity and fatherhood? To what extent do these practices and ideals reproduce traditional or new models of masculinity and fatherhood? Is this model 'tailor-made' for the needs of the upper middle class? Or, more specifically, is the model the reason why parents of the upper middle class (and higher classes) can embrace the new ideal of parenthood in the first place, simply because they have access to cheap migrant labour and can pay their way out of time-consuming domestic work and leave them with more 'quality time' at their disposal (see Kilkey et al., 2013)? If so, what implications does this hold for a notion of citizenship that calls for broader social participation and emphasises individual autonomy and empowerment throughout Europe, including the new European Union (EU) member states in the east?

I start by looking at the phenomenon of the male handyman in the German context, arguing that the term 'new butler' is useful for understanding their role. Next, I describe the changing policies relating to citizenship that are relevant to this phenomenon. I continue by showing how the models of citizenship (in particular those promoting gender equality) work to produce certain concepts of fatherhood and masculinity in contexts such as the outsourcing of male domestic work. After introducing the empirical study I draw on, I look at how the models of citizenship

10 Unequal Fatherhoods: Citizenship, Gender, and Masculinities... 219

under discussion frame the asymmetry of power between migrant handymen (and their families) and the households that employ them. Finally, I discuss the theoretical and political implications of the findings.

Polish Handymen in German Households: The Male Dimension of Social Reproduction?

The outsourcing of domestic work (often to migrants) has become increasingly common in Germany, as in Europe as a whole, especially among the middle class (Schupp, Spieß, & Wagner, 2006, p. 46). According to a 2009 survey, 4.5 million German households (approximately 11 % of households) purchased 'household-related services', of which 95 % did so informally (Institut der deutschen Wirtschaft Köln, 2009, p. 3). Cleaning was the most commonly outsourced task, followed by elderly care, with childcare and gardening outsourced to a lesser degree (Gottschall & Schwarzkopf, 2010, pp. 25–26). The demand for stereotypically male work is growing along with that of stereotypically female work (for example Traba, 2008).

According to my analysis of the Frankfurt registry of companies' records, there has been a steady growth, ethnicisation, and gendering of the male domestic services sector. Out of 2300 self-employed builders who registered or deregistered their business in 2009, 1200 (that is, more than 50 %) were male Polish citizens.[1]

Both government institutions and the involved parties (handymen and employers) usually refer to handymen services as 'building work', without distinguishing between work carried out in private households and work carried out in 'public' construction sites, with which the job description 'builder' is usually associated. I therefore initially assumed that the number of handymen services undertaken in private households was negligible and that these services were generally performed 'after hours'. However, both the qualitative research, based on interviews, Internet fora and advertisements, and the quantitative secondary analysis,

---

[1] Out of a total of 2344 self-employed persons in the building sector, 47 were women. There was no subdifferentiation according to gender.

based on records in the Frankfurt registry of companies, demonstrated that handymen services in private households are usually performed as full-time work and have developed into a rapidly growing, gendered, and ethnicised sector of the labour market.

The categorisation of handymen's work as 'domestic' work relates to the debate around the definition of care and domestic work, which has revolved around questions relating to the increased formalisation, professionalisation, and commodification of this type of labour. As previous research has demonstrated, the commodification of domestic work does not automatically entail its formalisation and professionalisation (Geissler & Pfau-Effinger, 2005). While the handymen are perceived and labelled (as well as labelling themselves) as 'construction workers'[2], I suggest that this term may suggest a greater degree of formalisation and professionalisation than the situation actually represents. Instead, I identify aspects of their work that set them apart from traditional tradesmen performing 'productive work' and highlight the similarity between their work and 'reproductive work'.

By 'reproductive work', I mean work that has traditionally been performed informally within families and neighbourhoods, or, in the case of paid reproductive work, work that has been poorly formalised and is typically performed by low-status groups such as (migrant) female domestic workers. In this context, I use Glenn's (1992, p. 1) definition of social reproductive work as 'activities and relationships involved in maintaining people both on a daily basis and intergenerationally [including] activities such as purchasing household goods, preparing and serving food, laundering and preparing clothing, maintaining furnishings and appliances, socializing children, providing care and emotional support for adults, and maintaining kin and community ties'.

In the context of the discussion on the commodification and outsourcing of stereotypically female domestic work and the return of the 'servant society' (Glenn, 2010; Näre, this volume), Lutz (2011) has proposed the term 'new maids' to refer to female migrants who perform domestic work

---

[2] See also Ringrose, this volume, for another example of how care and domestic work is being redefined as more 'masculine'.

that middle-class households no longer want to perform themselves. I suggest that the outsourcing of stereotypically male domestic work can be seen as analogous to that of outsourcing domestic tasks to the 'new maids', and that the term 'new butlers' can be considered to correspond to that of 'new maids'. As with 'new maids', 'new butlers' are permanently available (6–7 days per week), provide both unskilled and professional services 'from one source', and often find themselves in an asymmetric power relationship with their employers or clients (as a result of their citizenship, ethnicity, class, and gender) that makes them vulnerable to exploitation. While the situation of Polish handymen is more heterogeneous than that of Polish female domestic workers (see Palenga-Möllenbeck, 2013b), the majority of my respondents exemplified the characteristics of 'new butlers' to a more or less complete degree.

In the rest of the article, I discuss the side effects this type of outsourcing has in the context of fatherhood and family life. I argue that it engenders and rigidifies inequality between Western and Eastern Europe in terms of different access to social reproductive work. First, however, I examine three processes in the current conceptualisations of citizenship that, as I argue below, underpin the structure of inequality that frames the phenomenon of the 'new butler'.

Citizenship Perspectives: Expansion, Erosion, and Engendering

Even though the German labour market was closed to EU citizens from the A8 countries[3] until 2011, Polish citizens have been legally allowed to settle in Germany as part of the EU's eastern expansion since 2004, on the condition that they are self-employed. Thus, Poles became the largest group of migrants to register businesses in Germany, as this was their only legal access to the German labour market (with the only exception being workers posted by companies registered in Poland). This meant

---

[3] The Czech Republic, Estonia, Hungary, Latvia, Lithuania, Poland, Slovakia, and Slovenia.

that the Polish handymen sector, which had existed since the early 1990s, was becoming semi-legal.[4].

Despite this, as the present study shows, the majority of handymen services continues to be provided informally, as both employers and handymen prefer this mode of working. Moreover, the conditions under which migrants—including Polish migrants—work in this sector are extremely precarious, because of the widespread bogus self-employment practices and, not least, because of the informal subcontracting structures.

The work of Polish migrant handymen can be understood in the context of growing disparities related to 'expanding' versus 'eroding' rights of citizenship in Europe (Kivisto & Faist, 2007). This development can be linked to three dimensions of citizenship. The first, referred to as the 'expansion' of citizen rights, describes policies that give residents who do not have formal citizenship, rights to political and social participation (Soysal, 1994). Polish citizens working and living in Germany fall into in this category, which represents a particular form of supranational or 'nested' citizenship (Faist, 2001). Here, the relatively privileged status of EU citizenship is superimposed on member state nationality; freedom of movement and settlement is of central importance in this context (see also Cox and Busch, this volume). This situation privileges internal migrants in the EU over undocumented migrant workers, who form a large part, if not the majority, of migrant domestic workers worldwide (ILO, 2013).

The expansion of citizenship rights in the political sphere can lead to an 'ethnicisation' of certain labour market sectors, usually those with low-paid jobs and a relatively low access threshold (Sassen, 2001). In the case of the German domestic work sector, this has also led to 'transnationalisation' as migrants have left their families behind in Poland. This development in Germany has gone hand in hand with the erosion and replacement of the standard employment relationship with atypical employment relationships characterised by fixed-term contracts, part-time

---

[4] Until 2011, Polish handymen accessed the labour market indirectly by using the freedom of services rule provided by the EU (2006/123/EG) and the assignment guideline (96/71/EG). This practice was legally controversial (Dollinger, 2008, on binational placement agencies in elderly care), as most cases did not qualify as the provision of cross-border services. Likewise, many handymen working as independent contractors in the present sample did not meet the criteria for genuine self-employment (which consist of, essentially, having more than one client, working independently of detailed instructions and bearing entrepreneurial risk).

work, bogus self-employment, and contracts requiring an extreme degree of flexibility and mobility (Minssen, 2006, p. 173). Here, as with all large-scale societal developments, it is obviously difficult to identify cause and effect in the precarisation and transnationalisation nexus: the offer of precarious labour and the demand for it are mutually reinforcing.

The second aspect of citizenship that impacts Polish workers relates to the fact that the expansion of political citizenship rights has been accompanied by the 'erosion' of social citizenship rights in Germany. The model of citizenship based on formal political inclusion as well as on socioeconomic inclusion (Marshall, 1964) is gradually losing ground as a result of a deregulatory restructuring of the welfare state model. The role of the state is increasingly to enable and facilitate work, while social benefits relating to unemployment or incapacity are selective and reduced (Nail, 2004). However, if we look at the question of Polish handymen from a transnational perspective, we note that the labour market in Poland is comparatively less regulated (Portet, 2007) and the welfare state even less developed than that of Germany (Myant & Drahokoupil, 2011). This means that, from the perspective of Polish handymen in Germany, the 'lowered' standards of life and work in Germany are still considered relatively comfortable.

The third aspect of citizenship that sheds light on the question of Polish handymen concerns the dimension of gender and the adult worker model (Lewis, 2009; Lister, 2003)—an EU policy objective that has gradually been realised both in Germany and in Poland. According to this model, women and men are expected to engage in paid work to the same extent. At the same time, domestic work is supposed to be shared between women and men in heterosexual couples. While the specifics of the model are left to the individual member states, EU policy favours the Nordic model of broad institutional support for child and elderly care aimed at promoting the family–work balance (Eurofund-European Foundation for the Improvement of Living and Working Conditions, 2006). For the time being, this remains a mere policy objective, as Germany continues to represent a modified male breadwinner model, while Poland, with low female employment and a poorly developed care infrastructure, is a long way from reaching this goal (Plomien, 2009). However, even as a long-term objective, the adult worker model does not provide a solution to the question of how to fill the social reproduction gap that is left behind as a result of the devaluation of the maternal role and the pressure that the shrinking market for full-time labour exerts on the (male) breadwinner model (Van Walsum, 2013, pp. 3–4). This gap is, however, gradually becoming a 'private' problem as social reproductive work is being commodified in the sense that it is becoming yet another product on the market that only the more affluent part of society can afford. This brings us to the question of how policies work towards producing certain models of fatherhood and masculinity in contexts such as the outsourcing of male domestic work, in particular those promoting gender equality.

Gender Equality from the Perspective of Masculinity and Fatherhood Studies

As I will show, the 'new butler' model allows fathers who purchase male domestic services to fully commit themselves to their own paid work. Outsourcing stereotypically male work helps men solve the work–life conflict that arises from the clash of two contradicting norms of fatherhood: the 'new' father (see for example Bereswill, Scheiwe, & Wolde, 2006) and the 'main male breadwinner'. Men are increasingly involved in their children's education compared to fathers in the past (Sullivan, Coltrane, Mc Annally, & Altintas, 2009, p. 240). Unlike their parent's generation, 'new fathers' no longer define themselves exclusively in relation to their breadwinner role. Instead, they want to take an active part in their children's lives and education. However, German men tend to work as much or even more after they become fathers (Grunow, 2007), and are caught between traditional and modern patterns of masculinity (Bereswill et al., 2006). The ambiguity this engenders is not only the result of competing cultural norms of masculinity and fatherhood, but also the result of gendered welfare regimes and is further reinforced by the deregulation of working time regimes and the ever-longer hours that these men are expected to work (Kilkey & Palenga-Möllenbeck, 2013).

This, again, raises the question of whether labour market deregulation can be understood as a process that expands or erodes citizenship. Deregulation renders the migrant handymen's position on the labour market more precarious in terms of insecure and irregular employment. And from the perspective of employers, this means that work progressively intrudes into their private lives. The motivation to outsource male domestic work thus results from employers being torn between competing norms of fatherhood. At the same time, the outsourcing also produces inequality between fathers on opposite sides of the contract.

This takes us to the notion that the outsourcing of (mostly 'female') domestic work holds an emancipating potential for the women who are able to outsource the work, which is something that has been discussed in scholarly and political debates for a long time. It has been argued that outsourcing not only changes, but in fact increases gender inequality and can, at best, shift its burden to economically less-privileged women and female migrants (Ehrenreich & Hochschild, 2003). This criticism is confirmed by recent surveys that show how the outsourcing of domestic work deepens the gender and class gap (Goňalons-Pons, 2015). In spite of this, outsourcing domestic work remains the most common solution to achieve a tolerable work–life balance in the middle and upper class in Europe and many other regions of the world (Triandafyllidou & Marchetti, 2015). The causes and mechanisms of this phenomenon are well researched as far as women's motivations for delegating domestic work are concerned (see for example Triandafyllidou & Marchetti, 2015). By contrast, men's role in this process and their specific motivations remain relatively poorly researched. The same is true for the consequences of this process for both sides of the contract, that is, for men selling and buying 'male' domestic work (for an exception, see Kilkey et al., 2013). This raises the question of which understandings of masculinity lie beneath these competing norms of fatherhood, and what influence these understandings exert on intra- and intergender relations.

In this context, I draw on Connell's (1995) concept of 'hegemonic masculinity'. Connell describes masculinity as a socially constructed norm that changes depending on time and place. Hegemonic masculinity assumes power over both femininity (in the shape of patriarchy) and subordinate masculinities through marginalisation, subordination, and compliancy. The modern version of hegemonic masculinity is personified by the 'global manager', who is rooted neither in a specific place nor within a family. This male figure is extremely mobile, elitist, and hedonistic, and is able to successfully negotiate the uncertainties of the labour market (Connell & Wood, 2005). However, at the same time, 'new fatherhood' is becoming an equally attractive model of masculinity (Meuser, 2014). The question is how this model is put into practice: Does it fall back on a hegemonic understanding of masculinity or does it open itself towards gender equality (Connell & Messerschmidt, 2005, pp. 847–848)? Which concepts of fatherhood, masculinity, and gender relations can be found in the narratives of couples who outsource male domestic work? And what about the men who are unable to live up to the ideal of new fatherhood because their families are unable to outsource 'unpleasant' domestic work and they are absent from their families for long periods of time? What kind of relationship connects those two groups of fathers and families?

Empirical Basis

This chapter is based on an explorative study of Polish handymen in German households conducted in Germany in 2011 and 2012 and draws on semi-structured interviews with fathers and members of their families.[5] These include 19 interviews with Polish handymen and their partners and 17 interviews with families (fathers and/or mothers) contracting handymen. All interviews were conducted in Germany. The purpose of the study was to estimate the quantitative extent of the migrant handymen phenomenon in Germany, to understand how the handyman labour market sector works, for example, how employers and handymen find each other, and, finally, to analyse the circumstances that motivate households to outsource 'male' domestic work and motivate Polish migrants to offer these services.

---

[5] The study combined three methods: Secondary analysis of regional statistics on handyman activities in the labour market; analysis of 'brokering firms' and Internet fora used by handymen and households; and, finally, 37 in-depth interviews with Polish handymen, their partners (specifically, thirteen interviews with men, two with couples, and two with female partners), informal brokers, and companies in the handyman sector, and men and women in households with dependent children (six with couples, two with men and three with women) employing Polish handymen. Student assistant Paulina Talar was involved in the collection and analysis of quantitative and qualitative data.

Unequal Fatherhoods and Masculinities

Outsourcing Fathers

Outsourcing male work enabled some of the employers interviewed to live their lives according to a model of hegemonic masculinity termed modern 'transnational business masculinity' (Connell & Wood, 2005; see also Kilkey et al., 2013). Fathers employing 'new butlers' gain the opportunity to come close to this ideal. For those who most closely conform to the ideal of the 'global manager', stereotypically male domestic work (like other domestic work and, in part, family life) is rendered 'invisible'. In these cases, domestic work, both male and female, is outsourced without any participation from the fathers whatsoever. The handymen are hired to do work that would usually be done by the 'master', as in the popular cliché of the 'butler', but his everyday interaction is mostly with the 'lady of the house'.

The female partners assume full responsibility for the household, in some cases with assistance from family members or domestic workers. Martha, a 48-year-old part-time teacher, mother of four children aged 12–21 and wife of a physician, gave a typical example:

> Well, my husband is self-employed, and he went out of the house at seven in the morning and came back at eight in the evening. Whatever needed to be done in the house was my job. There was simply… there was no talking about it, no point in discussing it (…) I just knew that when I go back to work then it would be in addition to the things that I had to do anyway. So it had to be well organised and I needed help from outside. The children were taken care of and I had the household help.

Here we observe an allocation of roles that Martha does not question. The father's responsibility is earning an income. The mother also works, but her responsibility is looking after the family and the house, assisted by 'staff' consisting of Polish domestic workers. When the children were smaller they had nannies; up to the time of the interview, the family had employed cleaners and handymen who carried out 'male' domestic work. Martha emphasises that her husband pays for the domestic workers so that she may feel 'free' and live a more modern life than those in her parents' generation. She is financially independent from her husband and has a rewarding job—'adequate to the times we live in', as she puts it.

For all the 'modernity' that Martha represents—her type of motherhood appears perfectly aligned with the current neoliberal discourse on femininity in which mothers 'can have everything' (Rottenberg, 2014). Yet her family life conforms to the traditional heteronormative model of femininity and masculinity (Hirschauer, 2013). This model rests on a breadwinning, but absent, father and his female counterpart, who is expected to project what Connell (1987) defines as 'emphasised femininity'[6]. The one astonishing aspect about this 'modern' arrangement is the indispensable role of domestic workers—more specifically Polish migrants—who underpin it: they invisibly enable their 'master' to achieve a tolerable work–life balance. At the same time, his partner is the 'mistress' who again manages the household by coordinating the work of 'servants'. The main difference between this phenomenon and a traditional class-ridden society is the fact that in the modern version, the woman additionally works outside the house.

For the second group of men among my interviewees, outsourcing male domestic work (and domestic work in general) helped them realise an increasingly egalitarian model of partnership and new fatherhood. By outsourcing some domestic work, they could deal with the remaining work selectively. In other words, they could 'choose' portions of it that were less monotonous (see also Miranda, 2011; Wetterer, 2005). Furthermore, they could be involved fathers and partners who could spend 'quality time' with their partner, share certain parental responsibilities, and still have time left for their hobbies. One of my respondents, Stefan, put it in a nutshell:

> My wife and I, we are both working, we're not really into cleaning the house, doing repairs and stuff. That's why we're hiring someone to do it, so

---

[6] In the initial concept of 'hegemonic masculinity', Connell (1987) formulated the idea of 'emphasised femininity' as a female pendant to hegemonic masculinity that explains how heteronormative femininity support hegemonic masculinities ('women's conspiracy'). This part of the concept was not enhanced to the extent of the idea of multiple masculinities. Hence, this study aimed to explore the relationality of masculinities in both dimensions—within and between genders.

we have more free time (…) And we have to look after our son. He's 15 now, so he still needs a lot of support and attention after all. Even more so at the moment, because he's smack in the middle of puberty.

Stefan openly declares that he and his wife are simply 'not interested' in domestic work. This shows the essence of this contract: It is the outsourcing of domestic work (both 'male' and 'female') that makes egalitarian gender relations and modern fatherhood possible in the first place. The situation of the people selling these services is not discussed in this context; the issue simply remains outside perception for Stefan. As we will see below, this pertains to the domestic workers' status as 'non-citizens'—not only in legal terms, but also in terms of social recognition (Glenn, 2010).

For some employers, certain aspects of male domestic work may be experienced as a welcome change after long working days and demanding intellectual tasks. An example of this is provided by Torsten, who accomplished his 'ambitious projects' himself, such as technically or aesthetically 'challenging' tasks like renovating an antique garden bench, while leaving other less attractive chores, like cutting the hedge, to a Polish handyman. When I asked him where exactly he drew the line between tasks he reserved for himself and those he left to the handyman, Torsten explained it using an example from gardening:

> …It's somewhat tiring everything? And it's nothing that I would say is fun. In the meantime, [the hedge] is big, you need a ladder, and you have to keep setting up the ladder, and it's taking two or three hours, and at some point I said to myself it's OK if somebody else does it.

Torsten could afford to 'reserve' for himself the kind of domestic tasks that were 'fun' and confirm his identity rooted in middle-class masculinity—the attributes of being ambitious, 'creative', and resourceful. This is a typical narrative for a group of fathers who could carry out technical domestic work themselves, but usually do not because they lack the time or motivation. Moreover, the domestic work that Torsten did himself was not considered just another kind of work that needed to be done.

Rather, it was a welcome change from his desk job and provided instant gratification:

> By now it's something relaxing. You get something done; you see the result when you're finished. (…) When you're sitting in front of the computer all day, you keep getting new messages in your inbox, so you're never really done with your work.

Finally, as in Torsten's case, the outsourcing of certain 'male' work allows fathers to spend more time with their children. All this, however, happens under the condition that their 'hobbies' do not collide with their demanding paid work. Along with all the other employers, Torsten associated masculinity with traditionally paid male work. Moreover, with one exception, all of the fathers were the main breadwinners with their partners working part-time. In these households, the majority of stereotypically female work was undertaken by the female partners and by female domestic workers, as most of the interviewed households employed both a handyman and a female domestic worker. In these households, the women also dealt with managing the outsourcing of male work.[7] These factors suggest that the buying of domestic services can be considered a new way of balancing life and work, and one that preserves the hegemonic masculinity that is based on high economic status.

In this respect, the 'traditional' masculinity of absent fathers and that of 'involved' fathers are not significantly different: 'new fatherhood' and egalitarian gender relations are appreciated, as long as they do not collide with the traditional 'breadwinner masculinity', maintaining the previous economic status and the ideal of self-actualisation. Thus, men from both groups outsource stereotypically female tasks to their partners and female domestic workers, and unpleasant stereotypically male tasks to their handymen. They owe their lifestyle to the continued existence of gendered inequality in the sphere of domestic work, but also to women and other men who enter into these arrangements because of their lower social and ethnic status.

The subtle nature of the inequalities that are concealed behind the 'new butler's' job can be seen from the example of 52-year-old Thomas, who, for

---

[7] See also Kilkey et al. (2013) for the UK.

12 years had been outsourcing various chores around his house and garden to a 61-year-old Polish migrant, Zygmunt. Both men described their relationship as a friendship. For example, Zygmunt had a key to Thomas's house. Thanks to Zygmunt's work, Thomas, who was a teacher, could keep his house in good repair and realise some 'aesthetic' projects around the house. This is how Thomas described his working relationship with Zygmunt, which he saw as being based on 'reciprocal' benefits, or even a way of 'unselfishly helping' Zygmunt without seeking any benefit for himself:

> T: Well… I pay Zygmunt 10 euro an hour and I think it's… quite inexpensive, but that's also the reason why I'm having him do all these things, which perhaps I wouldn't have otherwise. For example, during a time when Zygmunt was out of work, he was doing all kinds of things, I had a lot of money, relatively speaking, I had taken a credit for the renovation, and then he was really working here for hours on end.
> I: So it was a deal, in your eyes, that you supported him?
> T. It was perfectly okay, I wouldn't have been able to do it at all if I'd had little money, well, so it simply all fell together, it was just the right thing at the time, and insofar it was okay, [I said] just go ahead… The fireplace out in the garden, for example, that was one thing I could have just as well done myself… but I said 'So what'… Or building the wooden house, well maybe not that one, but laying the stones down there, things like that, or plastering the walls, or… Oh, I don't really remember, it was so many things I really could have myself or that I'm still doing myself.

Here we observe how Thomas subtly justifies his unequal relationship with Zygmunt—he tries to frame it in the broad terms of friendship and emphasises their ostensibly egalitarian 'win–win' situation. This appears to be a typical narrative of the younger generation who outsource domestic work (see also Kristensen in this volume).

The New Butler

Zygmunt, a father of three adult children, came to Germany in 1987 as an ethnic German. He held German citizenship and thus, at least formally, had the most privileged status possible. Unlike most other handymen, Zygmunt had been in regular employment for most of his time in

Germany and had held down various handymen jobs after hours and on weekends, usually on Saturdays (while on Sundays he worked for a temporary work agency). At the time of the interview, Zygmunt had been on sick leave for several months. Meanwhile, his wife continued to work full time as a cleaner, as she had done for decades. Since Zygmunt was almost permanently absent from home, his wife did all the 'female' tasks around the house. Unlike his 'handyman employer', who actively spent his free time with his son, Zygmunt had been spending all his time off on various other jobs to achieve what he considered to be an acceptable standard of life for himself and his family. Asked about his experiences as a father, Zygmunt described his 'absentee' fatherhood:

> Everyone is happy when their child gets born and so on, but Dad isn't always the Dad he's supposed to be, right? Most of the time, my wife was doing everything with those kids. I mean, I did play with them, too, but there never was enough time, right? I'm trying to make up for it now that I have a grandson, I spend a lot more time with my grandson than I did back then with my children, now I've got the time.

In his narrative, Zygmunt adopts certain tropes from the 'new fatherhood' discourse. He regrets not having 'invested' more time in his children, and instead becoming just like his own father who never had time for him back when he had an agricultural business in Poland. On the other hand, he emphasises that he succeeded in supporting three children and securing their education thanks to his hard work, and that his family 'was functioning well'. At the time of the interview, Zygmunt was retired and chronically ill as a result of accidents he had suffered while working as a handyman. Looking back, he felt that he had fulfilled his role as a father well by being a reliable breadwinner, but was nonetheless pleased that he could now make the 'emotional investment' in his grandson which he had previously failed to make in his children.

What makes Polish handymen so attractive to their employers is the fact that they, unlike regular trade companies, offer an uncomplicated and unobtrusive 'all-in-one' type of service. Also, regular companies do not offer 'packages' of stereotypically male services. This is the particular domain of the 'new butlers', who either individually or as the head of a team are permanently on call and operate without requiring lengthy negotiations and detailed instructions. This is how Stefan puts it:

> There's always something that needs to be fixed or to be done somewhere in our house. Then I just call him and he gets it done. Yeah, and not only does he know the ropes, but he proactively puts forward good ideas… He also has good taste, I mean, he relatively quickly understood my taste and provided me with good tips then.

Interestingly, just like Torsten and Thomas, Stefan also subtly presents himself here as someone who is more 'distinguished' than the Polish handymen, in Bourdieu's terms of taste and habitus. The outsourcing of male domestic work is yet another example of masculinity being projected within an all-male frame of reference, where 'Male habitus is constructed and completed only in connection with the space reserved for men, the space in which the serious games of the competition are played among men' (Bourdieu, 1997, p. 203, quoted in Bereswill & Neuber, 2011, p. 77). Conversely, Polish handymen also construe their masculinity in opposition to that of their German employers, who are seen to have all sorts of tools in their houses but who are simply not 'man enough' to put them to use.

The fact that male tasks are increasingly being outsourced pertains to the availability of cheap, flexible, and skilled migrants[8] who accept precarious living and working conditions, such as a strong dependency on individual employers or clients inside subcontracting networks, group living in cheap housing and working as 'freelancers'. For these 'new butlers', the freelancer role is often a challenge. Self-employed work requires business know-how, contacts, language and social skills (articulateness and negotiation techniques), and, in some cases, capital. Only a small portion of my respondents were 'naturally born' entrepreneurs. The majority consisted of 'survivors' struggling with their dependency on other Poles, with 'difficult' clients and generally precarious economic, social, and family situations.

---

[8] For more on the role of ethnic (auto)stereotypes of Polish handymen as opposed to German companies, see Palenga-Möllenbeck (2013a).

At the same time, though, these precarious conditions take on a different meaning when we look at their alternatives in Poland. There, working on so-called 'junk jobs' is the order of the day and as a result, working conditions must be measured against the standards in both countries. As it turns out, Polish workers have the longest working hours in Eastern Europe (Chustecka, 2012, p. 30), so it comes as no surprise that they have less time to spend with children.

The work of Polish handymen is thus based on a regression (relative to the pre-transformation period) towards a traditional distribution of roles—a return to the patriarchal masculinity of the male breadwinner model, which had been on the wane under socialism. It is primarily this traditional male breadwinner model that motivates men's actions and is referred to in order to 'make sense' of biographical narratives. Regardless of age, my male respondents found themselves 'pushed' by their families and, above all, by themselves into the role of 'absent fathers' as a result of transnational migration.

This raises the question, which form of patriarchy—or rather 'transpatriarchy', as Hearn (2009) calls a type of patriarchy that is supported by a transnational lifestyle—is evolving from the practices of transnational fathers and their partners? Can this type of fatherhood really be called hegemonic?

This non-linear relationship between transpatriarchy and hegemonic masculinity is well illustrated in the case of Marek, a father to five children, four of whom were adults, including one university student and one 15-year-old living with his parents. One of his adult sons (now a father himself) lived and worked with Marek in Frankfurt. Marek's handyman career began in Austria as early as 1987, during a visit with his own father—attesting to the third generation of transnational migration. Marek had been working in Germany since 1991. He had spent the time between 2001 and 2005 back in Poland, but failed to establish a business operation there. At the time of the interview, Marek and his adult son lived in a two-room flat. Since his four-year break in Poland, Marek had been struggling to rebuild a pool of clients.

> I came for three months, but those three months turned into 20 years. And so it's dragging on, dragging on, dragging on. I also had many offers… In

Poland I could have set up a business. But I always listened to my wife: But go and stay there, that's where the money is, and so on. It was money, money, money, money. I've had it up to here, I'll tell you. And then the kids. They're grown up now. And I've hardly ever seen them. My wife was like, 'You'll go there, I'm pregnant, you'll come here', birth, baptism and off to Germany.

Marek was an unsatisfied and overworked father (like most handymen, he worked long hours, 6 days a week) who complained about how limited his role as a father was due to his being the main breadwinner. Marek blamed his wife, who had raised all five children alone, for maintaining a traditional distribution of gender roles. Marek and his wife's situation can be understood in the context of the regression towards the male breadwinner model in Poland.

During the systemic transformation beginning in 1989, unemployment hit women much harder than men (Kalwa, 2007, pp. 208–209). This was exacerbated by the refamilialisation of social policy, which pushed women out of the labour market (Szelewa & Polakowski, 2008, p. 117). In Poland today, labour markets and family-related policies continue to disadvantage women disproportionally. For instance, the day-care infrastructure is insufficiently developed and costly for parents. The result is that preschool attendance is very low, with only 3 % of under 3-year-olds (Bregin & Kmita, 2012, p. 124) and 41 % of 4-year-olds attending preschool (EACEA, 2009, p. 65). The work–life conflict is, as a result, a problem primarily faced by the less affluent majority of society. Women who do not work express a greater degree of life satisfaction than women who work. The latter cite both long commutes and long working hours as a direct consequence of the extremely deregulated working regime (Chustecka, 2012, p. 34).

The current regression towards the male breadwinner model is not occurring within a cultural vacuum. Even during socialism, gender equality in the sphere of work was not matched by the equal sharing of domestic obligations and the role of fathers was generally a non-topic within the official ideology of equal rights. During the transformation period, the gender contract underwent a retraditionalisation (for more, see Palenga-Möllenbeck & Lutz, 2016). However, despite the continued legacy of this return to tradition, there are changes within the Polish middle classes; more couples try to practice an equal partnership and modern forms of family life (see for example Sikorska, 2009).[9]

The migration of Polish handymen thus reinforces gender inequality within a patriarchal model of family life. This is confirmed by other research into the transnational migration of men and the gender relations in migrant families, which points to the fact that the majority of women with migrant partners have partners who are absent almost all of the time (Palenga-Möllenbeck, 2014). These women are totally economically dependent on their partners and take responsibility for all of the care work. Female partners either 'complicitly' encourage their husband to migrate (Connell, 1987) or even actively enforce it, as we see in Marek's case, as he described himself as his wife's 'cash cow'.

Although the family model that handymen conform to may, at first sight, appear to be much more traditional than that of their employers, it is not necessarily accompanied by a return to hegemonic masculinity. To be sure, some of my respondents did seem to aspire to a return to full-fledged masculine hegemony—in particular those who were businessmen working with German architectural firms and earning an above-average income.

I would argue, however, that the less advantaged handymen—the 'new butlers'—represent a marginalised masculinity. Although they present themselves as skilled tradesmen (Kilkey et al., 2013) who successfully compete with their 'incompetent' German equivalents, the vast majority resemble the traditional 'butler' cliché; that is, they are strongly dependent on their 'masters' and subordinate their own needs to those of their 'masters', particularly with respect to their family life. The competitive pressure on the labour market, which endangers their male breadwinner role, makes their masculinity similar to the marginalised masculinity of manual workers (Meuser, 2010; Paap, 2006). However, it additionally intersects with their status as migrants whose mobility is constructed as one of low-qualified workers.

As transnational migrants, unlike their employers, they cannot fully live up to the expectations of the modern father role and partnership,

---

[9] Also with the help of paid domestic workers from Poland and abroad, mostly from Ukraine (Kindler & Kordasiewicz, 2015; Lutz & Palenga-Möllenbeck, 2012).

which are based on the premise of being physically settled and close to family members, in order to share common time and to freely choose a lifestyle. Even though they try to compensate for this by communicating with their families using telecommunication technology, as in Marek's example, who, through his daily and extended contact via phone calls and text messages, practiced emotional fatherhood. However, such usage of communication technology can compensate for the lack of proximity only to a limited extent (Madianou & Miller, 2011). Thus, 'new butlers' cannot actually realise what can arguably be categorised as their 'intimate citizenship' rights, for example, family cohabitation and sexual consumption (Lister, 2003, p. 127; Plummer, 2003). Marek's fatherhood is based on the traditional male breadwinner role, which is associated more with financial success and less with maintaining care obligations at home. At the same time, this is an inevitable result of situatedness within a labour market sector that is a buyer's market marked by tough competition, lack of long-term security, engrained inequality along ethnic divisions, and, not least, legal inequality—for these migrants may legally remain in Germany only as long as they are in employment. It is these circumstances that lead them to become self-employed, with all the hardships for families that this entails.

A 'new butler's' relationship with his employer may be long term and perfectly amicable, as in the case of Zygmunt and Thomas, but this does not alter the fact that even this apparently symmetric relationship is rooted in power relations based on dimensions of gender, class, and citizenship that limit the handymen's and their family's freedom more than that of their employers.

Conclusion

The example of Polish handymen working in German households shows how the commodification and outsourcing of male domestic work is part of a broader structure of inequality based on dimensions of gender, class, and citizenship. The concept of the 'new butler' captures the power relations not only between buyers and sellers, but also between the families who are party to this type of working contract.

The changing interpretations of citizenship, that is, its expansion (EU mobility) and erosion (neoliberal transformation of welfare states), the new welfare regimes promoting the adult worker system, and the deregulation of labour markets are all imbricated in the growing demand for and supply of male domestic work.

Policy-makers may well consider the outsourcing of domestic work to be a viable solution to the work–family balance for some parts of the population and to unemployment for others. As I have shown, there are, however, serious side effects to this type of outsourcing.

Such outsourcing engenders and rigidifies inequality between Western and Eastern Europe in terms of access to social reproductive work. The case described in this chapter illustrates this: on both sides of the contract we observe 'unequal fatherhoods', where the supposedly 'modern' and gender-equal lifestyle of German middle-class fathers is dependent on the mobility and precarious working and living conditions of Polish fathers and, paradoxically, the gender-unequal relations in their own families. Furthermore, the commodification of domestic work—including male domestic work—only seemingly contributes to more gender equality, which is not only a paramount objective of EU policies, but also an ideal stated by many of my respondents, in particular, from the upper middle class.

If we adopt a broad understanding of citizenship, this finding has serious consequences. First, it points to a potential re-emergence of the private/public dichotomy that has been thoroughly criticised within elaborations of feminist concepts of citizenship (Lister, 2003), except that this time it is not just women who are confined to the 'private' realm as 'new maids', but also *men* who suffer this fate as 'new butlers'. Second, the mobility required of both migrant women and men poses a serious obstacle to their enjoyment of intimate citizenship rights. Taken together, these phenomena threaten to establish a new 'ethclass' (Gordon, 1964, p. 51) that is both confined to the private realm and under pressure to renounce intimate citizenship rights. Thus, they damage the ideals of an inclusive citizenship, where the categories of race and class that were supposed to lose political significance seem to be returning with a vengeance.

References

Bereswill, M., & Neuber, A. (2011). Marginalised masculinity, precarisation and the gender order. In H. Lutz, M. T. Herrera-Vivar, & L. Supik (Eds.), *Framing intersectionality: Debates on a multi-faceted concept in gender studies* (pp. 69–87). Farnham: Ashgate.

Bereswill, M., Scheiwe, K., & Wolde, A. (Eds.) (2006). *Vaterschaft im Wandel. Multidisziplinäre Analysen und Perspektiven aus geschlechtertheoretischer Sicht.* Weinheim and München: Juventa.

Bourdieu, P. (1997). Die männliche Herrschaft. In B. Krais & I. Dölling (Eds.), *Ein alltägliches Spiel. Geschlechterkonstruktionen in der Praxis* (pp. 153–217). Frankfurt am Main: Suhrkamp.

Bregin, D., & Kmita, D. (2012). Oferta opieki i wczesnej edukacji dla dzieci do 3. roku życia. *Małe Dzieci w Polsce, 1*(38), 123–129.

Chustecka, M. (2012). Kobieta kobiecie nierówna. Zróżnicowanie nieodpłatnej pracy kobiet. In A. Dryjanska (Ed.), *Nieodpłatna praca kobiet—różowa strefa gospodarki* (pp. 27–37). Warszawa: Heinrich Böll Stiftung and Fundacja Feminoteka.

Connell, R. (1987). *Gender and power.* Sydney: Allen and Unwin.

Connell, R., & Messerschmidt, J. W. (2005). Hegemonic masculinity: Rethinking the concept. *Gender & Society, 19*(6), 829–859.

Connell, R. W. (1995). *Masculinities.* Cambridge: Polity Press.

Connell, R. W., & Wood, J. (2005). Globalization and business masculinities. *Men and Masculinities, 7,* 347–364.

Cox, R. (2010). Hired hubbies and mobile mums: Gendered skills in domestic service. *Renewal, 18*(1–2), 51–58.

Dollinger, F.-W. (2008). *Von der Schwarzarbeit zur legalen pflegerischen Dienstleistung. Wie wir den Status der osteuropäischen Pflegerinnen legalisieren können.* In Gesundheitspolitisches Seminar, April 26, 2008. Konrad Adenauer Foundation.

EACEA, Agencja Wykonawcza ds. Edukacji, Kultury i Sektora Audiowizualnego, Fundacja Rozwoju Systemu Edukacji. (2009). Wczesna edukacja i opieka nad dzieckiem w Europie: zmniejszanie nierówności i społecznych i kulturowych. Retrieved May 9, 2016, from http://tinyurl.com/hbj5cdg.

Ehrenreich, B., & Hochschild, A. (Eds.) (2003). *Global woman: Nannies, maids and sex workers in the new economy.* New York: Metropolitan Press.

Eurofund-European Foundation for the Improvement of Living and Working Conditions. (2006). Working time and work–life balance in European companies. Establishment survey on working time 2004–2005. Retrieved January 17, 2013, from http://www.eurofound.europa.eu/pubdocs/2006/27/en/1/ef0627en.pdf

Faist, T. (2001). Social citizenship in European Union. Nested membership. *Journal of Common Market Studies, 39*(1), 36–60.

Geissler, B., & Pfau-Effinger, B. (2005). Change in European care arrangements. In B. Pfau-Effinger & B. Geissler (Eds.), *Care and social integration in European societies. Variations and change* (pp. 3–19). Bristol: The Policy Press.

Glenn, E. N. (1992). From servitude to service work: Historical continuities in the racial division of paid. Reproductive labor. *Signs, 18*(1), 1–43.

Glenn, E. N. (2010). *Forced to care. Coercion and caregiving in America*. Harvard: Harvard University Press.

Goñalons-Pons, P. (2015). Gender and class housework inequalities in the era of outsourcing. *Social Sciences Research, 52*, 208–218.

Gordon, M. (1964). *Assimilation in American life*. New York: Oxford University Press.

Gottschall, K., & Schwarzkopf, M. (2010). Irreguläre Arbeit in Privathaushalten. Rechtliche und institutionelle Anreize zu irregulärer Arbeit in Privathaushalten in Deutschland. In *Bestandaufnahme und Lösungsansätze*. Düsseldorf: Hans-Böckler-Stiftung. Retrieved September 29, 2012, from http://www.boeckler.de/pdf/p_arbp_217.pdf

Grunow, D. (2007). Wandel der Geschlechterrollen und Väterhandeln im Alltag. In T. Mühling & H. Rost (Eds.), *Väter im Blickpunkt. Perspektiven der Familienforschung* (pp. 49–76). Opladen and Farmington Hills: Budrich.

Hearn, J. (2009). Patriarchies, transpatriarchies, and intersectionalities. In E. H. Oleksy (Ed.), *Intimate citizenships. Gender, sexualities, politics*. New York and London: Routledge.

Hirschauer, S. (2013). Geschlechts(in)differenz in geschlechts(un)gleichen Paaren. *Special Issue of Gender Zeitschrift für Geschlecht, Kultur und Gesellschaft, 2*, 37–56.

ILO—International Labour Organization. (2013). Domestic workers across the world. Global and regional statistics and the extent of legal protection. Retrieved January 17, 2013, from http://www.ilo.org/wcmsp5/groups/public/—dgreports/---dcomm/---publ/documents/publication/wcms_173363.pdf

Institut der deutschen Wirtschaft Köln (IWK). (2009). Arbeitsplatz Privathaushalt. Ein Weg aus der Schwarzarbeit. Pressekonferenz, Berlin, February 24. Retrieved May 24, 2012, from http://tinyurl.com/ckfn4hr

Kalwa, D. (2007). "So wie zu Hause". Die private Sphäre als Arbeitsplatz. In M. Nowicka (Ed.), *Von Polen nach Deutschland und zurück. Die*

Arbeitsmigration und ihre Herausforderungen für Europa (pp. 205–226). Bielefeld: Transcript.

Kilkey, M., & Palenga-Möllenbeck, E. (2013). Fathers' time-bind and the outsourcing of "male" domestic work in Europe: The cases of UK and Germany. *Journal of International and Comparative Social Policy, 29*(2), 109–121.

Kilkey, M., & Perrons, D. (2010). Gendered divisions in domestic-work time: The rise of he (migrant) handyman phenomenon. *Time and Society, 19*(1), 1–26.

Kilkey, M., Perrons, D., & Plomien, A. (2013). *Masculinities, male labour and fathering in the UK and USA*. Basingstoke: Palgrave Macmillan.

Kindler, M., & Kordasiewicz, A. (2015). Maid-of-all-work or professional nanny? The changing character of domestic work in polish households, XVIII–XXI c. In D. Hoerder, E. van Nederveen, & S. Neusinger (Eds.), *Towards a global history of domestic and caregiving workers*. Leiden: Brill.

Kivisto, P., & Faist, T. (2007). *Citizenship: Theory, discourse and transnational prospects*. Oxford: Blackwell.

Lewis, J. (2009). *Work-family balance, gender and policy*. Cheltenham: Edward Elgar.

Lister, R. (2003). *Citizenship. Feminist perspectives* (2nd ed.). Basingstoke: Palgrave.

Lutz, H. (2011). *The new maids. Transnational women and the care economy*. London: Zed Books.

Lutz, H., & Palenga-Möllenbeck, E. (2012). Care work, care drain and care chains: Reflections on care, migration and citizenship. *Special Issue of Social Politics, 19*, 15–37.

Madianou, M., & Miller, D. (2011). Mobile phone parenting: Reconfiguring relationships between Filipina migrant mothers and their left-behind children. *New Media & Society, 13*, 457–470.

Marshall, T. H. (1964). *Class, citizenship and social development*. Garden City and New York: Doubleday.

Meuser, M. (2010). Geschlecht, Macht, Männlichkeit—Strukturwandel von Erwerbsarbeit und hegemonialer Männlichkeit. Erwägen, Wissen, Ethik (EWE), 21(3), 325–336.

Meuser, M. (2014). Care und Männlichkeit in modernen Gesellschaften— Grundlegende Überlegungen illustriert am Beispiel involvierter Vaterschaft. *Special Issue of Soziale Welt, 20*, 159–174.

Minssen, H. (2006). *Arbeits- und Industriesoziologie. Eine Einführung*. Frankfurt and New York: Campus Verlag.

Miranda, V. (2011). Cooking, caring and volunteering: Unpaid work around the world, OECD social, employment and migration. *Working Papers* 116. Retrieved September 27, 2012, from http://www.oecd.org/els/workingpapers

Myant, M., & Drahokoupil, J. (2011). *Transition economies: Political economy in Russia, Eastern Europe, and Central Asia*. Hoboken: John Wiley and Sons.

Nail, G. (2004). *Transformation of the welfare state: The silent surrender of public responsibility*. New York: Oxford University Press.

Näre, L. M. (2010). Sri Lankan men working as cleaners and carers: Negotiating masculinity in Naples. *Men and Masculinities, 13*(1), 65–86.

Paap, K. (2006). *Working construction: Why white working-class men put themselves—And the labor movement—In harm's way*. Ithaca, NY and London: Cornell University Press.

Palenga-Möllenbeck, E. (2013a). New maids—New butlers? Polish domestic workers in Germany and commodification of social reproductive work. In B. Aulenbacher & C. Innreiter-Moser (Eds.), *Making the difference—Critical perspectives on the configuration of work, diversity and inequalities*. Special issue of *Equality, Diversity and Inclusion: An International Journal, 32*(6), 557–574.

Palenga-Möllenbeck, E. (2013b). Care chains in Eastern and Central Europe: Male and female domestic work at intersections of gender, class and ethnicity. In A. Triandafyllidou & S. Marchetti (Eds.), *Migrant domestic and care workers in Europe: New patterns of circulation?* Special issue of *Journal of Immigrant and Refugee Studies, 11*(4), 364–383.

Palenga-Möllenbeck, E. (2014). *Pendelmigration aus Oberschlesien. Lebensgeschichten in einer transnationalen Region Europas*. Bielefeld: Transcript Verlag.

Palenga-Möllenbeck, E., & Lutz, H. (2016, forthcoming). Fatherhood and masculinities in post socialist Europe: The challenges of transnational migration. In M. Kilkey & E. Palenga-Möllenbeck (Eds.), *Family life in an age of migration and mobility: Global perspectives through the life course*. Houndsmills, Basinstoke, Hampshire: Palgrave Macmillan.

Plomien, A. (2009). Welfare state, gender, and reconciliation of work and family in Poland. Policy developments and practice in a new EU member. *Social Policy & Administration, 43*, 136–151.

Plummer, K. (2003). *Intimate citizenship: Private decisions and public dialogues*. Seattle: University of Washington Press.

Portet, S. (2007). Elastyczność zatrudnienia w Polsce, czyli o odkrywaniu rzeczy zakrytych. In M. Marody (Ed.), *Wymiary życia społecznego. Polska na przełomie*

XX und XXI wieku (pp. 116–137). Warszawa: Wydawnictwo Naukowe Scholar.

Rottenberg, C. (2014). The rise of neoliberal feminism. *Cultural Studies, 28*(3), 418–437.

Sarti, R. and Scrinzi, F. (2010). Men in women's job, male domestic workers, international migration and the globalisation of care. Special issue of *Men and Masculinities*, 13 (4).

Sassen, S. (2001). *The global city. New York, London, Tokyo.* Princeton, NJ: Princeton University Press.

Schupp, J., Spieß, C. K., & Wagner, G. G. (2006). Beschäftigungspotenziale in privaten Haushalten nicht überschätzen: Förderung und Ausbau familienbezogener Dienste sollte nicht in erster Linie ein arbeitsmarktpolitisches Instrument sein. In *Wochenbericht des DIW Berlin*, 4/2006 (pp. 45–52). Retrieved September 29, 2012, from http://www.diw.de/documents/publikationen/73/43982/06-4-1.pdf

Sikorska, M. (Ed.) (2009). *Być rodzicem we współczesnej Polsce. Nowe wzory w konfrontacji z rzeczywistością.* Warszawa: Wydawnictwa Uniwersytetu Warszawskiego.

Soysal, Y. N. (1994). *Limits of citizenship: Migrants and postnational membership in Europe.* Chicago: University of Chicago Press.

Sullivan, O., Coltrane, S., Mc Annally, L., & Altintas, E. (2009). Father-friendly policies and time-use data in a cross-national context: Potential and prospects for future research. *The Annals of the American Academy of Political and Social Science, 624*(1), 234–254.

Szelewa, D., & Polakowski, M. P. (2008). Who cares? Changing patterns of childcare in Central and Eastern Europe. *Journal of European Social Policy, 18*(2), 115–131.

Traba, L. (2008). *Haushaltsnahe Dienstleistungen in Hessen. Modul 1: Empirische Ermittlung des Bedarfs an haushaltsnahen Dienstleistungen.* Report No. 721. Wiesbaden: Hessen Agentur.

Triandafyllidou, A., & Marchetti, S. (Eds.) (2015). *Employers, agencies and immigration: Paying for care.* Surrey: Ashgate.

Van Walsum, S. (2013). Labour, legality and shifts in the public/private divide. *International Migration, 51*(6), 86–100.

Wetterer, A. (2005). Rhetorische Modernisierung und institutionelle Reflexivität: Die Diskrepanz zwischen Alltagswissen und Alltagspraxis in arbeitsteiligen Geschlechterarrangements. *Freiburger Frauenstudien. Zeitschrift für Interdisziplinäre Geschlechterforschung, Arbeit und Geschlecht, 11*(16), 75–96.

11

Buying and Selling Gender Equality: Concluding Reflections

Guro Korsnes Kristensen, Berit Gullikstad, and Priscilla Ringrose

The main aim of this book has been to contribute to existing scholarship on paid migrant domestic labour in various European contexts, explored through the concepts of gender equality and citizenship. It has also been an explicit aim to draw on the volume's multifaceted research material, with the complex intersections of gender, nationality/ethnicity/'race' and social class it brings to play, in order to cast a critical light on the political and cultural discourses of gender equality and citizenship unfolding in the different localised European contexts studied.

G.K. Kristensen (✉) • B. Gullikstad
Department of Interdisciplinary Studies of Culture, Centre for Gender Studies, Norwegian University of Science and Technology (NTNU), Trondheim, Norway

P. Ringrose
Department of Interdisciplinary Studies of Culture and Department of Language and Literature, Centre for Gender Studies, Norwegian University of Science and Technology (NTNU), Trondheim, Norway

© The Editor(s) (if applicable) and The Author(s) 2016
B. Gullikstad et al. (eds.), *Paid Migrant Domestic Labour in a Changing Europe*, DOI 10.1057/978-1-137-51742-5_11

The chapters in this book have documented a rich variety of contexts of domestic labour which illustrate some of the complexities involved when a highly gendered and classed form of labour becomes increasingly ethnicised as a result of international migration. In analysing these contexts, the contributors have adopted a contextualised and historicised approach by identifying local particularities, with reference to the organisation of domestic labour, the meanings that are attached to it, the relations that are produced when this form of work is outsourced, and the effects of both buying and selling have on both the perceptions and the 'doings' of gender equality and citizenship. The chapters have moreover demonstrated that while these phenomena are constituted in different ways, they bring to bear similar processes of minoritising and majoritising.

In the following, we discuss and synthesise the analyses presented in the chapters, and elaborate on what we consider to be the most important findings, both as regards to the European context and to ongoing theoretical discussions on gender equality and citizenship.

The European Context

The book's context is a changing Europe, where the steady rise in paid domestic labour is challenging the central values of citizenship and gender equality on the one hand, but also opening up a space for negotiating them on the other.

When paid migrant domestic labour, gender equality and citizenship are constituted in different localised ways, the forms they take on are, at least in part, shaped by the policies of migration, welfare and gender regimes. While in Spain, and to a lesser extent in Italy and in the UK, specific policies have been instigated to encourage migrant women to take on domestic and care work in private homes, this has not been the case in other countries, such as the Netherlands and Norway. While most Western European countries have opened up for a variety of tax relief initiatives and cash benefits for certain welfare services related to child, eldercare or other forms of dependent care, in Norway, there are few such systems in operation. And as far as gender regimes are concerned, the Nordic countries have focused on policies which have encouraged and

11 Buying and Selling Gender Equality: Concluding Reflections ...

led to a high participation of women in the labour force and to a higher birth rate compared to other countries in Western Europe.

At the same time, the contributions in this volume show that both policy development and cultural meaning making around paid migrant domestic work, gender equality and citizenship are characterised by widespread neoliberal thinking. While welfare services (benefits relating to childcare, care of the elderly and the disabled) are much more developed than they were 20 or 30 years ago, Europe has witnessed a trend towards the deregulation and the privatisation of these very same services. Finland is a good example of this trend, with public eldercare being increasingly performed by private actors, and where the tax system encourages the buying of both care and domestic labour services on private markets (Näre, Chap. 2). Another trend related to neoliberal processes concerns the deregulation of working life, which means that workers are expected to be more flexible as regards working hours and tasks, implying less economic security. This, combined with the free movement of workers in European Union (EU)/European Economic Area (EEA) countries, has led to large privatised markets which are largely unregulated.

In the UK, for example, the au pair sector is effectively a 'grey' market, which is protected neither by any specific regulation relating to au pairs nor by any general regulations related to domestic work (Cox and Busch, Chap. 5). Another example of this kind of 'grey' zone is found in Germany, where many male Polish workers provide domestic services on the German market in a self-employed capacity as 'handymen', within a sector characterised by a high level of informal labour and by a lack of state regulation (Palenga-Möllenbeck, Chap. 10).

Another feature of the neoliberal turn which the book has brought to light is the way in which the buying and selling of paid migrant domestic labour is perceived as a win–win situation. This is true of political argumentation, in popular culture and also amongst the buyers and sellers of paid domestic work. What is particular to this win–win narrative when related to the institution and practice of paid migrant domestic labour is that both those who are buying and those who are performing these services perceive the arrangement as positive. As such, there is a (false) understanding that the employer–employee relation is equal and symmetrical, and of mutual benefit to both buyers and sellers. Such an understanding of domestic labour is not only neoliberal, but also neocolonial, in that it is based on the presumption that the other, in this case the (often racialised) migrant domestic worker, is oppressed and needs 'help' from his or her benevolent employer. As several of the contributions show, the win–win narrative can be very concrete, for example, when buyers of cheap and badly organised cleaning and au pair services defend their decision to employ domestic workers not only by pointing to the benefits which are accrued to them, but also by citing the economic and symbolic advantages which the *sellers* get out of the 'bargain' (Kristensen, Chap. 8). But the perception that domestic labour is positive for the workers can also be more implicit, such as when the relations between buyers and sellers are subsumed under the rubric of friends and family, and when the benefits to the employer are expressed in terms which communicate that their 'generosity' makes them 'feel good', when in fact they are simply purchasing services which they in fact want and feel they need (Stubberud, Chap. 6; Marchetti, Chap. 7). The idea of a win–win situation can also hover below the surfaces as exemplified in the touching sentiments of bonding, expressed in the intimate relationship which develops between the wealthy white disabled man and his migrant/black care worker in the movie *The Intouchables* (Ringrose, Chap. 9).

The consequences of this win–win rhetoric is that asymmetries associated with gender, class, ethnicity/'race', age, disability and sexuality are unproblematised and made invisible, just as much in politics as in everyday life. This means, for example, that Norwegian au pair policy, with its emphasis on cultural exchange, can come across as inclusive because it does not *appear* to refer to services which are associated with inequalities based on gender, class and ethnicity (Gullikstad and Annfelt, Chap. 3). Similarly, the French understanding of citizenship is maintained despite the fact that in practice it covers up dissensions of class and 'race' (Ringrose, Chap. 9).

To summarise, the chapters in this book have shown that neoliberal politics, with its fervour for privatising welfare services and deregulating the labour market have made it more difficult, especially for women both in the global North and South, to combine care work with economic independence, and inclusive citizenship, thus opening up for the privatisation of the domestic sphere. Moreover, as many of the contributions show, a combination of privatisation and deregulation, and of neoliberal and neocolonial thinking, contributes towards making the problematic use of vulnerable migrants not only possible but acceptable, while effectively undermining the ideal of equality which is central to the concept of citizenship.

The Making of the Gender-Equal Citizen

This volume contributes to exploring a central paradox relating to paid migrant domestic labour. While this form of labour is a practice which is imbricated in the strong cultural and political focus on gender equality, it is also posing a serious challenge to that very focus. In other words, paid migrant domestic labour produces certain effects which undermine the ideals of gender equality.

As several of the contributors point out, the institution of paid migrant domestic labour is often perceived as facilitating the implementation of the dual *earner* part of the gender equality ideal—for both buyers and sellers. As such, it is seen to increase both ethnic nationals' and migrant women's access to formal and informal citizenship. This kind of understanding of paid migrant domestic labour is particularly evident in recent policy development. Most Western welfare states have been moving towards a new set of assumptions about the contributions that men and women make to families, based on the 'adult worker model' (Lister et al., 2007). This model, in theory, and to an extent in practice, signals a movement away from the traditional male breadwinner model, and towards 'greater symmetry in male and female roles and lifestyles' (Pfau-Effinger, 2005, p. 338).

The relation between the adult worker model and paid domestic labour is illustrated in Peterson's study of the gendered framings of work and care in policies relating to social citizenship in Spain. In the Spanish policy document aimed at 'reconciling work and family life', middle-class women's participation in paid work is represented as leading to gender equality. At the same time, since suitable welfare provision for child and eldercare and care for dependants has not been made available in Spain, such thinking implies a tacit condoning of low-paid and unregulated domestic work (Chap. 4).

Several chapters have also pointed to the fact that the adult worker model, with its ambitions to foster gender equality, is associated not only with the buyers of private domestic and care work, but also to the sellers, namely to migrant workers, who via this type of work are supposed to become independent citizens. This type of thinking is also commented on in Näre's chapter on neoliberal citizenship and domestic service in Finland, where policies start from the presumption that the privatisation of domestic and care services provides migrants (mostly women) with the opportunity of working, and of achieving economic independence, and gender equality (Chap. 2).

One variation of the adult worker model is 'the dual earner/carer model', a policy adopted in the Nordic countries and also to a greater or lesser extent in other European countries. The concept of the 'dual earner/ dual carer model' captures a certain ambition of gender equality, where women's participation in working life goes hand in hand with men's participation in family life (Ellingsæter, 2014). Just as with the 'adult worker model', the 'dual earner/carer model' can also be linked to the increased prevalence of paid migrant domestic labour, since when both men and women work, someone (usually a migrant woman) 'has' to perform the household tasks. The relation between the 'dual earner/carer model' and paid domestic work is interrogated in Gullikstad and Annfelt's study of the political regulation of the Norwegian au pair scheme. They show that by still clinging to au pairing as cultural exchange rather than regulating it as the 'proper work', these policies usefully mask what is, in effect in the Norwegian context, a form of culturally unacceptable 'servanthood'. This means that paid work for ethnic Norwegian women is considered so important that other inequalities are simply tacitly accepted as 'the price to be paid' (Chap. 3). In line with this, Kristensen's study of Norwegian employers of domestic services shows that the 'adult worker model' is so naturalised amongst middle-class citizens that it can be used to justify inequality along the axes of social class and nationality/ethnicity/'race'. At the same time, the interviews with employers in this same study show that the empowering dimensions of this kind of labour for domestic labourers (for example, enabling them to be the main provider in their own families) helps to mitigate the discomfort many employers may feel about outsourcing this type of work (Chap. 8).

These findings support the idea that gender equality—at least when understood as paid work for women—is perceived as an essential part of being a good citizen. By this, we mean that paid work has in effect become an important part of 'good citizenship' in contemporary Europe—both for the majority and for minorities. In other words, paid work is prioritised both when it comes to gender equality and as far as citizenship is concerned.

Majoritising and Minoritising Processes

As mentioned, this volume points to a nuanced and complex picture of the relation between paid migrant domestic labour and gender equality, and does not view this type of work as simply facilitating the cultural values, norms and political goals of gender equality. Moreover, just as the increased focus on gender equality has in many ways made way for *more* paid migrant domestic labour, the increased outsourcing of this highly gendered and classed work to other women, many of whom are migrants, raises questions about what 'good' gender equality is or is not, and about who has the 'right' to be or not to be gender equal.

A related effect of the return to a servant culture is the reproduction of the gendered dimension of domestic work. This concerns both care and domestic work which are traditionally perceived as feminised tasks, and traditionally masculinised household tasks such as repairs and garden work. But while the 'adult worker model' and the 'dual earner/dual carer model' can be read as attempts to transcend the traditional division of labour and gender stereotypes in working life, paid domestic work is moving in the opposite direction. For even though it is no longer wives and mothers who are doing most or all of the household tasks, or husbands and fathers who are doing most or all the repair and gardening work, these tasks are still highly gendered and the stereotypical divisions of labour still hold strong. In practice this means that gender equality is regressing.

This re-gendering or re-establishment of gendered stereotypes can also be identified in national policies, as is the case in Spain, where, as Peterson shows, care work is described in such a way that it is evidently naturalised as feminised (Chap. 4). Such gendered perspectives are also identified in the chapters focusing on buyers, who appear to take for granted that care workers and housekeepers are women and repair workers are men. Moreover, as Ringrose's analysis of the film *The Intouchables* shows, while men too can undertake care work, they often consider feminised tasks to be 'unnatural' and 'beneath their dignity' (Chap. 9).

Another point, which the volume draws attention to, is that gender, social class and ethnicity/nationality and 'race' intersect in paid domestic labour, and produce and reproduce hierarchies. Several chapters look at how the interplay between paid migrant domestic labour, gender equality and citizenship implies some kind of complying with colonialism. As an example of this, Gullikstad and Annfelt show that one effect of Norwegian au pair policy is to make au pairs 'invisible,' in the sense that there is no acknowledgement of this type of work as being proper work which should be paid. As such, au pairs are placed in a different category from 'Norwegian gender-equal women', who are expected to be economically independent. In other words, au pairs from the Global South are produced as 'the other' (Chap. 3). Another way of expressing this intersection of gender, social class and ethnicity/nationality and 'race' is to say that the unequal and unregulated field of paid migrant domestic labour and the discourses of gender equality and citizenship contribute to the majoritising of ethnic European employers and to the minoritising of migrant domestic workers. An example of these majoritising and minoritising processes can be found in Palenga-Möllenbeck's study of how fatherhood is 'done' by Polish handymen and their German employers. While the German employers outsource domestic tasks in order to have the opportunity to be present fathers, and as such to conform to the ideal of the good citizen (and are thus majoritised), the Polish fathers, who are also carers but who do not have the opportunity to be present fathers for their children, are minoritised (Chap. 10).

A final point which this volume brings to light is that care work, and especially housework, as an essential and widespread form of work, has become even more 'invisible' as a result of these minoritising processes.

11 Buying and Selling Gender Equality: Concluding Reflections ... 253

This kind of labour, largely thought of as 'dirty work' as Bridget Anderson termed it (2000), is considered by the buyers as clearly less valuable than other paid work, while at the same time contributing to maintaining the norms and standards of what is perceived as a successful middle-class lifestyle (Kristensen, Chap. 8). This means that paid housework in the form of au pairing escapes regulation (Cox and Busch, Chap. 5), that it is politically legitimate to operate with weaker social and labour protection than other kinds of work (Peterson, Chap. 4), and that it can evade the realm of policy, as in the Norwegian case (Gullikstad and Annfelt, Chap. 3). Introducing a tax refund scheme as in Finland nevertheless contributes towards making domestic work more visible, yet this does not mean that domestic work becomes the responsibility of the state (Näre, Chap. 2).

Agency and Negotiations

As we have seen, several of the book's contributions show that the field of paid migrant domestic labour is characterised by a whole set of problematic relations concerning working conditions, and migrants' position in their employers' homes and in wider society. They point to an increase in social, economic and relational inequalities, as well as to wider minoritising processes impacting on migrants' lived experiences and structural conditions, contributing to limited forms of citizenship. However, by including migrants' own perspectives on paid domestic labour, the volume has also demonstrated that such circumstances do not mean that migrants are passive victims. They should rather be viewed as active agents who are negotiating their positions in everyday life and looking to a better future, both in the countries where they are working and in their countries of origin.

Several chapters point to the fact that migrant domestic workers can negotiate their citizenship status in a variety of potentially empowering ways, for example, via intimate relations of mutual dependency with their employers, or with their romantic interests or partners, as demonstrated in Stubberud's chapter on au pairs in Norway (Chap. 6). Similarly, Marchetti (Chap. 7) shows how maternalistic relations between employers and employees can lead to the employers helping their employees with legal and bureaucratic challenges, such as applying for family reunification. However, as both Stubberud and Marchetti emphasise, while such tight bonds between employers and employees (sometimes expressed through the use of family metaphors) might be a way for migrant workers to avoid certain forms of exploitation, these types of relations are nevertheless asymmetrical, with the worker positioned as minoritised.

The 'helpful' and at times invasive attitudes at work in these maternalist and familial relations charted in Marchetti and Stubberud's chapters are mirrored in the approach of other buyers, as well as in that of authorities and policymakers, which are commonly characterised by good intentions and the perception that they are protecting domestic workers from violence and exploitation. This kind of attitude is identified in Gullikstad and Annfelt's analyses of Norwegian policy and media debates on the au pair scheme, where they point to the 2013 Norwegian Parliament's statutory provision which allows for the punishment of families who abuse the au pair scheme by temporarily disqualifying or banning them from hosting au pairs (Chap. 3).

Buyers, in contrast to migrant sellers, are (more) safely positioned within the nation state, not only as citizens but also as *good* citizens. This positioning is in part made possible by the migrant workers, who enable buyers to perceive themselves as 'helpers'. For despite engaging in unequal relationships and profiting both economically and socially from migrants' limited possibilities to resist their non-regular and exploitative working conditions, buyers come across as friendly helpers. We see this in stories of employers who offer their employees a whole string of opportunities; the possibility of conforming to the adult worker model, economic empowerment, facilitating their children's schooling, giving them greater self-confidence, freeing them from the limits of their gendered and classed positions and from the unfavourable life conditions in their homeland. Many employers directly claim that they make deliberate choices in the interests of their workers. A telling example of this can be found in Palenga-Möllenbeck's chapter on Polish handymen and their German employers, where one employer claims that he chooses to pay his Polish handyman to perform tasks which he could easily have undertaken himself, not only because he could afford this but also because the handyman needed the money (Chap. 10).

11 Buying and Selling Gender Equality: Concluding Reflections ...   255

As demonstrated in several chapters in this book, narratives of good intentions among employers can be interpreted as explanations which are used to justify the unequal relationships between employers and their domestic workers. However, the book also points to several examples where it is clear that in addition to the marginalisation at work, there is also a foundation for agency and empowerment enabling migrants to potentially access more secure forms of citizenship. This foundation, however, is mainly produced legislatively and structurally, rather than interpersonally. As such, paid migrant domestic labour is simultaneously producing both exploitation and empowerment, but it is up to policy makers to take responsibility for the inequalities that disproportionally affect migrant domestic workers.

Commonalities and Complexities: Localised Contexts and Global Challenges

As this book has shown, the phenomenon of paid migrant domestic labour is global in its geographical reach, in its production of particular kinds of migrants and in its transformation of transnational relations. At the same time, this type of labour takes place in local contexts and is influenced by national policies and a range of cultural ideals and practices in both sending and receiving countries. An important objective of the volume has been to investigate these localised contexts, using a wide set of approaches. Some chapters have investigated the ways in which different migration, welfare and gender regimes combine to produce employers and employees as very different types of citizens. Other chapters have explored the complexities of lived life both among and between buyers and sellers, in the light of cultural values, national policies and transnational exchanges of people, services and ideas.

By combining this empirical focus with a theoretically informed curiosity as regards to the concepts of gender equality and citizenship, the book as a whole has been able to identify national variations, as well as European commonalities. We have also been able to pinpoint important similarities between different national and cultural contexts, for example, in the ways in which policies, values and practices regarding gender equality and citizenship are produced and made legitimate, how they contribute to majoritising and minoritising processes, how these processes are negotiated, and—on the micro level—how they point to the ways in which agency is enacted.

Another important finding from the book, which draws on both the empirical results and the theoretically informed analyses, is that the phenomenon of paid migrant domestic labour needs to be understood in relation to political, social and economic processes. These processes 'transcend the boundaries of national states' and as such 'lie inside and beneath, as well as outside and beyond, national boundaries: in local, regional, international and transnational arenas and on various global levels' (Gingrich & Fox, 2002). By this we mean that the collection facilitates an exchange of ideas between thematic areas, which engage a variety of global, national and local processes. At the same time, the empirical and theoretical investigations also provide the opportunity to develop an exchange of ideas between different contexts with regard to the production of new equalities and inequalities at the intersections of gender, social class, nationality, ethnicity and 'race', and in this way open up for less minoritising, more secure forms of citizenship and a more gender-equal Europe for everyone.

References

Anderson, B. (2000). *Doing the dirty work. The global politics of domestic labour.* London and New York: Zed Books.
Ellingsæter, A. L. (2014). Nordic earner-carer models—Why stability and instability? *Journal of Social Policy, 43*(3), 555–574.
Gingrich, A., & Fox, R. G. (2002). *Anthropology, by comparison.* Oxon/New York: Routledge.
Lister, R., Williams, F., Anttonen, A., Bussemaker, J., Gerhard, U., Heinen, J., et al. (2007). *Gendering citizenship in Western Europe: New challenges for citizenship research in a cross-national context.* Bristol: PolicyPress.
Pfau-Effinger, B. (2005). Welfare state policies and the development of care arrangements. *European Societies, 7*(2), 321–347.

Index

A
Aalto, K., 40
Aarseth, H., 171
Abrantes, M., 38
abuse, 56, 69, 113, 143, 164, 254
acculturation, 205
Act for Effective Equality between
    Woman and Men (Spain), 93
Agrela Romero, B., 82
Alberge, D., 195
Alsop, R., 207
Alsos, K., 172
Anderson, B., 3–6, 10, 31, 33, 35,
    60, 102, 104, 106, 108,
    110, 113–14, 126, 149,
    151, 154, 209, 253
Annfelt, T., xiii, 8, 11, 16, 38,
    55–74, 93, 106, 128, 173,
    175, 184, 248, 250, 252–4
Anthias, F., 3, 60, 68
Arbeidsliv i Norden, 66, 69, 73

Ashcroft, B., 205
assimilation
    citizenship and, 22, 196–7, 201,
        213
    colonialism and, 202
    family and, 199
    French culture and, 196–7, 200, 205
    marriage and, 133
    masculinity and, 8, 197
au pair scheme, 6, 11, 13, 16–17,
    20, 55–74, 104, 107, 111,
    115, 118, 125–30, 142–3,
    173, 250, 253–4
au pairs, Norway
    analyzing cultural narratives of
        intimacy, 131–41
    citizenship, 127–8
    cultural exchange
        preventing servitude, 68–70
        as restricted gendered
            migration regime, 65–8

au pairs, Norway (*cont.*)
  formal citizenship, 128
  gender equality and citizenship, 58–60
  heterosexuality and, 130–1
  informal citizenship, 128–9, 139–42
  intimate citizenship, 129–31
  limits of belonging, 137–9
  loophole strengthening gendered citizenship, 70–4
  marrying "Dad", 134–7
  overview, 55–7, 125–7
  promising intimacy, 142–4
  queering independence, 132–4
  representations of au pair category, 62–5
  research methodology on, 60–1
  See also domestic service, Finland
au pairs, UK
  citizenship, gender, and domestic work, 105–7
  deregulation of, 107–9
  differences in home countries, 114–19
  equality and, 109
  nationality and, 110–14
  overview, 101–3
  research, 103–4

B

Bacchi, C., 8, 61, 81–3
Bakan, A., 33, 110
Balibar, É., 196–7, 199, 201
Barker, D., 93
Bauböck, R., 10, 152
Bauder, H., 128–9, 141
bayani, 156, 163–4

belonging
  au pairs and, 102, 128, 130
  citizenship and, 9–10, 19, 128, 130, 141
  domestic service and, 34–8
  intimacy and, 131, 142
  limits of, 137–9
  maternalism and, 150
  race and, 199
  sexuality and, 93, 126
  women and, 93
Benhabib, S., 10, 57
Bereswill, M., 224, 233
Berg, A.-J., 170–1
Berlant, L., 130, 144, 197, 199
Berry, J. W., 205–6
Bettio, F., 82
Bhambra, G., 32
Bikova, M., 3, 32, 55, 73, 173–5
Bird, S.R., 196
Boltanski, L., 42
Bosniak, L., 10–11, 35, 57, 59–60, 63, 128, 151, 174–5, 188, 190
Bourdieu, P., 128, 204, 233
Brah, A., 12–13
Brandth, B., 170–1
Bregin, D., 235
Brodin, H., 83
Brown, W., 36–7
Búriková, Z., 133
Busch, N., xiii, 13, 17–18, 57, 101–20, 222, 247, 253
Butler, J., 126

C

Calleman, C., 4, 15, 56, 69, 73
Carling, J., 60, 63–5
Cho, S., 7

Chow, R., 136
Christensen, H.R., 8
Chustecka, M., 234–5
Cingano, F., 33
citizenship
  agency in, 139–41
  assimilation and, 22, 196–7, 201, 213
  au pairs and, 19, 128–30, 139–42, 187–8
  belonging and, 9–10, 19, 128, 130, 137, 141
  care work and, 81–2
  defined, 127–8
  "denizen" concept, 10
  domestic work and, 83–95, 105–7
  families and, 19–20
  formal, 10, 13, 18, 59–60, 102, 105–7, 109, 111, 114, 120, 126–31, 222
  gender and, 14, 45–8, 55–74, 81–2, 101–20, 170
  informal, 125–31, 133–4, 139–41, 144
  intimate, 13, 126, 129
  intimate relations and, 125–44
  Intouchables and, 196–7, 200–1, 205, 210–13
  marketisation of, 34–8
  masculinity and, 217–38
  maternalism and, 147–65
  migrants and, 151–4, 174–6, 190
  neoliberal, 16, 32–50
  non-citizenship, 10
  Norway and, 55–74, 189–90
  paid domestic work and, 83–95, 174–6

partial, 10, 20, 60, 73, 152–4, 161–5, 196
policy and, 58–60
sexual, 210–12
social, 79–96
Spain and, 79–96
tax credit debate and, 42–5
women and, 175, 183, 249
Clarke, J., 37
colonialism, 3, 22, 33, 57, 71–2, 196, 201–2, 205–6, 213, 248–9, 252
Connell, R. 225–8, 236
Constable, N., 107, 151
Coser, L., 31, 49
Cox, R., xiv, 3–4, 7, 13, 17–18, 31, 56–7, 63, 74, 101–20, 143, 149, 217, 222, 247, 253
cultural exchange
  preventing servitude, 68–70
  as restricted gendered migration regime, 65–8

D

Daniel, J., 202
Danielsen, H., 170
Davis, K., 7
"denizen" concept, 10
Dependent Care Act (Spain), 80, 89–92
de-sexualization, 143. *See also* sexuality
Directorate of Immigration (UDI), 61, 64–8
dirty work, 6, 209, 253
disability
  dependent care and, 89, 91
  homosociality and, 210

disability (*cont.*)
  Intouchables and, 21–2, 195,
    206–8, 210–13, 248
  masculinity and, 207
  sexuality and, 197, 210–12, 248
  welfare and, 247
Dobrowolsky, A., 8–10
Dollinger, F.-W., 222
domestic service
  citizenship and, 34–8, 83–95, 174–6
  Finland and, 31–48
  gendered neoliberal citizenship,
    45–8
  Germany and, 217–38
  Intouchables and, 195–213
  Italy and, 155, 158–61
  Netherlands and, 154–65
  Norway and, 55–74, 125–44,
    169–90
  overview, 31–4
  paid household services, 38–41
  Spain and, 79–96
  tax credit debate, 42–5
  UK and, 101–20
  See also au pairs
dual earner/dual carer model, 7, 11,
  16, 21, 32, 42, 46–7,
  56–59, 171–3, 180, 182,
  187, 189–90, 249–51
Duarte, C.M., 116
Duffy, M., 82
Dusseut, A., 197

E
education
  au pairs and, 16, 57, 62, 64, 68,
    116, 119, 142

domestic work and, 182
gender equality and, 224
neoliberalism and, 33–4, 36
taxes and, 40
Eggebø, H., 9, 128–30, 133
Ehrenreich, B., 225
Einarsdottir, T., 8
Ellingsæter, A.L., 11, 57, 171, 250
empowerment, 21, 174, 187,
  189–90, 218, 250, 253–5
Engel, D.M., 207
Esping-Andersen, G., 15, 38
ethnicity, 7, 12, 14, 23, 57, 72,
  82, 92–3, 103, 105, 110,
  148, 155, 200–1, 219–2,
  230–3, 237, 245–6,
  248–50, 252, 256
European agreement on au pairing
  1969, 16, 56, 62
European Council's Convention
  1969, 57, 61, 64, 73
European Economic Area (EEA),
  65–7, 173, 247
European Union (EU), 7, 15, 17–18,
  32, 38–9, 44, 49, 60, 65–7,
  101–2, 104, 173, 218,
  221–3, 238, 247
Eveline, J., 8
exploitation
  au pairs and, 56, 60, 67, 69, 109,
    113, 115, 120, 184–6
  domestic workers and, 6, 20–1,
    174, 198, 221
  immigrants and, 109, 113, 115,
    117, 190, 255
  Intouchables and, 196
  maternalism and, 149, 154, 254
  women and, 60, 67

F

Faist, T., 218, 222
Fernández Cordón, J.A., 94
Filipina migrant domestic workers
  citizenship and, 151–4
  maternalism and "family analogy", 149–51
  maternalism from employers' perspective, 154–8
  negotiations around gratitude in views of employees, 158–64
  overview, 147–8
Finland, 15–16, 31–50, 247, 250, 253
Fjell, T.I., 32
Fortier, A.-M., 22, 126, 139, 199–200, 204, 213
Fournier, V., 36
France, 18, 22, 84, 101, 110, 115, 196–8, 200–2, 206–7, 210, 213
Fraser, N., 37, 43, 48, 83, 87, 152
Friberg, J.H., 60, 68, 74, 172

G

García Sainz, C., 80
Gavanas, A., 4, 15, 32, 34, 40, 94
Geissler, B., 220
gender equality
  agency and negotiations, 253–5
  citizenship and, 6–11, 13, 58–60, 70–4, 135–6
  commonalities and complexities, 255–6
  domestic work and, 45–6, 48–9
  ethnic inclusion and, 57
  European context, 246–9
  Finland and, 42–3
  majoritising and minoritising processes, 251–3
  making of the gender-equal citizen, 249–51
  masculinity and, 217–19, 221, 224–6
  neoliberalism and, 34–8
  Norway and, 56–74, 169–90
  overview, 245–6
  policy and, 2–3, 57, 80–2
  regimes and, 14–15
  rights and, 84–9
  Spain and, 79–96
gender regimes, 58–60, 71, 188, 246, 255
Germany, 22–3, 103, 109, 111–12, 117–19, 217–26, 231–8, 247, 252, 254
Gingrich, A., 256
Glenn, E.N., 81, 220, 229
Goñalons-Pons, P., 225
Goodwin, S., 83
Gordon, M., 238
Gottschall, K., 219
Grossman, J.L., 7
Grunow, W., 224
Gullestad, M., 170, 172–3
Gullikstad, B., xiv, 1–23, 38, 55–74, 93, 106, 126, 128, 175, 184, 245–56
Gutierrez-Rodriguez, E., 151

H

Hagelund, A., 59
Häkkinen Skans, 40
Hall, T., 9, 151

Halrynjo, S., 171
Halsaa, B., 9–10, 33, 128
Hammar, T., 10
health care, 33, 153, 162
Hearn, J., 234
Henriksen, K., 64, 68
Hess, S., 56, 143
heterosexuality, 127, 130–1, 134, 136, 139, 176, 206–7, 210, 223. *See also* sexuality
Hiilamo, H., 39
Hindess, B., 36
Hirschauer, S., 228
Hochschild, A., 12, 198, 225
homosexuality, 130, 207. *See also* sexuality
homosociality, 13, 21–2, 195–213
Hondagneu-Sotelo, P., 106
household employment, 83–9
Household Employment Act (Spain), 80, 84–8, 92
Hovdan, M., 55

I

Ibañez, Z., 80, 91
Immigration Act (Norway), 61, 73
interviews
 au pairs, 101–146
 domestic workers, 45–7, 158–64, 176–9, 202–13, 227–38
 employers and, 154–8, 177–88
intimacy, cultural narratives of, 131
intimate citizenship, 13, 126, 129
Intouchables, The (film)
 background, 197–202
 from colonial chains to homosocial bonds, 202–13
 overview, 195–7

Isaksen, L. W., 3–4, 7, 12, 15, 31, 55, 70, 172
Isin, E.F., 9, 151–2
Islam/Muslims, 131, 137–9, 201–2
Italy, 5, 18, 20, 110, 151–5, 158, 162, 246

J

Jokela, M., 49
Joppke, C., 9, 152

K

Kalwa, D., 235
Kaplan, E., 150, 210
kennedy-macfoy, M., 9
Keskinen, S., 3, 71–2
Kiesling, S.F., 206–7
Kilkey, M., 3, 5, 217–18, 224–5, 227, 236
Kittay, E.F., 81
Kitterød, R., 171–2
Kivisto, P., 218, 222
Kluge, L., 69
Knijn, T., 81
Kristensen, G.K., xiv, 1–32, 38, 46, 94, 149, 169–90, 231, 245–56
Kvist, E., 11
Kymlicka, W., 9

L

Lan, P.C., 6, 147, 149, 151
Lawler, J., 209
Le Nouvel Obserateur, 202
León, M., 80, 84, 86, 91
Lessa, I., 83

Lewis, G., 8, 12–13, 53, 72, 199
Lewis, J., 223
Liarou, E., 107–8
Lister, R., 3, 7–11, 15, 33–5, 58–9,
    63, 71, 81, 84, 94, 128, 152,
    172, 175, 218, 223, 237–8,
    249
Løvdal, L., 55
Lutz, H., 3–4, 7, 31, 59, 110, 151,
    198, 220, 235

M
Määttä, A., 32
Macklin, A., 11, 174
Madianou, M., 237
male breadwinners, 23, 56, 58, 94,
    173, 187, 223–4, 228–37,
    249
Manalansan, M., 7
Marchetti, S., xiv–xv, 3–6, 13, 18,
    20, 31, 57, 133, 147–65,
    225, 248, 253–4
Markkula-Kivisilta, H., 42–3
Marshall, T.H., 9–10, 105, 223
Martínez Buján, R., 91
masculinity, domestic work and
    citizenship and, 217–38
    gender equality, 224–6
    overview, 217–19
    Polish handymen in German
        households, 219–21
    research on, 226
Massey, D.S., 109
maternalism
    belonging and, 150
    "family analogy" and, 149–51
    from employers' perspective, 154–8
McCall, L., 7

McClain, L.C., 7
Mellström, U., 207–8
Meuser, M., 226, 236
migrants/migration
    care work and, 44, 81–2
    citizenship and, 32–5, 59,
        102, 128–30, 151–4,
        174–6, 190
    Filipina workers, 137–65
    Finland and, 44
    gender and, 57, 59–60, 64, 67–8,
        81–2, 94, 96, 174–6, 249–51
    home care and, 41, 44
    inequality and, 49
    Intouchables and, 196–203
    invisibility of, 72
    masculinity and, 217–28, 231,
        233, 236–8
    migration policies, 106, 110
    Norway and, 59–60, 67–8, 169–90
    rights and, 84–6
    UK and, 102–20
Miller, D., 133
Minssen, H., 223
Miranda, V., 228
Misra, J., 33–4
Mohanty, C.T., 13
Morel, N., 15, 32, 39, 49
Moss, P., 11
Mundlak, G., 106, 113
Murphy, R.F., 207–8
Murray-West, R., 116
Myant, M., 223
Myhre, A.S., 172

N
Nail, G., 223
Narayan, U., 12

Näre, L., xv, 4–6, 10, 15–16, 31–50, 149, 170, 175, 197, 207, 217, 220, 247, 250, 253
Nentwich, J.C., 8
Netherlands, 18, 148, 151–4, 156–63, 246
"new butlers", 218, 221, 224, 227, 230–8
Nilssen, E., 58
Norway, 11, 13–14, 16–21, 49, 55–74, 93, 125–44, 169–90, 246, 248, 250, 252–4

O

O'Connor, J., 81
Øien, C., 55, 60, 128, 173
Organisation for Economic Co-operation and Development (OECD), 33, 44
Orloff, A.S., 81
Oso, L., 94
Ozyegin, G., 106

P

Paap, K., 236
paid domestic work, Norway
 ambivalence toward, 183–9
 background, 170–4
 gender equality and citizenship, 174–6
 overview, 169–70
 positive view of, 177–83
 research, 176–7
paid domestic work, Spain
 debates surrounding social citizenship, 82–3

dependent care, 89–92
gendered social citizenship and care work, 81–2
household employment, 83–9
overview, 79–80
reconciliation of work and family life, 92–5
Pajnik, M., 9
Palenga-Möllenbeck, E., xv, 3, 5, 11, 18, 22–3, 31, 88, 94, 217–38, 247, 252, 254
Parreñas, R., 4, 6, 10, 12, 60, 147, 149–53, 156
Pelechova, L., 174, 180
Pérez Orozco, A., 79
Peterson, E., xv–xvi, 8, 11, 17, 38, 79–96, 106, 249, 252–3
Pfau-Effinger, B., 220, 249
Phoenix, A., 177
Platzer, E., 32
Plomien, A., 3, 217, 223
Plummer, K., 126, 129, 237
Poland, 66, 107, 221–3, 234–6
Portet, S., 223
Predelli, L.N., 10–11
professionalisation, 220
Purkayvastha, B., 7

Q

queering independence, 132–4

R

race, 6–7, 12–13, 22–3, 57, 60, 71, 82, 93, 105, 195, 204, 213, 238, 245, 248–52, 258
racism, 138–9, 199, 204–5

Razavi, S., 82
Reconciliation Act (Spain), 92–3
regulation
  au pairs and, 57–8, 61–3, 65–7, 72, 102–3, 106, 170, 173, 183
  citizenship and, 128
  deregulation, 6, 18, 102–3, 106–9, 120, 223, 235, 238, 247–9
  domestic sphere and, 6, 12, 39, 50, 153
  gender and, 224
  household employment and, 83–4, 87–8, 95
  migration and, 13, 21, 57, 61, 74, 144, 158
  policy and, 80, 83–4, 87
  reunification and, 162
  unregulated arrangements, 4, 56, 249–50, 252–3
  sexuality and, 130–1
Ringrose, P., xvi, 1–23, 195–213, 245–56
Rivas, L.M., 198, 209
Rodríguez, G., 91
Rodriguez, R.M., 33
Rollins, J., 149–50, 158, 174
Rose, J., 197, 200, 206, 213
Roseneil, S., 9–10, 33, 128
Rothenberg, P., 147
Rottenberg C., 228
Roy, A., 105

S
Sainsbury, D., 82
Sam, David L., 205–6
Saraceno, C., 81
Sarti, R., 151, 217

Sassen, S., 34, 222
Schupp, J., 219
Scrinzi, F., 197–9, 207–8, 217
Serrano, A., 89, 91
servitude, avoiding, 68–70
sexuality
  de-sexualization, 143
  disability and, 197, 210–11, 248
  domestic work and, 130–1, 143, 223, 237
  family and, 9, 92–3, 126, 170–1
  gender and, 7
  homosociality and, 206
  nonsexual attractions, 196
  normativities, 210–11
  sameness and, 201
  See also heterosexuality; homosexuality
sex workers, 37, 134
Shechory, M., 74
Shildrick, M., 210–11
Sikorska, M., 236
Smeby, K.W., 171
Smith, J.L., 102
Sogner, S., 172
Sollund, R., 55, 68–70, 173, 179
Somers, M., 10–11, 33, 35–6
Søndergaard, D.M., 13
Sørensen, S.Ø., 171
Soysal, Y.N., 222
Spain, 17, 38, 79–96, 103, 116–17, 119, 246, 249, 252
Special Regime for Domestic Workers (Spain), 84–5, 94
Squires, J., 8
Sri Lanka, 5
Stasiulis, D.K., 33, 110, 121
Staunæs, D., 13, 28

Stenum, H., x, 3
Stiell, B., 110
Strasser, S., 10
Stubberud, E., xvi, 4–6, 13–14, 19–20, 57, 66–8, 70, 107, 125–44, 149, 173, 175, 184, 248, 253–4
Sullivan, O., 224
Szelewa, D., 235

T

Tastsoglou,, E., 8–10
terrorism, 138
Tobío, C., 94
Traba, L., 219
Træen, B., 171
Triandafyllidou, A., xiv, xv, 3–6, 31, 151, 225
Tronto, J., 4–5, 11, 174, 176
Trygstad, S., 172–3
Turner, G., 9, 151, 196

U

unemployment, 18, 22, 33, 39, 84, 86, 114, 116–17, 119–20, 196, 223, 235, 238
United Kingdom, 17–18, 101–20, 246–7
unpaid care work, 79–82, 92, 95

V

Vaage, O.F., 171
Van Walsum, S., 57, 151, 224

Varjonen, J., 40, 45–6
Verloo, M., 8
violence, vii, 138, 254
Vuorela, U., 71

W

Wærness, K., 81
Walby, S., 8, 105–6
Waquant, L., 36
Weissberg, J., 204
welfare regimes, 34, 38, 224, 238
Wetterer, A., 228
whiteness, 13, 72, 204
White Paper for Dependent Care (2005), (Spain) 90
Williams, F., 34, 94, 110
Williams, L., 128
Williamson, H., 9, 151
Wolkowitz, C., 209

X

xenophobia, 199

Y

Yeates, N., 7, 151
Yeoh, B., 107
Young, I.M., 152
Yuval-Davis, N., 8–9, 57, 128, 152

Z

Zaidman, C., 197
Zontini, E., 151

The manufacturer's authorised representative in the EU is Springer Nature Customer Service Centre GmbH, Europaplatz 3, 69115 Heidelberg, Germany. If you have any concerns regarding our products, please contact ProductSafety@springernature.com

Printed and bound by CPI Group (UK) Ltd, Croydon, CR0 4YY
23/03/2026
02076460-0003